THE ESSENTIALS OF THE VINAYA TRADITION

THE COLLECTED TEACHINGS OF THE TENDAI LOTUS SCHOOL

BDK English Tripiṭaka 97-I, II

The Essentials of the Vinaya Tradition

by

Gyōnen

Translated from the Japanese

(Taishō, Volume 74, Number 2348)

by

Leo M. Pruden

The Collected Teachings of the Tendai Lotus School

by

Gishin

Translated from the Japanese

(Taishō, Volume 74, Number 2366)

by

Paul L. Swanson

Numata Center
for Buddhist Translation and Research
1995

First Printing, 1995
ISBN: 0-9625618-9-4
Library of Congress Catalog Card Number: 94-068461

Published by
Numata Center for Buddhist Translation and Research
2620 Warring Street
Berkeley, California 94704

Printed in the United States of America

A Message on the Publication of the English Tripiṭaka

The Buddhist canon is said to contain eighty-four thousand different teachings. I believe that this is because the Buddha's basic approach was to prescribe a different treatment for every spiritual ailment, much as a doctor prescribes a different medicine for every medical ailment. Thus his teachings were always appropriate for the particular suffering individual and for the time at which the teaching was given, and over the ages not one of his prescriptions has failed to relieve the suffering to which it was addressed.

Ever since the Buddha's Great Demise over twenty-five hundred years ago, his message of wisdom and compassion has spread throughout the world. Yet no one has ever attempted to translate the entire Buddhist canon into English throughout the history of Japan. It is my greatest wish to see this done and to make the translations available to the many English-speaking people who have never had the opportunity to learn about the Buddha's teachings.

Of course, it would be impossible to translate all of the Buddha's eighty-four thousand teachings in a few years. I have, therefore, had one hundred thirty-nine of the scriptural texts in the prodigious Taishō edition of the Chinese Buddhist canon selected for inclusion in the First Series of this translation project.

It is in the nature of this undertaking that the results are bound to be criticized. Nonetheless, I am convinced that unless someone takes it upon himself or herself to initiate this project, it will never be done. At the same time, I hope that an improved, revised edition will appear in the future.

It is most gratifying that, thanks to the efforts of more than a hundred Buddhist scholars from the East and the West, this monumental project has finally gotten off the ground. May the rays of the Wisdom of the Compassionate One reach each and every person in the world.

NUMATA Yehan
Founder of the English
Tripiṭaka Project

August 7, 1991

Editorial Foreword

In January, 1982, Mr. NUMATA Yehan, the founder of the Bukkyō Dendō Kyōkai (Society for the Promotion of Buddhism), decided to begin the monumental task of the complete translation of the Taishō edition of the Chinese Buddhist canon into the English language. Under his leadership, a special preparatory committee was organized in April, 1982, and by July of the same year the Translation Committee of the English Tripiṭaka (Scriptures) was officially convened.

The initial Committee consisted of the following thirteen members: HANAYAMA Shōyū (Chairman); BANDŌ Shōjun; ISHIGAMI Zennō; KAMATA Shigeo; KANAOKA Shūyū; MAYEDA Sengaku; NARA Yasuaki; SAYEKI Shinkō; (late) SHIOIRI Ryōtatsu; TAMARU Noriyoshi; (late) TAMURA Kwansei; URYŪZU Ryūshin; and YUYAMA Akira. Assistant members of the Committee were as follows: KANAZAWA Atsushi; WATANABE Shōgo; Rolf Giebel of New Zealand; and Rudy Smet of Belgium.

Holding planning meetings on a monthly basis, the Committee has selected one hundred thirty-nine scriptures and texts for the First Series of translations, an estimated one hundred printed volumes in all. Scriptures and texts selected are not necessarily limited to those originally written in India but also include works written or composed in China or Japan. All the volumes in the First Series are scheduled for publication within the twentieth century. While the publication of the First Series proceeds, the scriptures and texts for the Second Series, which is expected to be published in the following ten- or twenty-year period, will be selected from among the remaining works; this process will continue until all the scriptures and texts, in Japanese as well as in Chinese, have been published.

Frankly speaking, it will take perhaps one hundred years or more to accomplish the English translation of the complete

Chinese and Japanese scriptures and texts, which consist of thousands of works. Nevertheless, as Mr. NUMATA wished, it is the sincere hope of the Committee that this project will continue unto completion, even after all its present members have passed away.

It must be mentioned here that the final object of this project is not academic fulfillment but the transmission of the teaching of the Buddha to the whole world in order to create harmony and peace among mankind.

More than eighty Buddhist scholars in the West and in the East, all well qualified to be translators of the Chinese and Japanese scriptures and texts, have agreed to translate certain selected works. It is really a great pleasure for the Committee to announce that more than forty-five translations have already been received as of the end of September, 1992.

The present members of the Translation Committee of the BDK English Tripiṭaka are HANAYAMA Shōyū (Chairman); BANDŌ Shōjun; ISHIGAMI Zennō; ICHISHIMA Shōshin; KAMATA Shigeo; KANAOKA Shūyū; MAYEDA Sengaku; NARA Yasuaki; SAYEKI Shinkō; TAMARU Noriyoshi; URYŪZU Ryūshin; and YUYAMA Akira. Assistant members are WATANABE Shōgo and SUZUKI Kōshin.

Commemorating the ninety-fourth birthday of Mr. NUMATA Yehan, the Committee published the following three texts in a limited edition in April, 1991:

(1) *The Lotus Sutra* (Taishō No. 262)
(2) *The Sutra on Upāsaka Precepts* (Taishō No. 1488)
(3) *The Summary of the Great Vehicle* (Taishō No. 1593)

In December, 1991, the Publication Committee headed by Prof. Philip Yampolsky was organized. New editions of the above volumes and the remaining texts will be published under the supervision of this Committee.

HANAYAMA Shōyū
Chairman
Translation Committee of
the BDK English Tripiṭaka

September 10, 1992

Publisher's Foreword

In December, 1991, at the Numata Center for Buddhist Translation and Research in Berkeley, California, a publication committee was established for the purpose of seeing into print the translations of the Buddhist works in the BDK Tripiṭaka Series. This committee processes the translations forwarded for publication by the Translation Committee in Tokyo. It performs the duties of copyediting, formatting, proofreading, indexing, consulting with the translator on questionable passages—the routine duties of any publishing house. No attempt is made to standardize the English translations of Buddhist technical terms; these are left to the discretion of the individual translator. Represented on the committee are specialists in Sanskrit, Chinese, and Japanese who attempt to ensure that fidelity to the texts is maintained.

The Publication Committee is dedicated to the production of lucid and readable works that do justice to the vision of the late Mr. NUMATA Yehan, who wished to make available to Western readers the major works of the Chinese and Japanese Buddhist canon.

Dr. Leo M. Pruden, the translator of *The Essentials of the Vinaya Tradition (Risshū-Kōyō),* passed away in October, 1991. Thus there was no opportunity to consult with him during the preparation of the manuscript for publication. The manuscript, however, remains substantially as Dr. Pruden left it.

In some instances an important text is too brief to justify publication as a separate volume. This is the case with Professor Paul L. Swanson's translation of *The Collected Teachings of the Tendai Lotus School (Tendai Hokke-shū Gishū),* which is also included in this volume. There is no direct connection between the two works except that they were both written by Japanese monks and are both contained in volume 74 of the Taishō Tripiṭaka; they are printed together here as a matter of convenience.

"Taishō" refers to the *Taishō Shinshū Daizōkyō* (Newly Revised Tripiṭaka Inaugurated in the Taishō Era), which was published during the period from 1924 to 1934. This consists of one hundred volumes, in which as many as 3,360 scriptures in both Chinese and Japanese are included. This edition is acknowledged to be the most complete Tripiṭaka of the Northern tradition of Buddhism ever published in the Chinese and Japanese languages. As with all books in the BDK Series, the series number on the spine and title page of each work corresponds to the number assigned to it by the Translation Committee of the BDK English Tripiṭaka in Tokyo. A list of the volumes is appended at the end of each volume.

Those participating in the work of the committee are Diane Ames, William Ames, Brian Galloway, Nobuo Haneda, and the Reverend Kiyoshi S. Yamashita.

Philip Yampolsky
Chairman
Publication Committee

July 1, 1995

Contents

BDK English Tripiṭaka 97-I

THE ESSENTIALS OF THE VINAYA TRADITION

by

Gyōnen

Translated from the Japanese

(Taishō, Volume 74, Number 2348)

by

Leo M. Pruden

Numata Center for Buddhist Translation and Research

1995

Contents

Translator's Introduction

The monastic life of the Buddhist Sangha has always been the framework within which the great Buddhist masters and teachers have developed their dogmatic systems. Given the emphasis on the three learnings, *śīla, samādhi,* and *prajñā* (precepts on morality, meditation, and wisdom), by all schools of Mahayana Buddhism, the study of the monastic precepts forms the traditional starting point of the formal study and practice of Buddhism.

Regardless of this, Western scholarship, perhaps looking for points of similarity with Western theology, has laid almost exclusive emphasis on the transcendental or abstract aspects of the Buddhist religion and has almost completely ignored Buddhist insights into ethics and morality.

Buddhist scholarship in recent years has flourished largely in Japan. Yet while the Japanese lead the world in Buddhist scholarship, their work often reflects social trends within their country. With the decline and virtual disappearance of Buddhist monasticism in Japan, the attention of Japanese Buddhist studies has turned away from this once important aspect of their tradition. Today studies of Buddhist ethics, of Buddhist monastic institutions, and of the Vinaya tradition are almost completely lacking in Japan.

In September of 1960 I began my formal study of Buddhism in Los Angeles by reading, with a group of friends, Gyōnen's *Essentials of the Eight Traditions* (*Hasshū-Kōyō*). This work has long been considered a standard introductory text with which to begin the study of this religion and its various philosophies. The reading was conducted under the guidance of the then Mr. and now Dr. UNNO Taitetsu, who gave unselfishly of his time to us three students. My curiosity was aroused as I read the section of the *Hasshū-Kōyō* on the *Risshū* or Vinaya tradition of Japan. From that time on, regardless of the press of other studies, I kept searching for some further reference work or study on this tradition. Since I had acquired an acquaintance with Gyōnen's writing style through the *Hasshū-Kōyō,* in September of 1964 I read his *Essentials of the Vinaya Tradition* (*Risshū-Kōyō*) for the first time and found that as far as my interests were concerned, an understanding of this work would serve admirably as a guide to the study of the Vinaya tradition. It was with this thought that I began this present work.

In October of 1964 I was privileged to be able to go to Japan for further study of Buddhism; and from September of 1965 I was able to read the *Risshū-Kōyō* with Professor HIRAKAWA Akira of the Department of Indian and Buddhist Studies at Tokyo University. It is his encyclopaedic knowledge of the Vinaya tradition that has made this translation possible. This present work is cordially and warmly dedicated to him, with the realization that the errors it contains are my own responsibility.

It would not be out of place here to mention a few of the *kalyāṇa-mitra*s who have indirectly contributed to the realization of this project: Professor Stanley Weinstein, presently at Yale University, who, while not directly connected with my studies, has often encouraged me through his infectious enthusiasm for the study of Mahayana Buddhism; Professor NAGATOMI Masatoshi, who, despite a pressing teaching and research program, always found time to give me very sound corrections and suggestions; the Rev. Dr. HIRAOKA Jōkai, incumbent of the Kami-no-bō of the Tōdai-ji temple, who on several occasions treated me with graciousness and courtesy and who helped me greatly with facts about the Tōdai-ji temple; and numerous other friends and students, whose interest in the study of Buddhism makes our efforts worthwhile.

The Life of Gyōnen

Gyōnen (March 6, 1240–September 5, 1321), the author of the *Risshū-Kōyō,* was born in the province of Iyo, on the island of Shikoku, of reputed Fujiwara lineage. At the age of eighteen he formally entered the religious life under the tutelage of the master Enshō of the Kaidan-in temple in the huge monastic complex of the Tōdai-ji temple. It was here that he received full ordination (*gusoku-kai*) at the age of twenty. Gyōnen studied Vinaya texts under the masters Shōgen and Jōin, *Tendai* and *mikkyō* under the master Shōshū, and *Kegon* under the master Shūshō. Consequently when Gyōnen speaks of these men with reference to the *Risshū* tradition in Kamakura Era Japan, he is speaking of men he knew personally.

In 1259 or 1260 he returned to Enshō in the Kaidan-in. Thereafter for a period of approximately ten years Gyōnen shared his masters' tasks of lecturing and teaching.

In 1276 Gyōnen lectured on the *Hua-yen-ching* (Jp. *Kegon-gyō*) in the main sanctuary, the Daibutsu-den, of the Tōdai-ji. In the following year, he succeeded to the abbotship of the Kaidan-in upon the death of Enshō. Gyōnen then devoted himself to lecturing and administering the precepts. His fame in scholarship attracted the attention of the ex-Emperor Go-Uda, who on one occasion lodged in Gyōnen's temple, and who received the Mahayana precepts from him. Gyōnen thus received the title of "kokushi" or "National Imperial Teacher." On one occasion Gyōnen was invited to the Palace and there lectured on the *Hua-yen-ching Wu-chiao-chang.*

In 1291 Gyōnen gave a well-attended series of lectures on the *Lotus Sutra* at the Kongōzan-ji near Nara.

In 1316 Gyōnen succeeded Shinjō as abbot of the Tōshōdai-ji, a position he held for five years. In 1320 Gyōnen returned to the Kaidan-in, where he died the following year at the age of eighty-two. His ashes were divided; part rest even today behind his beloved Kaidan-in, and part rest next to his master Enshō on Mt. Jūbi.

Gyōnen's Literary Works

Although Gyōnen's life would appear dull if judged by worldly standards, his intellectual life and written output were tremendous. The *Shōshūshōshō-roku* (a two-*kan* bibliography of various monks' writings compiled in 1790 by one Kenjun), written 469 years after Gyōnen's death, ascribes to him a total of 94 works in 918 *kan,* including works dealing with *Kegon* (31 works in 469 *kan*), *Risshū* (34 works in 223 *kan*), *Jōdo* (16 works in 116 *kan*), *Hossō* (8 works in 84 *kan*), and *Shingon* (5 works in 36 *kan;* all of Gyōnen's *Shingon* works are commentaries on select volumes of Kūkai's *Jūjūshinron*). The *Honchō-Kōsōden* (*Dai Nippon Bukkyō Zensho* CII, pp. 246–47) lists 21 works attributed to Gyōnen; the *Ritsuon-Shōbōden* (*DNBZ* CV, pp. 278–79) lists 33 such works.

The Kaidan-in burned down in a fire on the 23d of July, 1567, and a large portion of Gyōnen's manuscripts were permanently lost. Of a recorded total of some thirty-four works dealing with the Vinaya tradition or *Risshū,* only some six remain, and two of these are incomplete.

The first is the *Un'u-shō* in one *kan* (*DNBZ* CV). Written in 1276, this work is a history of the Vinaya tradition with reference to the role of the Dharmaguptaka Vinaya.

Second is the *Bommō-kyō-sho Mokujushō,* originally in eighty *kan.* The fifty-one extant *kan* are in *T.* 62, No. 2247; forty-four *kan* in Gyōnen's own hand exist in manuscript in the Tōdai-ji Library. Composed by Gyōnen in 1277 and revised by him in 1284 and again in 1319, this is a subcommentary on Fa-tsang's commentary on the *Bommō-kyō* (*Fan-wang-ching*).

Third is the *Risshū-Keikanshō,* originally in sixty *kan.* Only one *kan,* the sixth, is extant (see the *DNBZ* CV). The extant volume (dated February 1306) gives an exhaustive bibliography of works written by various masters of the Lü-tsung (Vinaya tradition, *Risshū*) in China and of the Vinaya masters' transmission of this tradition from India to China and Japan. By September, 1368, it was lamented that only one *kan* remained of this work; see the *Busshō-kaisetsu-daijiten* XI, 208d. This work is close to the *Risshū-Kōyō* in language and in content. Is the *Risshū-Kōyō* an abbreviated version of this work?

Fourth is the *Tsūju biku zange ryōji fudōki* in one *kan;* written in 1306, it is now preserved in *T.* 74, No. 2355. This work is about the *zange* or confession ceremonies composed by Kakujō (of the

Tōshōdai-ji) and Eison (of the Saidai-ji), and how they agree in doctrine but differ in externals. Its first printed edition is dated 1618, and it is this printed edition that serves as the basis for the *Nippon-daizōkyō* edition.

Fifth is the *Risshū-Kōyō* in two *kan*. It was composed in 1306 (Kagen 4), and the (first?) printed edition is dated 1660 (Manji 3). KITAGAWA Chikai mentioned by way of a commentary to this work a *Risshū-Kōyō kage* (by himself? See the *Busshō-kaisetsu-daijiten* XI, 209a). This 1660 edition and the edition in the *Taishō Shinshū Daizōkyō* (*T.* 74, No. 2348) are the editions used in this present translation.

Sixth is the *Shibun-kaihon-sho San-shū-ki* in twenty *kan*, preserved in the *Nippon-daizōkyō Shōjō-ritsu-shōshō*, Vol. 1. This is Gyōnen's subcommentary on Ting-pin's (see the Twenty-ninth Question) commentary on the Dharmaguptaka *prātimokṣa*. Of these twenty *kan*, the first ten were written in 1310, the remaining ten in 1312.

The Contents of the *Risshū-Kōyō*

The contents of the *Risshū-Kōyō* are broadly divided into two parts, the doctrines of the *Risshū* and its history.

Gyōnen's Preface deals with the significance of *śīla* (precepts) within the overall scheme of Buddhism and especially within the Mahayana. The First Question deals with the relationship of the threefold pure precepts to the three learnings of *śīla*, *samādhi*, and *prajñā*; and the scriptural sources of the learning of the precepts.

The Second Question introduces the ways of receiving the precepts: receiving all of the threefold pure precepts at once, or receiving only the first of these threefold precepts, the precept that embraces all the rules of discipline. The precept that embraces all the rules of discipline is discussed with reference to the seven types of Buddhist believers, from laymen to fully ordained monks or nuns (Third Question), and with reference to the Hinayana precepts of the *śrāvaka* (Fourth Question). The Fifth Question deals with the difference between receiving all of the threefold pure precepts and the receiving of only the precept that embraces all the rules of discipline.

The Seventh Question deals with the scriptural sources of the threefold pure precepts.

The Eighth Question treats of the differences between the threefold pure precepts as taught in the *Ying-lo-ching* and as taught in the Chinese translation of the *Yogācāra-bhūmi,* the *Yü-ch'ieh-lun.* This is followed by an elucidation of the differences between the precept that embraces all the rules of discipline in the *Ying-lo-ching* and the one in the *Yü-ch'ieh-lun.*

The Ninth Question deals with mental action and its relation to the threefold pure precepts.

There now follows a discussion of variant traditions of the minor precepts found in other Mahayana works: the relationship between the forty-eight minor precepts of the *Fan-wang-ching* and the forty-four minor precepts of the *Yü-ch'ieh-lun* (Tenth Question); the "eighty-four thousand rules of conduct" (Eleventh Question); the relationship between the four major precepts and the forty-four minor precepts (Thirteenth Question); and the four hundred bodhisattva precepts taught in the *Yao-shih-ching* (Fourteenth Question). This section ends with a discussion of the various types of minor bodhisattva precepts (Fifteenth Question) and of the teaching of receiving only the precept that embraces all the rules of discipline (Sixteenth Question).

The subject matter now shifts to the *chiao-p'an* (Jp. *kyō-han*) or doctrinal classification that the *Lü-tsung* or Vinaya tradition in China establishes. This is introduced by an enumeration of the masters or patriarchs of the *Lü-tsung* in China, followed by Tao-hsüan's doctrinal classification of the four teachings, the three insights, and the three traditions (Eighteenth Question), and his view of the three learnings in the Mahayana.

The Nineteenth Question deals with the major orthodox texts of the *Lü-tsung,* and the Twentieth Question gives ten reasons for the Buddha's promulgating *śīla* and the *Vinaya Piṭaka.*

Tao-hsüan's teaching of the three insights is now taken up again (Twenty-first Question) in greater detail, followed in the Twenty-second Question by a discussion of what Dharma it is that constitutes the teaching of the Buddha.

There now follows a more detailed study of the precepts; why one would undertake the precept that embraces all the rules of discipline in lieu of all the threefold pure precepts (Twenty-third Question); an etymology of the threefold pure precepts (Twenty-fourth Question); etymologies of *Vinaya, śīla,* and *prātimokṣa* (Twenty-fifth Question); and an enumeration of the seven classes of persons that constitute the Sangha (Twenty-sixth Question).

Here follows a discussion of the *chieh-t'i* (Jp. *kai-tai*) problem, i.e., what *dharma* it is that constitutes the essential existence of the precepts (Twenty-seventh Question). The concept of "substance" or "nature" is viewed in the context of *dharma,* nature, practice, and external features; its nature, *vijñapti,* and *avijñapti-rūpa* are discussed, as is the nature of the precepts embodied in the *prātimokṣa.* This section concludes with a discussion of variant theories concerning the nature of the precepts (Twenty-eighth Question), and with mention of the nature of all the threefold pure precepts.

The Twenty-ninth Question addresses itself to the *Vinaya Piṭaka,* specifically to the precept that embraces all the rules of discipline, the purport of the Dharmaguptaka Vinaya, the purport or content of one's receiving all the threefold pure precepts (Thirtieth Question), and the inner structure of the Dharmaguptaka Vinaya Piṭaka (Thirty-first Question).

The religious path relevant to the *Lü-tsung* is now presented: on the basis of the premise that all sentient beings possess the Buddha nature (Thirty-second Question), the religious path is divided into either four or fifty-two stages (Thirty-third Question); and their interrelationship is discussed (Thirty-fourth Question). The practice of all four stages is discussed; the stage of understanding (Thirty-fifth Question), the stage of insight, the stage of meditation, and the stage of the Ultimate.

Since, in Buddhism, progress in the religious life is described with reference to the quantity and the quality of the hindrances temporarily put down or totally extirpated, the Thirty-sixth Question introduces the topic of those hindrances: the two bodies within which one cuts off the hindrances; the hindrances of illusions (*kleṣa-āvaraṇa*) and the hindrances of knowledge (*jñeya-āvaraṇa*) (Thirty-seventh Question); the four abiding realms of delusion; the separate passions of discrimination; the accompanying passions; the hindrance of knowledge; the grossness or minuteness of these two types of hindrances; the putting down and cutting off of the hindrances; those hindrances that are cut off; and the truths one is enlightened to in the stage of insight, in the stage of meditation, and in the stage of the Ultimate.

The second major division of the *Risshū-Kōyō* is the section dealing with the history of the Vinaya tradition in India, China, and Japan.

The transmission of the Vinaya lineage in India is narrated (Thirty-eighth Question), and the narration is then supplemented by quoting the sectarian lineages given in the Mahāsāṅghika Vinaya and in the *Shan-chien-lun,* the Chinese translation of the *Samānta-pāsādikā.* These are contrasted with a similar Dharma lineage of the Sarvāstivādins.

The early development of a Vinaya tradition in China is traced, beginning with the introduction of Buddhism into China and the first ordination of *bhikṣu*s and *bhikṣuṇī*s (monks and nuns). The early practices of ordaining monks and nuns according to the Dharmaguptaka *karma-vacana* and of simultaneously reciting the Mahāsāṅghika *prātimokṣa* at the twice monthly *uposatha* are mentioned, as is the eventual translation of the complete texts of various Vinaya Piṭakas.

Studies of the Dharmaguptaka Vinaya resulting in the crystallization of a Dharmaguptaka Vinaya sectarian tradition are related; the accepted lineage of the nine Dharmaguptaka Vinaya tradition's masters or patriarchs is given; and this tradition's division into the three scholastic traditions of Tung-t'a, Hsiang-pu, and the Nan-shan Lü-tsung is described.

The traditional account of the introduction of Buddhism into Japan continues the narration, followed by Tao-hsüan and Chien-chen going to Japan. The establishment of first the Kaidan-in and subsequently the Tōshōdai-ji is narrated, followed by a description of the construction of the three official ordination platforms (*kai-dan*) in Japan, as well as that of the ordination platform of the Tōshōdai-ji.

The lineage of *Risshū* masters in Japan in the generations after Chien-chen is given, special attention being paid to the activities of Jippan, Jōkei, Kakujō, and Eison. Kakujō's major disciples are listed as well as the major disciples of Eison. This section of the *Risshū-Kōyō* then concludes with a narration of the activities of Shunjō and his major disciples.

Preface

5a The great Vinaya Piṭaka assembles all the teachings and cannot be fathomed; the broad practice of *śīla* embraces all the *pāramitās* and is difficult to calculate. The five realms of delusion are quickly extinguished by means of the practice of the precepts; the mental entanglements of the two types of death are forever cut off by means of the *prātimokṣa*.

The precepts are a bejewelled boat to cross the river of desire, a divine carriage to traverse the mountains of hatred, a proximate cause of entering the citadel of Enlightenment (*bodhi*), and a direct path leading to the realm of the Buddhas. Further, because of the precepts, the sustaining power of the Three Jewels leading all sentient beings to Enlightenment is ever new; the saving virtue of the vehicles of the five classes of beings is tremendously great.

The spreading about in the world of the scriptures and their commentaries is due solely to the power of the Vinaya; the cutting off of doubts by meditation and wisdom is due exclusively to the power of practicing the precepts. The precepts are truly the essentials by which the teaching is protected and the Sangha is kept in order. They are the model for teaching and saving all sentient beings. They are the level path to Enlightenment and Nirvana. They are an excellent model of the four wisdoms and of the three bodies [of the Buddha].

It is only the teachings of the precepts that in large measure penetrate to the most subtle points. Now we shall present these teachings in outline and roughly reveal their principles. The establishment of the purport of the teaching has significance.

The forest of the Dharma is luxuriant, and the rain clouds of the principles are torrential, but out of this [teaching that is likened to a] forest and [to] billows of waves we can only narrate [this work] by discussing the "leaves" [of the forest] and other such traces.

5b A complete outline of the precepts and of the Vinaya Piṭaka is extremely deep and very broad; the universe constitutes its object, and all of space constitutes its measure. It permeates both phenomenon and noumenon; it embraces both outer characteristics and inner nature. It envelops both the Absolute and the Conventional [levels of Truth]; nothing is omitted. It includes both emptiness and existence; nothing is left out.

The empyrean is deep and profound, embracing everything within it. Since it is the Ultimate, [we can only say] that it is contained herein [i.e., in the study of the precepts].

Now the teachings of the true Way of the Mahayana are vast and numerous; in the quest of the religious life, the minds of all men are varied and different. The perfect tradition is broad and vast; the vehicle of the Buddha is profound and mysterious. In sudden Enlightenment, when one's capacity matures, the One Path is straightaway revealed; but when one's nature and [external] conditions have not yet matured, then a separate "expedient means" is set up.

For this reason, within the One Buddha Vehicle, the three vehicles are preached. On the basis of these individual three vehicles, one's nature and capacities are trained, and finally the great Way of the basic One Vehicle is entered. Although the appropriate conditions differ for sudden Enlightenment and for a gradual progression, both are reconciled in the One Vehicle, and all enter into the One Nature.

The purpose of the Tathāgata's appearing in the world, his Enlightenment, his conversion of mankind—the purport of all these lies in the Vinaya Piṭaka. The follower of the Mahayana enters speedily into the Great Path. Producing the mind of Enlightenment, he looks forward to Buddhahood. With broad and expansive compassion he establishes relations with all sentient beings.

He practices the six *pāramitās*, the four universal vows, the three learnings, the fourfold [means for the salvation of all sentient beings], and the benefitting of himself and others. His vows and their subsequent practices are perfected.

When both his cutting off [of passions] and his Enlightenment are totally completed, then Buddhahood is accomplished. When the four wisdoms are perfected, when the four qualities are perfectly arranged, and when the three bodies [of the Buddha] are fully possessed, then the great functioning [the activity that proceeds from Enlightenment] will always appear.

This is none other than the perfect teaching of the One Vehicle. If the mind of Enlightenment is awakened, spiritual progress in the religious life is far-ranging and broad, automatic and unhindered. The great functioning is without limits, and the work of salvation is never completed.

Although the characteristics of the numerous practices of benefitting [oneself and others] are without limit, they always follow the three learnings [i.e., the precepts, meditation, and wisdom]. When one possesses them fully, one progresses [in the religious life]. The grades of practice in religious training are truly thus.

When one first enters into the Dharma of the Buddha, faith is to be regarded as primary. Next one receives the precepts in order to guard against actions of evil. If the bulwark of the precepts is firm, then the waters of meditation will be calm and clear. Putting down passions and delusions and not letting them arise again will cause the great, pure wisdom to appear automatically. The seeds of delusion are soon cut off without any exception whatsoever.

As for this marvellous wisdom, when one is enlightened to these principles, a profound fusion [between the object thus perceived and the subject of this perception] takes place. The meritorious actions of the three teachings in the Mahayana are thus.

The learnings of the bodhisattvas' precepts fall into three groups. As it says in the first volume of the *Kuei-ching-i:*

> Should we now begin [our religious practice], we should first venerate the tradition of the precepts. Of the precepts there

are basically three, the causes of the three bodies [of the Buddha].

> First is the precept that embraces all the rules of discipline, which may be said to cut off all evil. This is none other than the cause of the Dharma Body. This is because the Dharma Body is essentially pure, but if obscured by evil it is not revealed; so if one practices successfully this separating from evil, such qualities [as the Dharma Body] will appear.
>
> Second is the precept that embraces all good dharmas, which may be said to be the practicing of all acts of good. This is none other than the cause of the Body of Recompense, for recompense is attained by the accomplishment of all good. In the accomplishment of good, there is nothing higher than the ceasing of evil and the doing of good. Now, it is the practice of the two good acts of ceasing from evil and doing good that bring about the conditions for the Buddha of Recompense.
>
> Third is the precept that embraces all sentient beings, which is none other than having compassion and the desire for the salvation of all sentient beings. The merit of this brings about the cause of the Buddha of Transformation. The Buddha of Transformation, without conscious effort, responds according to the feelings of all sentient beings; hence the great compas-
> 5c sion of one practicing this precept saves all sentient beings. His intention and his activities are equal.

All practices are embraced within these threefold precepts.

The precept that embraces all the rules of discipline is the path of putting an end to evil. From the first production of mind [i.e., the first thought directed to attaining Enlightenment] up to the result that is Buddhahood, evil action is guarded against, and all infractions [of the moral code] are ended. The seeds of delusions are crushed, and their appearance is not generated. Truly, the seeds of delusions are cut off, and any remaining influences are completely eliminated.

Even the casting off of one's mortal body [subject to the] permutations [of the mind], and subject to [karmic] retribution, and the casting off of *dharmas* that, although unhindered, are impure, etc.—all these are characteristics of the practice of the precept that embraces all the rules of discipline.

The precept that embraces all good *dharmas* is the path of practicing good. From the first production of the mind [of Enlightenment] until the final, ultimate result is attained, all good acts are embraced and practiced and various practices are cultivated. Of all practices, of all good deeds, none are omitted.

Stillness of mind, wisdom; the path of ceasing evil, the path of putting down, of cutting off; the path of action, the path of good—all these are the instruction of cultivating the practice of good. The twofold adornments of fortune and wisdom, practices generated by a bodhisattva having the four wisdoms that are acquired through the attainment of Enlightenment, teachings revealed by the Absolute Truth of the two emptinesses—all these are obtained with Enlightenment. Such teachings as these are all the precept that embraces all good *dharmas*.

The precept that embraces all sentient beings: all practices are the path of action, as the ways of benefitting (i.e., saving) all sentient beings are numberless and varied. They are all produced [by the bodhisattva]. Acquired wisdom; relative wisdom; skill in expedient means; saving all sentient beings and embracing all beings; the great compassion of the bodhisattva replacing pain—such actions are all the precept that embraces all sentient beings.

These are called the threefold pure precepts of the bodhisattva. Both broad and profound, they are likened to mountains and seas.

All actions are embraced within these threefold [precepts]. All virtues are included; this constitutes the teaching of the precepts.

First Question

If all learnings are included within the learning of the precepts, what constitutes the learnings of meditation and wisdom?

Answer: The contents of the three learnings of the Mahayana include one another; when one is raised, all the others are included within it without any exception.

In general, the learning of the precepts embraces all actions; the learning of meditation also embraces all actions; and the learning of wisdom embraces all acts of good.

Each separate teaching [in Buddhism] is common to the three learnings. So although we may speak of the "three learnings," they are individually made up of all actions. But because the paths to Enlightenment differ, they [all actions] have been divided into the "three learnings." Within the rules for the prohibition of evil, there are the teachings of positive good—this is meditation and wisdom. Within meditation and wisdom there are the teachings of the prohibition of evil—this is the learning of the precepts. All the characteristics of the various phenomena interpenetrate one with another; they are definitely not separated one from another.

Right mindfulness and right intention create the supreme benefit [Enlightenment]; to reside in right views benefits all sentient beings. Accordingly, as they benefit all sentient beings, right mindfulness and intentions constitute the learning of meditation and wisdom. It is for this reason that benefitting all sentient beings is called the learning of meditation and wisdom. Right views and right thoughts themselves benefit all sentient beings. Never to abandon the basic principles of supreme meditation and supreme wisdom is none other than the task of supreme mercy and the supreme conversion of all sentient beings.

From the first thought of Enlightenment, one gradually and more profoundly evolves toward the Supreme. Both inner nature and outer activities become firm and immovable; they are mutually penetrating and mutually inclusive—unhindered, one strives freely.

Now, within the one true Mahayana teaching it is said of the precepts that one precept is identical to all the precepts and that
6a the learning of meditation and wisdom does not exist without the learning of the precepts.

The mind of one is the mind of all; the learnings of the precepts and wisdom do not exist without the learning of meditation.

The wisdom of one is the wisdom of all; the learnings of the precepts and meditation do not exist without wisdom.

The precepts, meditation, and wisdom are all obtained within one mind. One thought and all the three learnings are mutually interpenetrated without hindrance. One act constitutes all actions, and one instant (*kṣaṇa*) may span many aeons.

The one and the many completely embrace one another; an instant and an aeon mutually interfuse. They enter into all quarters perfectly and completely.

Because of this principle, the threefold division of all actions constitutes the learnings of meditation and wisdom. The aspects of meditation and of wisdom of all the various good actions constitute the threefold division of the precepts.

Although all actions are completely embraced within this threefold division of the precepts, it is because the precepts [primarily] constitute this path that this is called the Vinaya tradition.

Of all the teachings or practices of the Mahayana, each teaching or practice possesses the teaching of the precepts.

Among the various scriptures and commentaries, many speak thus about the characteristics of all the various actions.

Beginning with the Three Refuges, and finally ending in Buddhahood, each of the various stages of the bodhisattva's path has its practice of the precepts.

In the various stages of the bodhisattva who is still in the causal state, the causes of the precepts are perfected. The result of the practice of the precepts is perfected in the highest realm, the stage that is the result [Buddhahood].

Among the seven holy gifts is the holy gift of the precepts. Among the ten inexhaustible stores is the store of the precepts. Among the three learnings, the learning of the precepts is the first. Among the six *pāramitās*, the *pāramitā* of the precepts is the second. Among the ten stages of faith is the mind of the precepts.

In the *Hua-yen-ching,* the sermon on the ten faiths has a chapter on pure conduct; the sermon on the ten abodes has a section on divine conduct; and among the ten types of divine conduct, the precepts are the essence of practice. Of the ten *pāramitās* within these ten grades of conduct, the second is the *pāramitā* of the precepts.

As for the ten *pāramitās* of the ten realms, [as one advances spiritually] one totally possesses all previous *pāramitās*. Each stage contains all other stages to perfection. Before the stage of faith, in the stage of faith, and in the threefold wise stages and the ten realms, each and every stage in the bodhisattva's career contains the practice of the precepts.

Not for one moment, not for one instant, are they separated from the precepts, for without the precepts there are no bodhisattvas. When one arrives at the realm of Buddhahood, all the various practices are perfected, their many qualities are perceived, and they are all completely perfected. These many qualities that constitute the result [Buddhahood] all come from the practice of the precepts.

Buddhahood contains all the various aspects of the precepts. The fivefold Dharma Body has a Precept Dharma Body.

Among the adornments of fortune and wisdom is the adornment of the precepts. In attaining the thirty-two major marks of a Buddha, there are no separate causes to be practiced. The precepts are its essence. These are the marks of the Transformation Body [of the Buddha].

When one has attained the body [of the Buddha] which is attained for the enjoyment of others, there are eighty-four thousand marks and rays of light emanating from his [thirty-two] major and [eighty] minor marks. In attaining the infinitely vast number of characteristics of the Tenfold Lotus Flower Enclosure [of Vairocana Buddha], there are no separate causes to be practiced, for they are all due to the power of the precepts.

Yet among the various separate causes [leading to the attainment of the thirty-two major and eighty minor marks of a Buddha] is the merit of the precepts.

In this way, the meritorious teachings of cause and effect all [come down to] the practice of the precepts and are created by the qualities of the precepts.

In the causes and the result of the bodhisattva's career, both his internal Enlightenment and his external benefitting of all sentient beings are created through his practice of the precepts.

Second Question

What a bodhisattva of the perfect One Vehicle tradition [of Mahayana Buddhism] receives [as precepts] and what he practices as the marvellous cause [leading to] Buddhahood are these great threefold precepts. What are the characteristics of his receiving of these precepts?

Answer: A bodhisattva's aspirations are broad and deep; his practice and understanding are lofty and far-reaching. He does not
6b discard any single precept that is to be received; he does not neglect any single practice that is to be practiced. All the practices, and the vast number of *pāramitās*, are to be practiced. The precepts must be universal and without limit, all-embracing, and inexhaustible. The characteristics of the principles of the Mahayana are truly thus.

Based on these principles, there are two methods of carrying out the rituals of receiving these great precepts.

First is the "general receiving," so called because all the threefold precepts are received. This is none other than the *karmavacana* ritual. The master Uijŏk established this name because it appeared in the *Chan-ch'a-ching.* This is also called "receiving all the precepts," since one receives all the threefold precepts. The Ts'u-en master [K'uei-chi] and T'aehyŏn initiated the use of this term.

Second is the "separate receiving of the precepts." From among the threefold precepts, only the precept that embraces all the rules of discipline is undertaken, as this one precept exhausts all aspects of the bodhisattva's religious practice. All teachers together have established the usage of this term.

Third Question

Why is it that only the precept that embraces all the rules of discipline can be received separately? Why is it that the other two groups of precepts—those that embrace all good *dharmas* and all sentient beings—cannot be received separately?

Answer: The one precept, the precept that embraces all the rules of discipline, sets up seven groups of persons within the Sangha. The Buddha, for the sake of the *śrāvakas*, pointed out that within the One Vehicle this precept legislates all the precepts. The seven groups of persons within the Dharma of the Buddha are established in this manner.

Now the bodhisattva has always possessed all the precepts of this one group within the threefold precepts. Originally the precept that embraces all the rules of discipline of the threefold precepts sets up the seven classes of persons. The teachings of the "general receiving" of all the threefold precepts is thus also classified into its various grades.

Neither the precept that embraces all good *dharmas* nor that which embraces all sentient beings possesses this principle. Hence these latter two are not received separately.

Fourth Question

In receiving all the threefold precepts, the seven groups of persons are already delineated within the Sangha. Why then is it necessary to receive the "separate ordination"?

Answer: The ritual of the "separate receiving of the precept that embraces all the rules of discipline" is the same as [the ordination ritual] of the *śrāvaka*s. The reason it is the same [for the followers of the Mahayana] as three vehicles is because such is the custom of this Sahā world.

Fifth Question

Of the two types of receiving the precepts—the "general receiving of all the threefold precepts" and the "separate receiving of the precept that embraces all the rules of discipline"—which is of long duration, and which is of short duration?

Answer: The ritual receiving of all the threefold precepts lasts forever. The separate receiving of the precept that embraces all the rules of discipline lasts only for the lifetime of the individual.

Sixth Question

Why would the bodhisattva make use of a teaching that lasts only one lifetime?

Answer: Both the practice and the understanding of the bodhisattva are broad and deep; he may practice endlessly; such would be his long practice. However, there is also the teaching that lasts only one lifetime. The bodhisattva is free to choose a precept that lasts either a long or a short time. He may accomplish its practice in any way he intends, because, be it one teaching or many teachings, there is no limitation for him.

Should he wish to practice it forever, he makes use of the receiving of all the threefold precepts. Should he wish to practice for just one lifetime, he makes use of the separate receiving of the precepts.

Whether it be for a long or for a short duration, he follows his own intentions, and the teaching [i.e., the precept] will correspond to this.

Seventh Question

The threefold pure precepts are based upon what texts?

Answer: The threefold precepts have their origin in the *Hua-yen-ching,* but a fuller explanation of their characteristics is taught in various places in later Mahayana scriptures and commentaries.

The *Hua-yen-ching* speaks of three types of precepts, but their
6c names are not given. Commentators upon this scripture, however, narrated the principles of the threefold precepts.

The *Fan-wang-ching* contains the principles of the threefold precepts, but it does not specifically give their names. The various masters who have commented upon this text and the principles of this scripture explain in greater detail the aspects of the threefold pure precepts.

The Hsien-shou master [Fa-tsang], commenting upon the *Fan-wang-chieh-ching,* said, "All the threefold pure precepts constitute the Vinaya tradition." He made a correspondence between the ten major prohibitive precepts given in this scripture and the threefold precepts.

The master T'aehyŏn, in commenting on the scripture of the forty-eight [minor precepts, i.e., the *Fan-wang-ching*], stated that each one of the forty-eight precepts fully contains the teachings of the threefold precepts.

The *Fan-wang-ching* was the first sermon of the Buddha; the *Ying-lo-pen-yeh-ching* was preached twenty-eight years after the Enlightenment of the Tathāgata.

In the chapter "On the Names of the Wise and Holy" in the first volume of this [i.e., the *Ying-lo-ching*] scripture, the ten major precepts are preached, while in the chapter "On Cause and Result" in the last volume the six *pāramitās* are taught. Within these precepts the threefold precepts are elucidated in greater detail;

these are "the self-nature precepts," "the precepts to receive the good *dharmas*," and "the precept to benefit all sentient beings."

In the chapter "Instruction for the Multitude" it says:

> O sons of the Buddha! Now on behalf of the various bodhisattvas I shall compile the fundamentals of all the precepts. These are the so-called teachings on receiving the threefold precepts.
>
> "The precept that embraces all good *dharmas*" is the teaching of the eighty-four thousand *dharmas*.
>
> "The precept that embraces all sentient beings" refers to compassion, mercy, joy, and equanimity and to extending one's converting influence to all sentient beings and thus causing them all to obtain [the ultimate] bliss.
>
> "The precept that embraces all the rules of discipline" refers to the ten *pārājikas*.

The threefold precepts are taught in the *Shan-chieh-ching;* however, there are extended and abbreviated editions of this precept scripture. The extended text in nine volumes teaches the six *pāramitās* in full. The chapter on the precepts is in the first half of the fifth [volume]. In "The *Pāramitā* of the Precepts" it is taught that there are nine characteristics. The second characteristic is called "all precepts." Within these all the threefold pure precepts common to both monks and laity are taught. In explaining these threefold precepts it states, "First, there are the precepts; second, there is the precept [about] receiving all the good *dharmas*; and third, there is the practice of the precepts in order to benefit all sentient beings." Here the characteristics of the threefold precepts are taught in detail.

There is also the one-volume *Shan-chieh-ching* scripture. It is this scripture that the Hsien-shou master [Fa-tsang] referred to by the name *Ch'ung-lou chieh-ching* [The Precept Scripture Likened to a Double-Storied Pavilion].

As that scripture teaches, after one receives the three groups of precepts—the five precepts, the ten precepts, and full ordination—one then receives the bodhisattva's precepts. Here the bodhisattva's precepts mean all the threefold precepts. In presenting the threefold precepts it says, "the precept that embraces all paths to Enlightenment, and the precept that benefits all living sentient beings. . . ." These are none other than the two precepts that embrace all good *dharmas* and that embrace all sentient beings.

This scripture has its origins in the *karma-vacana* ritual in the ordination ceremony [in which one takes] the bodhisattva precepts. Consequently it only presents the twofold [precepts, as above] and abbreviates the precept that embraces all the rules of discipline. Thus it follows from the above sentences that one receives everything [when one receives] the bodhisattva's precepts.

This scripture teaches an abbreviated outline of the *karma-vacana* ritual. A description of the precepts is more fully presented within the eight major precepts of the monastic bodhisattva. These correspond to the four major precepts taught throughout the *Fan-wang-ching*. Later [in the *Fan-wang-ching*] some forty-odd items of the minor precepts are taught. These are in large measure identical to the minor precepts taught in *Yü-ch'ieh-lun*.

The expanded version of the *Shan-chieh-ching* expounds in greater detail the threefold precepts, and yet it does not teach the characteristics of the four major and forty minor precepts. These
7a characteristics of the threefold precepts are largely similar to those taught in the *Yü-ch'ieh-lun* and the *Ti-ch'ih-lun*.

The threefold precepts are taught in the *Chan-ch'a-ching*. In narrating the threefold precepts it states, "the precept that embraces all the rules of discipline, the precept that embraces all good *dharmas*, and the precept that embraces and converts all sentient beings. . . ."

These are explained more fully in the first volume of this scripture. The bodhisattva produces the mind of Enlightenment and learns the Way of the Mahayana; confessing his transgressions, he extirpates his transgressions. He makes a self-vow and [by means of this self-vow, he] receives all the threefold pure precepts.

When he has received the fundamental ten major prohibitive precepts of the bodhisattva, the teaching of the precepts is completed. This is none other than being called a *bhikṣu, bhikṣuṇī, śrāmaṇera,* or *śrāmaṇerikā,* etc. Each one studies the Vinaya Piṭaka of the *śrāvaka*s as well as the *Mātṛkā* of the bodhisattvas, etc.

The description of the practice of receiving all [the threefold precepts] is now clearly understood and given in ample detail.

The threefold precepts in other scriptures, whether stated in the text or implied in principle, are scattered throughout various texts and are in no way unified. However they may be known through this [description given above].

The threefold pure precepts of the various Mahayana commentaries are very broad in their terminology, their principles, their practice, and their explanations. Nevertheless, they are most profound when taught in the *Yü-ch'ieh-lun.* This is the fundamental *Mātṛkā.*

In the first, the "Pen-ti" section [of this commentary], the six *pāramitā*s in the realm of the bodhisattva are taught in full.

Within the *pāramitā* of the precepts, a ninefold classification of the precepts is taught. [The one called] "all the precepts" is the threefold precepts. These are the precepts kept by both lay and monastic bodhisattvas. Each one receives the threefold precepts and practices them in all its aspects. The text of the "Chüeh-tse" section on the *pāramitā* of the precepts goes into very great detail and illustrates it quite clearly.

The precepts are discussed in detail in other portions of the text too, wherever there is need for it.

The *Ti-ch'ih-lun* is a variant translation of [the section that deals with] the realm of the bodhisattva in the "Pen-ti" [i.e., the first] chapter of the *Yü-ch'ieh-lun.* For this reason it does not have the [following] "Chüeh-tse" chapters, etc.

In the chapter on the teaching of the precepts in the *She-ta-ch'eng-lun,* [the precepts are] regarded as "distinguished" (*vaśiṣta*). Here too the threefold precepts are taught.

In the ninth volume of the *Ch'eng-wei-shih-lun,* the threefold precepts are explained in their essentials in an abbreviated form.

Also in the section dealing with the second realm in the *Shih-ti-lun,* as well as in other commentaries, wherever there is an opportunity, the precepts are taught in either an expanded or an abbreviated manner.

Both the expanded and the abbreviated versions of the *Shan-chieh-ching* are the same as the *Yü-ch'ieh-lun.* Both texts of the *Shan-chieh-ching* are the preaching of the Tathāgata himself.

The *Yü-ch'ieh-lun* and the *Ti-ch'ih-lun* were preached by Maitreya. The reason that these are the same [in their teachings regarding the precepts] is because when the Tathāgata initially preached the *Shan-chieh-ching,* Maitreya heard it in person. Some nine hundred years after the extinction of the Tathāgata, Maitreya transmitted to the world this teaching that he had personally heard while the Buddha was in this world. It is for this reason that the *Yü-ch'ieh-lun* is identical to the *Shan-chieh-ching.*

Broadly speaking, the precept section of the *Yü-ch'ieh-lun* assembles all the teachings of the precepts taught by the Tathāgata throughout all the Mahayana scriptures and so constitutes one large store of teachings about *śīla.* In it, the ninefold [classification of the precepts] and the threefold precepts are enlarged upon and reconciled [into a harmonious whole] without hindrance.

It is both broad and deep, and all [teachings of the precepts] are included within it. It is not only the Mahayana but also the Vinaya legislated by the Hinayana. This is because the precept that embraces all the rules of discipline is made up of the precepts binding upon the seven groups of persons that constitute the Sangha. The Mahayana includes the Hinayana, as the three vehicles [i.e., the teachings of the *śrāvaka,* the *pratyekabuddha,* and the bodhisattva] are all practiced [by the Mahayanist]. [Hinayana precepts] have always been the bodhisattva's own Dharma; the Hinayana is identical [in this sense] to the Mahayana; and [the Mahayanist] does not see the [precepts as] Hinayana. It is for these reasons that the precept that embraces all the rules of discipline in the *Yü-ch'ieh-lun* is completely given over to the Vinaya Piṭaka [of the Hinayana].

Therefore, as it says in the seventy-fifth volume of this text,
7b "And again you must know that the Vinaya of the bodhisattva is in outline the threefold precepts. First is the precept that embraces all the rules of discipline. This group of Vinayas is the practice of the Vinaya that the Blessed One preached for the benefit of all sentient beings to be converted by the *śrāvakas*. Know then that this is none other than this group of Vinayas [i.e., the first of the threefold]."

This means that all precepts taught in the various Vinayas, such as the Fourfold [Dharmaguptaka Vinaya] and the Fivefold Vinaya [of the Mahīśāsakas], are identical to the precept that embraces all the rules of discipline. The characteristics of this precept and of the practices [of the Hinayana *Vinaya Piṭakas*] are very much the same.

Eighth Question

In what ways do the threefold precepts differ, and in what ways are they similar, within the various teachings?

Answer: The scriptures give the basic teachings of these principles. In essential outline they are explained in the *Ying-lo-pen-yeh-ching.*

The Abhidharma literature has produced an expanded commentary and an analysis of these precepts, the nature of which is exhaustively probed in the *Yü-ch'ieh-lun.*

Both texts of the *Shan-chieh-ching* were preached by the Tathāgata himself. Maitreya, being entrusted with this teaching, taught the *Yü-ch'ieh-lun;* hence the *Yü-ch'ieh-lun* is completely identical to the *Shan-chieh-ching.*

The *She-ta-ch'eng-lun* and the *Ch'eng-wei-shih-lun* are completely identical to the *Yü-ch'ieh-lun* in that the various teachings of the precepts that embrace all the good *dharma*s and that embrace all sentient beings do not vary [in the two texts].

However, the precepts that embrace all the rules of discipline taught in the *Ying-lo-pen-yeh-ching* and in the *Yü-ch'ieh-lun* differ [from one text to the other]. The differences are as follows.

In the *Ying-lo-pen-yeh-ching,* the ten major precepts constitute the precept that embraces all the rules of discipline. The first four major precepts are practiced in common [with the *śrāvaka*s], while the latter six are practiced not in common but exclusively by the bodhisattva. In the *Yü-ch'ieh-lun* [the precepts practiced by] the seven groups of persons who make up the Sangha constitute the precept that embraces all the rules of discipline. These are practiced in common with the *śrāvaka*s and are identical to the former four major precepts and various other minor items.

The precept that embraces all the rules of discipline in the *Ying-lo-pen-yeh-ching* is as quoted above. The precept that embraces all the rules of discipline in the *Yü-ch'ieh-lun* is as quoted in volume forty of that work: "The precept that embraces all the rules of discipline is the rules of discipline leading to separate deliverance [i.e., the *prātimokṣa-śīla*] for the seven groups of persons who make up the Sangha, as undertaken by all bodhisattvas. These are the precepts for *bhikṣu*s, *bhikṣuṇī*s, *śīkṣamāṇā*s, *śrāmaṇera*s, *śrāmaṇerikā*s, *upāsaka*s, and *upāsikā*s.

"These seven groups are based upon the two divisions: laity and monastics.

"In this way, know then that this is called the precept that embraces all the rules of discipline of the bodhisattva."

These are precisely the same as those precepts for the seven groups of persons who make up the Sangha, as undertaken by the *śrāvaka*s.

The threefold precepts in the *Chan-ch'a-ching* are the same as those in the *Yü-ch'ieh-lun*. The precept that embraces all the rules of discipline in the threefold precepts is made up of the precepts for the seven groups of persons that make up the Sangha. However, the [*Chan-ch'a-ching*] also teaches the ten fundamental precepts of the bodhisattva, which are the ten major precepts [mentioned above]. This constitutes the precept that embraces all the rules of discipline [In this respect, this text] is exactly the same as the *Ying-lo-pen-yeh-ching*.

Ninth Question

The precept that embraces all the rules of discipline [that is] taught in the *Ying-lo-pen-yeh-ching* and the one taught in the *Yü-ch'ieh-lun* differ. What is the reason for this?

Answer: The teaching of the *Ying-lo-pen-yeh-ching* is about Absolute Truth, while the *Yü-ch'ieh-lun* is about Conventional Truth.

Within the precept that embraces all the rules of discipline, there are precepts that pertain to the three kinds of action [of body, speech, and mind].

The precepts of body and speech are held in common [with the *śrāvaka*s], but the precepts pertaining to mental action are not held in common with the *śrāvaka*s [i.e., are unique to Mahayana bodhisattvas].

The precept not held in common with the *śrāvaka*s is the precept for the automatic ceasing of evil.

In the *Ying-lo-pen-yeh-ching* it is taught that the precept that embraces all the rules of discipline fully contains these three aspects of action. The precept that embraces all the rules of discipline [that is] taught in the *Yü-ch'ieh-lun* belongs to the precepts held in common with the *śrāvaka*s.

Therefore the precept that pertains to mental action is included in which group [of the threefold precepts]?

The purport of the *Wei-shih-shu* by the Tz'u-en master K'uei-chi was to clarify the difference between those precepts held in common and those not held in common with the *śrāvaka*s. K'uei-chi judged that those precepts [that are] held in common constitute the precepts that embrace all the rules of discipline, while the precept for the automatic ceasing of evil [i.e., the precept unique to Mahayana bodhisattvas] is included within the second of the

threefold precepts, the precept that embraces all good *dharmas*.
7c This is because the precept that embraces all good *dharmas* is common to the three aspects of action, for its principles are broad and all-encompassing; and because [the two precepts] to embrace all good *dharmas* and to embrace all sentient beings are not held in common with the *śrāvakas*.

Based upon the Absolute Truth, however, behind the precept to embrace all the rules of discipline, as it is not held in common with the *śrāvakas*, the precept for the automatic ceasing of evil is included within the category of the precept to embrace all the rules of discipline.

For this reason, the principle is identical to that taught in the *Ying-lo-pen-yeh-ching*. The precept that pertains to mental action is identical to the four major precepts in the *Yü-ch'ieh-lun:* namely, those precepts that follow [the prohibition against] "praising oneself and slandering others." In addition to these four major precepts, this text also teaches forty-two minor precepts. [There may be forty-three, -four, or -five interpretations of the minor precepts according to different interpretations.] They are all, however, the precepts of bodhisattvas and are not held in common with *śrāvakas*.

Tun-lin, by way of commentary, says, "The four *pārājikas* and the forty-two minor precepts of the bodhisattvas are all included either in the precept that embraces all good *dharmas* or in the precept that embraces all sentient beings. This precept [i.e., that embraces all good *dharmas*] was set up in this way. This is not the precept that embraces all the rules of discipline."

The master T'aehyŏn judged that the four major precepts not held in common with the *śrāvakas* constituted the basis of the threefold precepts, and that they were included within all of these threefold precepts.

The Hsien-shou master Fa-tsang has two explanations concerning the ten major precepts of the *Fan-wang-ching*.

First, reasoning from the position of the Absolute Truth, these ten major precepts are included within the precept that embraces all the rules of discipline, as both [precepts] are designed to put an end to evil.

Second, from the standpoint of commonly held principles, they are contained within all the threefold precepts. That is, if one does not violate any one [of these major precepts], then they are included within the precept that embraces all the rules of discipline; if one practices them to put [a stop to] the ten evil deeds, then they are included within the precept that embraces all good *dharmas*. If these two precepts are the means by which to convert all sentient beings, and if they are self-initiated action, then they constitute the precept that embraces all sentient beings.

Tenth Question

How do the forty-eight minor precepts taught in the *Fan-wang-ching* differ from, and how are they similar in aspect and in practice to, the forty-four minor precepts taught in the *Yü-ch'ieh-lun?*

Answer: The minor precepts of the *Yü-ch'ieh-lun* largely [concern] those in monastic life, while the minor precepts of the *Fan-wang-ching* are common to both monastics and laity.

Some of the minor precepts in this [the *Fan-wang-ching*] scripture and in this [the *Yü-ch'ieh-lun*] commentary are the same, and some are different.

The minor precepts of the *Yü-ch'ieh-lun* are legislated within the two precepts that embrace all good *dharmas* and that embrace all sentient beings. This commentary is similar to this scripture in the [above] latter two groups of precepts.

The precept that embraces all good *dharmas* legislates offenses against the six *pāramitās*; the precept that embraces all sentient beings legislates offenses against the four[fold means for the salvation of all sentient beings.]

The Hsien-shou master Fa-tsang, Uijŏk, Fa-hsien, and Sheng-chuang all made correspondences between the minor precepts of the *Fan-wang-ching* and those of the *Yü-ch'ieh-lun.* All those items that do not correspond are all thus distributed, and all the other items, be they existent or not, are all specifically amplified upon and explained.

As in the case of the scripture's [i.e., the *Fan-wang-ching*'s] precept against not paying respect to an elder, which corresponds to the third precept in the commentary [i.e., the *Yü-ch'ieh-lun*], the precepts against not confessing and repenting correspond to the seventh precept in the commentary; the precept against not being able to preach the Dharma corresponds to one portion of the third precept of the commentary; the precept against not hearing the scriptures and the Vinaya corresponds to the thirty-second precept in the commentary; the precept against turning one's back on orthodoxy and embracing heresy corresponds to the twenty-seventh precept in the commentary; the precept against ignoring sickness and pain corresponds to the thirty-fifth precept of the commentary; the precept against a pupil rebelling against what he has been taught corresponds to the thirty-sixth precept in the commentary; the precept against begrudging the Dharma corresponds to the sixth precept in the commentary; the precept against having an ignorant person as one's teacher corresponds to the eleventh precept in the commentary; the precept against not being able to save all sentient beings corresponds to the fifteenth precept in the commentary.

Such are the characteristics [of the precepts]. We have given them in this abbreviated manner for fear of being prolix.

Such precepts as those against the consumption of alcoholic
8a beverages, meat, and the five strong seasonings are not in the commentary.

Further details may be known by referring to the texts themselves.

Eleventh Question

The eighty thousand rules of conduct, as mentioned in both the *Fan-wang-ching* and the *Ying-lo-ching,* are included within which of the threefold precepts?

Answer: The eighty thousand rules of conduct are an elaboration of the ten major precepts. They adorn these basic major precepts and cause them to be more strongly upheld. They are entirely the same as the precept that embraces the two hundred fifty precepts [of the monastics]. In type, these precepts belong to the four basic major precepts; they adorn the major precepts and thus clarify these basic items.

Twelfth Question

If this is the case, then the two hundred forty-six precepts [of the *Ying-lo-ching*] should be contained within the eighty thousand rules of conduct, as they adorn the former four major precepts.

Answer: Whether they are thus contained or not is difficult to know, as they have not yet been transmitted [to China or Japan]. As for whether [the eighty thousand rules of conduct and the two hundred forty-six precepts] are the same or different, both these [positions] cannot be objected to.

Thirteenth Question

Do the forty-four minor precepts of the *Yü-ch'ieh-lun* therefore correspond to an elaboration of the latter four major precepts?

Answer: If one closely examines the text, these principles should be there. However, this question has not been decided, as there are many differences of interpretation.

Here, the latter four major precepts belong to the latter two [of the threefold pure precepts]; it is because of this that we arrive at this decision in this question and answer. If the latter four major precepts belonged to the precept that embraced all the rules of discipline, then they would not be able to be included in the teachings of the *Yü-ch'ieh-lun.*

Nevertheless, the Hsüan-yün master Tao-shih, on the basis of the *Ti-ch'ih-lun,* decided that the latter four major precepts constitute the precept that embraces all the rules of discipline. This would be [just as is taught in] the *Ying-lo-pen-yeh-ching.* On the basis of this, we may know that any elaboration of the latter four major precepts is entirely different from the fivefold division [in the precepts] of the *śrāvaka*s, as it is the teaching of precepts not held in common with the *śrāvaka*s.

The precepts that are elaborations upon the former four major precepts contain precepts not held in common with the *śrāvaka*s, as these former basic major precepts themselves are of a teaching not held in common with the *śrāvaka*s.

"One needle, one blade of grass" is legislated and this [precept against stealing] constitutes a major *pārājika* rule. Anything that destroys life in the six realms of rebirth [is the subject of a] *pārājika* rule.

Worldly gossip is legislated to constitute a major *pārājika* rule. In this way [bodhisattva precepts] differ from the precepts of the *śrāvaka*s.

Fourteenth Question

In the *Yao-shih-ching* it speaks of the four hundred precepts of the bodhisattva. What are they?

Answer: In his *Yao-shih-ching shu,* Tun-lin says:

> [A]s to the meaning of the four hundred precepts of the bodhisattva, in the [Liu-]Sung dynasty text it speaks of "twenty-four precepts of the bodhisattva Good Faith." It also says, "As for the bodhisattva's precepts, the Sui dynasty text speaks of 'one hundred four precepts.'"
>
> In I-ching's translation of the scripture, it speaks of "the four hundred precepts of the bodhisattva."
>
> When the Liu Sung text says "the twenty-four precepts," it means that the bodhisattva Good Faith is a woman householder, as taught in the *Shan-hsin p'u-sa-ching* and the *Chou hsiao-chou-ching.*
>
> In the second volume it says, "[A]s for the bodhisattva precepts, they are the bodhisattva precepts of monastics." Both the T'ang and Sui dynasty texts do not specifically explain this; we can only say that they explain laymen's precepts. The T'ang dynasty text says, "the four hundred precepts."
>
> The master Fa-tsang said, "The bodhisattva precepts have as their basis the ten virtues. The ten virtues are the five faculties, faith, etc., the three roots of good, lack of greed, etc., as well as humility and timidity; altogether these form the ten virtues. Each of the ten virtues passes through these ten, and thus they constitute one hundred. Each of these has
> 8b four aspects: (1) the self-keeping of these precepts, (2) the other-keeping of these precepts, (3) praise, and (4) sympathetic joy. In this way, they make up four hundred precepts."

> The Sui dynasty scripture speaks of "one hundred four precepts," as this has been mistakenly written and the character "four" has been placed on the bottom. However, this is not the orthodox teaching; we do not yet know what is decidedly true.

The master Fa-tsang imagined four hundred precepts. This Fa-tsang is the Hsien-shou master.

This should be the so-called "bodhisattva Vinaya Piṭaka" passage, yet this passage occurs nowhere in the *Fan-wang-ching shu* [of Fa-tsang]. That passage of Fa-tsang's comments upon the precepts of the various teachings in a general manner.

There are many [instances] in which this passage is referred to in the *Fan-wang-ching shu.* Although this quotation says that "we do not yet know what is decidedly true," we may provisionally take this definition to [describe] the characteristics of the practice [of the four hundred precepts in the *Yao-shih-ching*], as there are no variant characteristics given in the commentaries of any other masters.

Fifteenth Question

Minor bodhisattva precepts are taught in various other teachings. In general, how many differences are there in their number and in their characteristics?

Answer: The Hsien-shou master, Fa-tsang, explained the characteristics of the minor precepts in his tenfold teaching. These are the forty-four minor precepts of the *Yü-ch'ieh-lun* and the *Ti-ch'ih-lun*. The *P'u-sa-nei-chieh-ching* has forty-two minor precepts. The *Shan-sheng-ching* has, in addition to its six major precepts, some twenty-eight minor precepts.

According to the Vaipulya [i.e., miscellaneous Mahayana] scriptures, there are, besides the twenty-four precepts, twenty-five types [of minor precepts] that legislate against what is not to be done. All the scriptures after the above *P'u-sa-nei-chieh-ching* largely contain precepts of the laity. The *Yü-ch'ieh-lun* and the *Ti-ch'ih-lun* largely contain precepts of the monastics.

The forty-eight minor precepts of the *Fan-wang-ching* make up one hundred precepts when they are analyzed in more detail within this scripture. These two [divisions, i.e., into forty-eight and into one hundred precepts] are those that are kept by both laity and monastics.

The eighty thousand [i.e., the eighty-four thousand] rules of conduct have a separate chapter; there may be one hundred thousand as in the *She-ta-ch'eng-lun,* which quotes the *Vinaya-ghoṣala-sūtra;* or there may be a number ten times the number of [grains of] dust or sand, as is taught in the *Ta-chih-tu-lun.*

If, however, we rely upon a general, inclusive [definition of all such minor precepts], then the precepts of the *śrāvaka*s taught in the Vinaya Piṭaka consist of 246 precepts, 340 precepts, and

500 precepts, within which are the sixty thousand or the one hundred twenty thousand minute precepts.

These are all of the bodhisattva's precepts that are held in common with the *śrāvakas*. Such is the practice of the precept that embraces all the rules of discipline.

Sixteenth Question

As for the various masters in China who studied the Mahayana and who, understanding the Vinaya Piṭaka, kept the precepts and spread its teaching, did these masters rely upon the "general receiving of all of the threefold precepts" or upon the "separate receiving of the precept that embraces all the rules of discipline"?

Answer: All the various masters of the past have relied upon the "separate receiving" in their keeping of the Vinaya Piṭaka and in their propagation of the precepts.

In this tradition the Mahayana is studied, and the various masters have spread the teachings as was appropriate, so that their practices have been indefinite.

Their precepts are the threefold marvellous precepts, and their teachings on meditation and wisdom are of existence, emptiness, and the middle path.

It is solely the precept that embraces all the rules of discipline [and which is received in the "separate receiving"] that spreads the Vinaya Piṭaka. All the various masters of the past have [belonged to the] group [that has advocated this].

Seventeenth Question

Who is regarded as the chief master of this Vinaya tradition?

Answer: It is Tao-hsüan of Mount Chung-nan, the bright shining bodhisattva possessing Dharma-wisdom, who is regarded as the chief master of the Vinaya tradition. This master of Mount
8c Chung-nan, Tao-hsüan, was born during the Sui dynasty and spread his converting influence during the T'ang dynasty. He was a bodhisattva who spread the scriptures by means of the four supports, a patriarchal master who kept the Vinaya during the three periods of life. Living on Mount Chung-nan, he greatly spread the Vinaya Piṭaka. He was foremost in converting and embracing all sentient beings and in keeping the precepts.

His name flew to India in the west, and his fame bounded to eastern lands. He completely probed the profound depths of Mahayana principles. By writing a commentary on the *Lotus Sutra,* he spread forth the One Vehicle. By preaching on the *Parinirvāṇa-sūtra,* he spread the school of Buddha nature. By lecturing on the *Laṅkāvatāra-sūtra,* he revealed the principles of consciousness only. By mastering the *She-ta-ch'eng-lun,* he manifested its perfect principles. In commentaries he probed the *Ch'eng-shih-lun,* and in the Vinaya he spread the Fourfold [Dharmaguptaka Vinaya].

He served as a model [of conduct during the Period of] the imitation teaching, and he upheld the Dharma bequeathed by the Buddha.

In setting up a teaching, in explaining this tradition, and in showing forth its nature and teaching its function, he was so vast it is hard to think of him, so awe-inspiring it is impossible to calculate concerning him.

Eighteenth Question

How did the chief master of the Vinaya tradition, the great master of Mount Chung-nan Tao-hsüan, divide and classify the various teachings of the Buddha, and how did he propagate the Vinaya Piṭaka?

Answer: The blessed elder of Mount Chung-nan established this tradition by a doctrinal classification of four teachings. He relied upon conditions according to what was appropriate, and the permutations of his teaching were many and varied. Nevertheless, this master's intention lay in nothing other than the principles of the three insights and the three traditions.

As for the teaching of conversion, it is [the three insights of] nature, characteristic, and consciousness only, the insight into and understanding of which probe the most profound.

As for the teaching of legislation, it is [the three traditions] of existence, emptiness, and the perfect tradition, within which the nature of the precepts completes all reasoning.

The three insights are truly [i.e., are primarily] concerned with meditation and wisdom, but in addition include the nature of the precepts. The three traditions are truly concerned with the nature of precepts, but in addition include insight and understanding.

If, however, we were to make a more direct classification, then the three traditions are the learning of the precepts, in which both the Mahayana and the Hinayana are made manifest; the three insights are the learning of meditation and wisdom, in which both the partial and the full teachings are illumined.

The three learnings of the Hinayana and the three learnings of the Mahayana definitely have both their differences and their similarities since they are Mahayana and Hinayana. The doctrinal classification of the master Tao-hsüan probes all principles to the utmost.

If we should rely upon [classification to determine whether the teachings of the three insights and the three traditions are] equal, we must say that they are [rather classified into] subordinate versus primary teachings. Nevertheless, the three insights include the three learnings of both the Mahayana and the Hinayana, and the three traditions include both the partial and the full teachings. This definition is in reference to the teaching of the Buddha during his lifetime.

According to the purport of the master Tao-hsüan, [this doctrinal classification] lies solely within the Mahayana.

The nature of the precepts in the perfect tradition is the learning of the precepts [one of the three learnings so-called] of the Mahayana. Perfect insight into consciousness only is the [learnings of] meditation and wisdom in the Superior Vehicle. It is with such opinions that Tao-hsüan propagated and transmitted the Vinaya Piṭaka.

One should remember that the principles of the nature and of the practice, etc., of the precepts within the Fourfold [Dharmaguptaka] Vinaya tradition all go to create the perfect, unhindered marvellous precepts. By means of the deep the shallow is determined, by means of the superior the inferior is determined, by means of the broad the narrow is embraced, and by means of the perfect the partial is embraced.

Perfectly sudden, perfectly interpenetrating, it is the teaching of perfection. Consciousness only, mind only—such principles as these probe widely into the nature [of all things]. Being most profound, they exhaust the mysterious.

Differing doctrinal classifications have been numerous in different ages. Some have maintained that the three wheel [turnings] embrace all of the Buddha's teaching; some, that it is the two teachings of converting and of action [that do]. Some have maintained that converting and legislating embrace all of the teaching; some, that it is the two teachings of legislating and permitting.

Some maintain that Buddhism is the two teachings, gradual and sudden; the two Piṭakas of the Mahayana and the Hinayana; the three Piṭakas, the four Piṭakas, or the eight Piṭakas. Some quote the doctrines established by others, and some proclaim doctrines established by themselves. Some speak of the Vinaya tradition [as belonging] to the Hinayana; some [say] that it is common to both the Mahayana and the Hinayana. Some speak of the Vinaya tradition [as belonging] to the teaching of legislation only; some [say] that it is common to the teachings of conversion and legislation. Such principles are numerous, and the calculations are many.

9a According to the age, persons have classified the Vinaya tradition and have thus promoted the Great Way [i.e., the Mahayana].

Nineteenth Question

How many scriptures generally constitute the basic teachings of the Vinaya tradition? How are they classified?

Answer: It was the belief of the chief master Tao-hsüan that the Mahayana was unique and ultimate, transcendent, superior, and both broad and profound. [It was by] relying solely upon the mutually interpenetrating scriptures of this, the One Vehicle, that Tao-hsüan first conceived the thought of Enlightenment, thus studied and practiced, and kept [these precepts].

It is the *Lotus,* the *Parinirvāṇa,* the *Laṅkāvatāra,* and the *She-ta-ch'eng-lun* that constituted his practice and the basis of his propagation of the teaching. This highest Way of the One Vehicle is none other than the three learnings, which successively, one after the other, will speedily lead one to Buddhahood.

The learning of discipline in the Mahayana is constituted *in toto* by the threefold pure precepts because within these threefold pure precepts all practices [relating to discipline] are embraced. All precepts taught within the various Mahayana teachings are taken to constitute the teaching that is the support [of the Vinaya tradition]. [Examples are] those various places where the precepts are taught in the *Fan-wang-ching,* the *Ying-lo-ching,* the *Shan-chieh-ching,* and the *Shan-sheng-ching;* and in the *Ti-ch'ih-lun,* the *Yü-ch'ieh-lun,* the *Shih-ti-ching-lun,* and the *She-ta-ch'eng-lun.*

Those aspects of practice within the precept that embraces all the rules of discipline held in common with the *śrāvaka*s are completely identical with those aspects of practice taught in the various Vinaya Piṭakas. Therefore, in order to establish these actions [of the Mahayana precepts], the Vinaya Piṭaka is thus quoted and used.

Among all the various Vinaya Piṭakas of the Hinayana, the one truly used is the Fourfold [Dharmaguptaka] Vinaya, which, in addition, has points in common with all the other texts [of the Hinayana Vinaya Piṭaka].

Because of this, then, we may say that the teachings of the Vinaya tradition are a collection and an anthology of those precepts taught in both the Mahayana and Hinayana Piṭakas, which make up the [present] tradition of precepts and Vinayas.

With respect to the practices [of the Vinaya tradition], we may say that the full teachings of consciousness only, the one, true Mahayana, the marvellous traditions of perfection and suddenness, constitute the basis [of this Vinaya tradition].

It is the precepts and the Vinayas of the Ultimate One Vehicle that are upheld. Thus the practices of the Vinaya Piṭaka used [by this tradition] are all the highest, unhindered traditions of the Mahayana.

This is what is called the scriptural classification of the Vinaya tradition.

In the broad outlook of the One Vehicle, there is basically no distinction between Mahayana and Hinayana, as persons with a Hinayana capacity are basically of the One Vehicle; the teaching, the principles, the practice, and the result contained within the Hinayana are essentially those of the One Vehicle. For this reason, the Vinaya tradition is the perfect and sudden Mahayana. Both broad and deep, it is an unhindered great storehouse.

In the past, Buan *sōjō* (archbishop) of the Tōshōdai-ji composed, by imperial order, the three volume *Kairitsu-denrai-ki,* thus determining the doctrinal classification of the Vinaya tradition. This text says:

> *Question:* Is the Vinaya tradition included within the Mahayana or the Hinayana teachings?
>
> *Answer:* The learnings of all the various precepts are taken as a whole to constitute this one tradition.
>
> In our land [i.e., Japan], there have only been bodhisattva [i.e., Mahayana] Vinaya masters; there have never been any who, because of clinging to false views, perceived only the Hinayana.

In general, all the precepts in both the Mahayana and the Hinayana are brought together and are named the One Mahayana Vinaya tradition. They largely correspond to the profound thoughts of the *Yogācārabhūmi*.

The chief master Tao-hsüan, in his preface to the *Commentary on the Karma-vacana [Ritual],* said, "During the lifetime of the master, his idea was to save the one person. The apparent intent of his great teaching consists in revealing the one principle."

The "one person" is the oneness of those persons, namely, those who may be transported [to Enlightenment]. The "one principle" is the oneness of all principles. The "great teaching" is the
9b oneness of all teachings. All practices are embraced within the teaching, and the result [i.e., Enlightenment] is embraced within the principle.

"Practice" as related in the [above mentioned] preface means both the practice of stopping evil and the doing and maintaining of good. "Result" means the ultimate result of the most superior Enlightenment as quoted in the *Hua-yen-ching.*

In volume six of the *Nei-tien-lu* [a catalogue of Buddhist texts], it says, "In what is generally called the Mahayana, there is no teaching that is not embraced; on the basis of this, we must say that there is no separate Hinayana."

In the Chia-hsiang master Chi-tsang's *Nieh-p'an shu* (Commentary on the *Parinirvāṇa-sūtra*), quoting the teachings of the Hsing-huang master Fa-lang, it says, "Basically there are no Hinayana precepts; there are only Mahayana precepts."

Speaking more broadly this is precisely the meaning of "In all the Buddha-lands within the ten directions there is only One Vehicle; there are not two, there are not three—with the exception of the teaching of expedient means."

Now then, the explanation propounded by the Nan-shan master, Tao-hsüan, is also thus. Hence in his *Commentary on the Karma-vacana [Ritual],* as well as in his *Nei-tien-lu,* he quotes the passage "the Buddha-lands visible within the ten directions . . ." from the *Lotus Sutra* in order to establish his teaching of the precepts of the Unique One Vehicle.

The principles of the Hsiang-hsiang master, Fa-tsang, and the Ch'iu-lung master, Yüan-hsiao, are also the same [as the above].

From ancient times up to the present [these teachings have been considered] the Ultimate One Vehicle. The teachings of the precepts are likewise only the precepts of the One Vehicle.

For the sake of all those of Hinayana capacity, portions of the Mahayana are pointed out [to them as Hinayana], but those of Mahayana capacity see that this basic teaching has always been the One Vehicle.

In the *T'an-hsüan-chi* by the Hsiang-hsiang master, Fa-tsang, a passage from the *Scripture Preached in Response to a Request by Mañjuśrī* is quoted: "The eighteen sects of the Hinayana as well as the original two [sects, the Sthaviravāda and the Mahāsāṅghika] all emerged out of the Mahayana."

The Kuryong master, Wŏnhyo of Haedong, only explains the principles of the precepts of the Unique, One Mahayana in his *Commentary on the Śrīmālā-devī-sūtra.*

The Nan-shan master, Tao-hsüan, in his *Commentary on the Prātimokṣa,* quotes only the passage, "The eighteen as well as the original two [sects of Buddhism] all emerged out of the Mahayana."

These various principles [given above] are of one flavor and are equal one with the other.

In volume one of Tao-hsüan's *Hsing-shih-ch'ao,* the author profoundly demolished [the opinion that would] recognize the precepts and the Vinaya as being Hinayana. In this work he sets up the theory that in principle there is no gulf between the Mahayana and the Hinayana, and that enlightened understanding lies in the mind, not merely in the teaching.

In his preface to the *Chiao-chieh-i,* Tao-hsüan again demolishes those who hold the Vinaya to be Hinayana.

Know then that the tradition of the precepts as established by the Nan-shan master, Tao-hsüan, is the ultimate [tradition] of the Higher Vehicle, the purport of the One Vehicle, the perfect interpenetration of ultimate consummation, and a great store of the precepts.

Twentieth Question

For what reason did the Tathāgata appear in the world and legislate the precepts?

Answer: The Tathāgata, in accord with the needs of the world, legislated the precepts and the Vinaya in order to cause all sentient beings to experience the ultimate result which is Enlightenment. The bodhisattva generates the mind of Enlightenment, and, having Buddhahood as his aim, practices the ten thousand practices, benefitting himself and others.

The three learnings in the Mahayana form a gradual ascension. Of these three, one first decorates himself with the learning of the threefold precepts. Only afterwards can one succeed in the learnings of great meditation and great wisdom. When these threefold precepts are perfected, the result is that the three bodies [of the Buddha] are attained. But as for meditation and wisdom, only when there is need do they combine with the threefold precepts.

The bodies, the Dharma Body, the Recompense Body, and the Transformation Body, are the Absolute and the Ultimate.

If we speak generally of why it is that the Tathāgata taught the threefold precepts, we say that it was to cause all sentient beings to return to the source from whence they came.

If we speak specifically, we should say in short that there were ten reasons.

First, it was because he desired to reveal the marvellous result that is the three bodies of the self-enlightenment of the Tathāgata, in order that all sentient beings should believe, understand, practice, and be enlightened to it.

9c Second, he wished to cause sentient beings to realize the three causes of the Buddha nature inherent in their own minds.

Third, it was in order to cause sentient beings to produce the three minds. The three minds are a straightforward mind, a profound mind, and a mind of great compassion. The three minds in this order are the cause of the ultimate result.

Fourth, it was in order to cause sentient beings to realize the great outstanding qualities of the nature, characteristics, and function of the Absolute.

Fifth, it was in order to cause sentient beings to [engage] in the three types of marvellous practice: the cutting off of evil, the cultivation of good, and the saving of all sentient beings.

Sixth, it was in order to cause sentient beings to fulfill the three "transferences of merits," namely, the transference of merits to reality [i.e., to help achieve one's own Nirvana], the transference of merits to *bodhi* [i.e., to strengthen one in the quest for Enlightenment], and the transference of merits to all sentient beings [i.e., to aid them in their quest for Nirvana].

Seventh, it was in order to cause sentient beings to be enlightened in part to the three bodies [of the Buddha].

Eighth, it was in order to cause sentient beings to attain the Buddhahood of the perfect three bodies [of the Buddha].

Ninth, it was in order to cause sentient beings to experience the qualities of the Dharma Body, *prajñā,* deliverance, the cutting off [of delusions], wisdom, and compassion.

Tenth, it was in order to cause sentient beings to cut off and remove the three hindrances, passions, actions, and evil rebirths, both inside and outside of the three realms [of desire, form, and nonform].

The teachings of the threefold precepts taught in all the Mahayana teachings, such as the *Fan-wang-ching,* etc., are as given above. These are the teachings of the "general receiving" of all of the threefold precepts.

The teachings of the "separate receiving" of the first of the threefold precepts are none other than the teachings of all the Vinayas.

In the case of the Fourfold [Dharmaguptaka] Vinaya, it was in order to cause the complete extirpation of the three poisons [of greed, anger, and ignorance] that the learning of the precepts was legislated. This was done in order that the undefiled Way of saintliness might be attained; it was not in order that worldly fortune or pleasures might be obtained.

An ultimate result (i.e., Enlightenment) in the Hinayana completely cuts off the hindrance of passions. The bodhisattva also completely cuts off the hindrance of passions. The Enlightenment inherent in those rules [of discipline] undertaken in common with the *śrāvaka*s must of necessity be obtained and understood. Those precepts that are not undertaken in common with the *śrāvaka*s and that provide for the automatic stopping of evil are those *dharma*s that by themselves cut off passions.

These *dharma*s thwart the ten [evil] deeds and crush the two hindrances; they cut off the seeds of the two hindrances and remove any influences of the two hindrances. The precepts undertaken in common, and those not undertaken in common, the general practice and the separate practice, these fuse together and mutually establish [one another]; and the great event [i.e., the attainment of Buddhahood] is perfected.

Twenty-first Question

What are the characteristics of the previously mentioned teaching of the three insights of the grand master of Nan-shan, Tao-hsüan?

Answer: The three insights are first, the teaching of the emptiness of nature. A perception of this principle of emptiness puts an end to belief in the soul and in *dharmas*. Those with Hinayana natures are dull and are unable [to perceive] "emptiness-in-identity." Although the belief in a permanent personal nature is destroyed, belief in the permanent nature of *dharmas* is only set aside. But as regards the emptiness of the *dharmas* and of the self, this teaching regards emptiness as its major principle.

Due to the insight and understanding of this teaching, the defilements are extirpated, one is enlightened to the principles of extinction, and one obtains the result of each one of the three vehicles. This teaching is [made up of] the four *Āgamas* and other works; the Mahāsāṅghika Vinaya, the Fourfold [Dharmaguptaka] Vinaya, and other works; and the *Abhidharma-kośa,* the *Ch'eng-shih-lun,* and other commentaries. All the various teachings of the Hinayana are embraced in this [teaching].

Second, the teaching of the emptiness of characteristics. This destroys the belief in the characteristics of the soul and of *dharmas*. The nature and characteristics of the soul and of *dharmas* [believed in] by non-Buddhists and by common persons are [seen to be] eternally "identical-with-emptiness." This teaching is the teaching, principles, practice, and result of the minor bodhisattvas.

This is all in the *prajñā-pāramitā* scriptures as well as the commentaries on these texts. It is taught that characteristics are empty. This is none other than the insight into and the understanding of emptiness. All such scriptures are embraced within this teaching.

Third, the teaching of consciousness only. All the various
10a dharmas are in their outward appearance basically nonexistent. In reality, only consciousness exists. Nature and characteristic are perfectly interfused.

This is the most profound, most marvellous practice of the great bodhisattvas. This is all in the perfectly ultimate, most subtly marvellous scriptures, Vinayas, and commentaries of the Mahayana, such as the *Hua-yen, Laṅkāvatāra, Lotus, Nirvāṇa, She-ta-ch'eng-lun,* and others. All are embraced within this teaching.

This teaching of the three insights embraces all the teachings [of the Buddha] during his lifetime. In such a doctrinal classification nothing at all is omitted.

The teaching of the emptiness of nature corresponds to the first period of the *Fa-hsiang* [in which a vast number of teachings were taught]; the [*Piṭaka*] teachings of the *T'ien-t'ai;* and the Hinayana teachings of stupid Dharmas [as defined by] the *Hua-yen.*

The teaching of the emptiness of characteristics corresponds to the teachings of emptiness of the second period of the *Fa-hsiang;* the pervasive teaching of the *T'ien-t'ai;* and the initial teaching of Mahayana emptiness coupled with the teaching of existence in the *Hua-yen.*

The teaching of consciousness only corresponds to the truth of the middle path of the third period of the *Fa-hsiang;* the separate and perfect teachings of the *T'ien-t'ai;* and the three teachings of finality, of suddenness, and of perfection in the *Hua-yen* tradition.

Twenty-second Question

What [element] is it that constitutes the nature of such a sealike teaching [of Buddhism] as is expressed in the teaching of the three insights and in the Tripiṭakas of the Mahayana and the Hinayana?

Answer: The element that constitutes the nature of the teaching being expressed is not always the same.

If we refer to the three teachings in order to clarify the essence of its nature, then within the teaching of emptiness, the tradition is divided into existence and emptiness. There are four aspects to the classification of nature in the Abhidharma tradition of existence. These are voice (*śabda*), name (*nāma*), sentence (*pāda*), and letter (*vyañjana*).

The sound that is produced when the four major elements collide is called 'voice.' The principle of its activity or function, which is called 'name,' etc., is established with respect to 'voice.'

In the *Mahā-vibhāṣā,* the theories of two masters are given. One says, "[The *dharma*] 'voice' constitutes the nature of the twelvefold teachings [of the Buddha]." Another says, "The Dharma taught by the Buddha has as its nature the elements 'name,' 'sentence (*pāda*),' and 'letter.'"

These two principles are in the *Fa-chih-pen-lun.* So for this reason, commentators have taken individually [whatever they wished] to constitute the nature [of the teaching]. However, it is a principle of the school of critics that 'voice' constitutes its nature.

In the *Cheng-li-lun* and the *Hsien-tsung-lun* 'name' is held to constitute the nature [of Buddhism]. In the *Tsa-hsin-lun* and the *Abhidharma-kośa* both principles are presented together, and no choice is made between them. Hence both are used here [in these texts]. In the tradition of "Temporary Names"—the Dharmaguptakas, the Sautrāntikas, and the *Ch'eng-shih-lun,* 'voice' is held to constitute the essence of the nature of Buddhism.

If we resort to the principle of inclusion [which is designed to include disparate elements into one comprehensive definition], then this would embrace [the *dharmas* of] 'name,' 'sentence ,' and 'letter.' In the first part of the first section of Tao-hsüan's *Yeh-shu,* where the author narrates what the nature of the teaching of the *karma-vacana* is, he says, "However, the Dharma of this teaching truly depends upon the accomplishment of subordinate conditions. Subordinate conditions are common to the spheres inside [the three worlds of desire, form, and nonform] and outside of them. If we were to define their natures, then we would become prolix. The principle of asking the consent (*kṣānti*) of the Sangha is none other than regarding a succession of the material characteristics of 'voice' as its nature."

This is the definition of nature in the *Ch'eng-shih-lun* tradition. Truly it may be said to be 'voice'; that is to say, the nature has 'voice' [as its essential element].

Should we definitely judge what the nature of the teaching of the Tripiṭaka of the Mahayana and the Hinayana as preached by the Tathāgata is, it is the same as this [above].

Within the Mahayana the perfect teaching of consciousness only does not appear in the master Tao-hsüan's doctrinal classification. On the basis of his principles, however, we may narrate one [for him]. The difference between provisional and real is clear. [*Dharmas* in] the form of 'name', 'sentence (*pāda*)', and 'letter' constitute the nature of Buddhism. Embracing the provisional and proceeding from the real [i.e., from the standpoint of the Absolute], 'voice' constitutes its nature. Embracing the spheres [perceived by the senses] and proceeding from the mind, consciousness only
10b constitutes its nature. Embracing the [various] characteristics and referring to nature, Ultimate Reality constitutes its nature here. When these four terms harmoniously fuse, the Mahayana teaching is formed. To mention one is to embrace them all.

When the various characteristics are destroyed, and when one enters into emptiness, then the negation of these four terms constitutes the nature [of the teaching].

Twenty-third Question

What are the steps by which the practitioner of the Mahayana attains the purport of the *Vinaya Piṭaka?*

Answer: If a person attains the purport of the Vinaya texts, then he will progress from the general [receiving of all of the threefold pure precepts] to the separate [receiving of the precept that embraces all the rules of discipline], from the broad to the narrow, for it is the narrow that perfects the broad.

An expectation directed toward the three learnings constitutes the gradual origin of this practice. One vows to uphold the threefold precepts and thus embraces all practices.

The separate receiving of the precept that embraces all the rules of discipline completes the practice of those precepts held in common with the *śrāvaka*s. All the various precepts that are thus held in common form, every one of them, the threefold precepts.

The expanded practice of these threefold precepts includes meditation and wisdom.

The Vinaya master Chih-shou, in the first volume of his *Ssu-fen-lü shu* (Commentary on the Fourfold Dharmaguptaka Vinaya), says, "The bodhisattva has threefold precepts: the precept that embraces all good *dharma*s, the precept that embraces all sentient beings, and the precept that embraces all the rules of discipline.

"There are three types of precepts that embrace all the rules of discipline: first, the *dhyāna* rules of discipline, which are the precepts that accompany [the state of] meditation; second, the undefiled rules of discipline, which are the precepts that accompany [entry into] the path; and third, the rules of discipline of separate deliverance (*prātimokṣa*), which are the five precepts, the eight, the ten, and all the precepts." The Vinaya master Chih-shou looked to the *Chan-ch'a-ching* in his explanation of the Dharma of the Mahayana.

The threefold pure precepts are either vowed by oneself or received from others. Such are the *dharmas* of the two types of receiving [of the threefold precepts].

If one receives the threefold precepts in a general manner, then from among [the three] one relies upon the precept that embraces all the rules of discipline, and that applies to the seven classes of beings in the Sangha: *bhikṣus*, *bhikṣuṇīs*, etc. This is as given in that commentary [above], volume one, which quotes the teaching of the scripture [i.e., the *Chan-ch'a-ching*], thus causing the practitioner to search out this scripture [for himself]. Therein the characteristics of the practice of the two types of receiving of the precepts, the general receiving and the specific receiving, are fully and completely provided.

The various masters of the New School of Translation [i.e., post-Hsüan-tsang] opened up in great detail the portals [of this teaching]. The various masters of the Old School of Translation likewise grasped these profundities.

The grand master Chih-shou was one from whom the Nan-shan master, Tao-hsüan, and the Hsüan-hui master, Tao-shih, received their teachings. Both teacher and pupil were fragrant [in the Dharma] and upheld the principles [of the teaching].

As the Nan-shan master, Tao-hsüan, pointed out in his *Kuei-ching-i,* the receiving and following of the threefold precepts in the correct practice of Buddhism are nothing other than the general receiving of all of the threefold precepts. Such are the characteristics of the perfect teaching.

However, the characteristic of this practice as explained in the three major works [of Tao-hsüan] is none other than the separate receiving [of the first of the threefold precepts, that precept that embraces all the rules of discipline]. This is the Way of practice of both stopping evil and doing good. Both phenomenon and principle are in perfect supply; there is nothing at all lacking.

Twenty-fourth Question

Why are these threefold precepts called the precepts that embrace all the rules of discipline, etc.?

Answer: There are rules for departing from evil, and these are called "all the rules of discipline" (*saṃvara*). Within all these rules of discipline are embraced many [rules], which however are contained within this one term. This is what is meant by "embraces." [The many rules contained within the precept that embraces all the rules of discipline are classified into three], namely, meditation, purity, and separate deliverance.

The rules of discipline are none other than this precept, so it is called the precept [that embraces] all the rules of discipline, a *karmadhāraya* [compound].

There are rules for following [the teaching] and benefitting [oneself and others]. These are called the "good *dharma*s." The good *dharma*s are numerous and are all embraced in this teaching. This is what is meant by the term "embraces."

Nothing other than this precept embraces [all] the good *dharma*s, [so it is called the precept that embraces all the good *dharma*s], a *karmadhāraya* [compound]. Those who are produced by multiple conditions are termed "all sentient beings," and the term "embraced" means that they are led to revert to good. Embracing all sentient beings is none other than this precept, [so it is called the precept that embraces all sentient beings]: a *karmadhāraya* [compound].

The reason why they are in general called "the threefold [pure] precepts" is that "three" is a number; a collection of elements is called "-fold"; separating from error is called "pure"; and, guarding
10c against evil constitutes "precepts." It is a *dvigu* [compound] that receives its name from its function.

Twenty-fifth Question

The precept that embraces all the rules of discipline refers in general to the *Vinaya Piṭaka.* How many names are there for the precepts taught in this *Vinaya Piṭaka?*

Answer: The term Vinaya precepts has numerous meanings, but broadly speaking, [its meanings] do not exceed three.

First, it is called the Vinaya, which translated [into Chinese] becomes "rules." The rules mean the Dharma, so it thus gets its name from its teachings.

Second, it is called *śīla,* which translated means "precepts." [The meaning of *śīla*] is "to admonish" and refers to both good and evil. The good precepts guard against [evil] wrongdoing and thus encompass the three types of actions [i.e., of body, speech, and mind].

Third, it is called the *prātimokṣa,* which translated means "separate deliverance." [Various] precepts separately guard against wrongdoing; and according to the sphere [to which each precept applies], one attains deliverance. Deliverance is the result. Thus while [the practitioner is] still within the causal state, the result is taught.

Twenty-sixth Question

What are the seven classes of persons that make up the Sangha within the precept that embraces all the rules of discipline, and what are their *dharma*s?

Answer: Bhikṣu, bhikṣuṇī, śikṣamāṇā, śrāmaṇera, śrāmaṇerikā, upāsaka, and *upāsikā;* these are the seven classes of persons. *Bhikṣu*s and *bhikṣuṇī*s receive the full ordination (*upasampadā*); *śikṣamāṇā*s undertake six *dharma*s; *śrāmaṇera*s and *śrāmaṇerikā*s undertake the ten precepts; and *upāsaka*s and *upāsikā*s both undertake the five precepts.

The eight precepts of abstinence are the *dharma*s of "residing near" [to the life of the monks, *upavasatha*]. According to the Abhidharma, this lies outside of the seven groups of persons. This one is added to the other seven, and then this is called the eight types of rules of discipline. According to the *Ch'eng-shih-lun,* however, these eight *upavasatha* precepts are included within the category of [the precepts of] laymen of pure faith [i.e., *upāsaka*s and *upāsikā*s].

All these various precepts are called the *dharma*s of the seven groups of persons who make up the Sangha. Those who practice the Buddha's Dharma, whether they be Mahayana or Hinayana, are to be found only within these seven groups of persons and nowhere else.

Now what we have explained here are the seven groups of bodhisattvas. Those precepts held in common [by the bodhisattva] are identical with those of the *śrāvaka*s.

But the precept that embraces all the rules of discipline and that is not held in common with the *śrāvaka*s is that which is upheld by the seven groups of bodhisattvas.

The precept that embraces all good *dharmas* and the precept that embraces all sentient beings are the precepts that are held by these seven groups [of Mahayana bodhisattvas] and are not held in common with the Hinayana *śrāvakas* but are practiced above and apart from them. Indeed, all practices are practiced by these seven groups [of Hinayanists]; so those who practice the Mahayana also must not fail in this.

Twenty-seventh Question

What constitutes the nature of those precepts received and upheld by the seven classes of bodhisattvas, whether generally or separately received?

Answer: The teaching concerning the nature of the precepts is the very eye of the Vinaya tradition, the bone and marrow of the learning of the precepts.

It is by this nature that one who practices these precepts is enabled to perceive sentient beings minutely. The purport of the precepts upheld by the student lies in this teaching. It is that from whence all practices emerge, the object of reverence and veneration of a multitude of virtues.

There is a fourfold division [of the precepts]; their content, their nature, their practice, and their characteristics.

Their content is the rules instituted by the Buddha; their nature is that which is undertaken by the person who practices the precepts; their practice is that which is embraced by the practitioner; and their characteristics are the attributes of the precepts that are practiced. When all the fourfold divisions of these marvellous precepts appear at one time, then one's intention is fulfilled, and all their lovely qualities are made perfect.

Within this fourfold division of the precepts, the teaching of the nature of the precepts is the most essential; indeed, it is the very basis of their origins. This nature of the precepts is called [an element that is both] "active and nonactive." It is also called "productive and nonproductive." The masters of the New School of Translation have called it [an element that is] seen and unseen [i.e., *vijñapti-avijñapti-rūpa*].

The active precepts are the path by which this nonactive [element] is generated, since it is from the active element that the

nonactive element is produced. The nonactive element is a nature
11a that is produced by the active element. It is always arising and eternally continuous, having as it does a superior ability [for such activity]. Within the threefold pure precepts there is both the active and nonactive element; this is the nature of the precept that is subsumed within the threefold [pure] precepts. Within the precept that embraces all the rules of discipline, all the precepts of the seven classes of persons that make up the Sangha have both these active and nonactive elements. Each one of these aspects of the nature [of the precepts] applies to the teaching of the separate receiving of these precepts.

The terms "seen" and "unseen" apply to both its particulars and its principles.

In the *Hsing-shih-ch'ao* of the grand master of Nan-shan, Tao-hsüan, the nature of the precepts as given in the *Ch'eng-shih-lun* is directly presented. In his *Yeh-shu* he fully presents the nature of the precepts as taught in the two traditions of existence and emptiness. Consequently he has related the opinions of these two traditions. Finally, Tao-hsüan narrates his own opinion and calls that principle the correct principle, the marvellous tradition that decides [all questions] and sunders [all doubts].

Setting up the doctrinal classification of the three traditions, he judged the depth or shallowness of the teaching. The traditions of existence, of emptiness, and of the perfect teaching are called the three traditions. The marvellous ideas of the patriarchal master Tao-hsüan, his decisions and his judgements, lie herein. It is by means of the deep that one decides what is shallow, and thus one proceeds to the limits of the Mahayana.

We shall now directly present the perfect teaching. The idea of the perfect is universally comprehensive, and its principles embrace everything. The Mahayana of the threefold pure precepts is fundamental among all Buddhists. This is none other than the perfect teaching, which has an exhaustive and final, marvellous nature.

For this reason, the precept that embraces all the rules of discipline has an independent ordination. In its nature, its characteristics are identical [one with another]. This is the most perfect, swift, and marvellous nature of the precepts. Thus Tao-hsüan originally propagated this separate ordination.

Now we shall clarify the nature of the perfect teaching by explaining the position of the Vinaya within the Fourfold [Dharmaguptaka] Vinaya tradition.

One who is a bodhisattva produces the mind of the One Vehicle and, relying upon the *Vinaya Piṭaka* of the Hinayana, receives all the precepts [*upasampadā*] in a *karma-vacana* ordination ritual. The precepts that are thus received accomplish the most profound and most broad, perfect nature [of these precepts]. The ritual of the *karma-vacana* ordination is basically a One Vehicle Dharma performed by a person who practices the perfect teaching.

One who attains sudden Enlightenment practices this Dharma of receiving the precepts according to the degree to which it was originally innate in him. It is thus that he receives the marvellous, unhindered precepts of the Mahayana.

It is the ritual of the separate ordination that accomplishes this tradition of the perfect teaching, as it is the one true nature of the precepts. Obtaining the *karma-vacana* ordination perfumes the storehouse consciousness (*ālaya-vijñāna*). The marvellous relationships of the *karma-vacana* perfume to perfection the nature of the storehouse [consciousness]. It is thus by reason of the arising of the perfect ideas of the Mahayana.

It was by means of the perfect teachings of consciousness only that Tao-hsüan explained in a straightforward manner the nature of the active and nonactive elements of the precept leading to separate deliverance within the precept that embraces all the rules of discipline.

Now we shall also explain the nature of the precepts leading to separate deliverance according to those texts of Tao-hsüan. Later we shall explain in greater detail the nature of the active and nonactive elements with reference to all the threefold pure precepts.

First, the nature of the precepts leading to separate deliverance [i.e., the *prātimokṣa*] within the precept that embraces all the rules of discipline means that when one receives the precepts, there is action of body and of speech. Prostrations and bows, lowering the head and raising the hands in veneration, are all actions of the body. Asking for the precepts, and answering one's teacher in a quiet location are actions of speech. Thus a thought that causes the body to move is considered to be of the nature of the element of action with regard to the body. Likewise, a thought that produces speech is considered to be of the nature of the element of action with regard to speech.

The ritual of receiving the precepts is completely perfected when these three items [in the ordination ceremony] are finished [i.e., the elements of body, speech, and thought].

The element of nonaction (*avijñapti-rūpa*) means that when the third item [of the above three] is finished, when the ritual of receiving the precepts is perfected, then the element of nonaction is produced. It possesses the ability to guard against distant [future error]. One [moment of] thought at this time accomplishes these two types of nature [of the precepts], namely action of body and speech, and the nature of nonaction.

Both body and speech have the ability to guard against [future error] and so both are said to constitute the precepts.

In one moment of thought, the active element disappears. Then it is only the nonactive element that thereafter evolves. When this active element is perfected, then the seed (*bīja*) that has been
11b perfumed upon a thought of good comes to be of the nature of these precepts. It serves to guard against error for the lifetime of the individual and continues in this function for a long time. The place where this perfumed seed resides is the eighth consciousness. This constitutes the place that has been perfumed.

The self-nature of the *ālaya* [i.e., the storehouse consciousness] maintains [this seed], and it is never lost.

Both [the teaching] set up by Tao-hsüan and [the teaching] established by the words of the texts truly take this seed as the nature of the precepts. However, this seed-nature must of necessity possess potentiality. When this potentiality is revealed, it is truly revealed in subsequent action. Nevertheless, it is not dependent upon subsequent action; rather, there is the quality of guarding [against future error] in this perfumed seed-nature. It is this quality of guarding [against future error] that is regarded as constituting the nature of the precepts.

This is embracing the peripheral and proceeding to the basic. Thus the seed-natures constitute the nature of the precepts. The basic and the peripheral are separately explained.

Regarding this potentiality as the nature [of the precepts] is [the teaching] set up by the Tz'u-en master K'uei-chi and others of the New School of Translation. They discuss this potentiality separately with regard to whether it is basic or peripheral, and thus they regard it as the nature [of the precepts].

Twenty-eighth Question

Are there examples of this in the commentaries of other masters?

Answer: The Hsiang-hsiang master, Fa-tsang, in propounding the nature of the precepts, said, "The precepts are established with regard to the seed-natures of thought. Hence these seed-natures of thought constitute their nature." This is discussing the seed-natures by "embracing the peripheral and proceeding from the basic."

This is exactly the same as Tao-hsüan's regarding the seed-natures as being the nature of the precepts; for in his *Yeh-shu* he says, "In the storehouse of basic consciousness the seeds of good are produced; these are the nature of the precepts."

Also the Dharma master Sheng-chuang said:

> If we regard the seed of the thought of a superior long-range vow as constituting the nature of the nonactive rules of discipline this would be because such [rules] are provisionally established by the seeds of such thoughts. Such a teaching teaches [us] to embrace the provisional and proceed to the real.

This is clearly and decidedly what is called proceeding to the real. This is exactly the same as the understanding of the master Tao-hsüan.

Although Fa-tsang and Sheng-chuang regarded thought as the nature [of the precepts], still their real opinion was that potentiality constituted its nature.

The master Tao-hsüan held that the seeds constitute the nature of the precepts; he made this judgement of principles because [in his thinking] he embraced the provisional and proceeded to the real. The seeds must of necessity have potentiality, so guarding against wrong constitutes their nature. The texts of the Old School of Translation discuss the nature of the precepts in this manner.

The teachings and commentaries of the New School of Translation narrate this in great detail; the *Ch'eng-wei-shih-lun* and other works reveal its fine points very thoroughly. As given above, it is with reference to the precepts leading to separate liberation within the precept that embraces all the rules of discipline that the nature of the precepts is explained.

The nature of the precepts of the whole of the threefold pure precepts lies in guarding against evil and producing good on the part of the seeds. Here the nature of these precepts does not differ [from the above].

The storehouse consciousness in the aspect of its holding these seeds is the same. Although in general receiving all the precepts differs from independent receiving of the precept that embraces all the rules of discipline, their structures and their functions are the same.

The nature of the threefold pure precepts in this perfect teaching is exactly one and the same as the nature of the precept that embraces all the rules of discipline.

The characteristics of the nature of the threefold pure precepts need not be separately discussed. However, it is receiving the precept that embraces all the rules of discipline with perfect intentions that constitutes the nature of all of these threefold pure precepts. Indeed, is it not a fact that the precept that embraces all the rules of discipline is the perfect product of all of the threefold pure precepts? As their principles are in mutual harmony, their reasons interpenetrate, and they possess each other to completion.

This perfect teaching is basically the teaching of the threefold pure precepts; and the precept that embraces all the rules of discipline is perfectly produced out of this basic, perfect [teaching].

For this reason, the nature of the precepts, whether it is generally received with all the threefold precepts, or with the independent receiving of the precept that embraces all the rules of discipline, is the same. Only the [element of] action or nonaction of thought has been added.

The above quotation from Sheng-chuang is a narration of the nature of the threefold pure precepts. [This has been a quotation] from a portion of his text.

The explanations of the Hsiang-hsiang master, Fa-tsang, are an elucidation of the precepts of the *Fan-wang-ching;* and this is none other than a narration of the nature of the threefold pure precepts.

11c The master Fa-hsien has said, "The three[fold pure precepts] rely upon the Mahayana. The active precepts have as their nature the thought that brings into action the three actions [of body, speech, and mind].

"The two actions of the body and speech have for their nature the thoughts that initiate movement, and mental action has for its nature the two thoughts of observation and of judgement."

The *Ch'eng-wei-shih-lun* says, "Thought that activates the body is called bodily action; thought that initiates the action of speech is called vocal action. As the two thoughts, observation, and judgement are conjoined with the mind, and as they activate the mind, they are called mental action.

"The precepts of nonaction have as their natures the capability of guarding against evil that is possessed by the mental seeds of the three actions [of body, speech, and mind].

"From the mind of a bodhisattva, one produces a mental vow; consciousness is perfumed and seeds are produced that extend to later ages. And entering into the stages of residual-mind, no-mind, etc., cannot be called 'losing the precepts.'"

This completely explains the nature of all of the threefold pure precepts. If we, however, individually elucidate the natures of the [various units within] the threefold pure precepts [we should say the following]:

[First], the nature of those precepts held in common with the *śrāvaka*s within the precept that embraces all the rules of discipline is none other than the seeds of the above-mentioned perfect teachings. Even if they are obtained in but an instant, they complete those precepts that are not held in common with the *śrāvakas*.

Although this precept has an independent ordination, it fully accomplishes the three actions. In addition, the precept that embraces all the rules of discipline contains the principles of all the threefold pure precepts.

[Second], the precept that embraces all good *dharmas* is the action of practicing all good. Meditation and wisdom are practiced by the three actions [of body, speech, and mind]. All the many practices of the six *pāramitās* are the constituent elements of Enlightenment.

As taught by the *Yü-ch'ieh-lun,* the nine good actions, i.e., the three wisdoms, the three actions, right meditation, right knowledge, right actions, etc., are contained within the precept that embraces all good *dharmas*. These are the characteristics of the active keeping [of this precept] that prohibits and guards against the sin of not cultivating all good *dharmas*.

It is the capability of guarding against evil and producing good on the part of the seeds of good thoughts that constitutes the nature of the precept that embraces all good [*dharmas*].

[Third] is the precept that embraces all sentient beings; these are all actions—the four means by which all beings are saved, the four unlimited [hearts]—that save all sentient beings. These are the characteristics of the active keeping of this precept.

As taught in the *Yü-ch'ieh-lun,* the salvation of all sentient beings has eleven characteristics; these are, however, only the four means by which all beings are saved. According to need, these characteristics are amplified.

This precept prohibits the transgression of not working for the benefit [i.e., the salvation] of all sentient beings. Here, too, it is the capability to guard against evil and produce good with respect to the seeds of good thoughts that constitutes the nature of the precepts that embrace all sentient beings. The natures of the last two of the threefold precepts contain in each of them all the threefold pure precepts.

Of the two teachings—of receiving all the threefold pure precepts, and of receiving only the precept that embraces all the rules of discipline—if one is mentioned, all are included. Each separate characteristic contains in itself all the threefold pure precepts.

Twenty-ninth Question

Within the precept that embraces all the rules of discipline, which element is it that constitutes the tradition as expressed in the Fourfold [Dharmaguptaka] Vinaya?

Answer: The different explanations of the various masters who set up the tradition of the Fourfold Vinaya of old are many and various. In abbreviated form, ten schools may be given.

(1) A certain master held that ceasing evil and doing good constitute this tradition.

(2) The Vinaya master Tao-hui held that receiving and following the precepts constitute this tradition.

(3) A certain master held that the stopping of evil constitutes this tradition.

(4) Fa-yüan and Chih-shou both held that the teaching and its practice constitute this tradition.

(5) A certain master held that cause and effect constitute this tradition.

(6) The Vinaya master Tao-yün did not specifically set up a tradition.

(7) The Vinaya master Fa-li held that ceasing evil and doing good constitute this tradition.

(8) The Vinaya master Tao-hsüan held that the threefold pure precepts constitute this tradition. The characteristics of the practice taught in the Fourfold [Dharmaguptaka] Vinaya are the two precept texts [i.e., the *prātimokṣa* of monks and nuns]
12a and the twenty *dharmas* [i.e., the *Skandhakas*], etc. Of all these, there are none that do not teach the threefold pure

precepts. In the "Extolling the Tradition" chapter in his *Hsing-shih-ch'ao,* Tao-hsüan maintains that in initiating all the many practices, it is the precepts that constitute the purport of this tradition. This is the conclusive proof [of Tao-hsüan's position].

(9) The Vinaya master Huai-su held that the practice of the precepts constitutes this tradition.

(10) The Vinaya master Ting-pin truly taught that the Vinaya constitutes the message of this tradition.

Now the master Tao-hsüan held that the precepts constitute this tradition, and it is keeping these precepts and [not committing] transgressions [against them] that Tao-hsüan primarily elucidated.

Thirtieth Question

What constitutes the teaching of the general receiving [of all the threefold pure precepts]?

Answer: The teachings of the general receiving [of all the threefold pure precepts] are various teachings scattered throughout the Mahayana scriptures and commentaries. The various texts that specifically teach [this general receiving of all the precepts] all hold that these are the threefold pure precepts. This is an established principle; there are no variant teachings.

Thirty-first Question

What are the various classifications of the teachings of the *Vinaya Piṭaka?*

Answer: The *Vinaya Piṭaka* is very extensive. Now by reference to the text basic [to the Chinese and Japanese Vinaya tradition], the Fourfold [Dharmaguptaka] Vinaya Piṭaka, we shall explain the various principles as they are arranged in the text itself.

This literary corpus embraces thirty-seven *dharma*s. The teachings of these six volumes do not exceed these. The thirty-seven are the eight divisions of the *bhikṣu*s' precepts, the six divisions of the *bhikṣuṇī*s' precepts, the twenty *skandhaka*s, the narration of the compilation [of the text], the section on "putting down," and the section [in which the numbered categories are] "increased by one."

The various masters of old made such a division. But if we add the preface and expand it by [the narration of] the compilation [of the text] by the Assembly of the Five Hundred and by the Assembly of the Seven Hundred, then it forms thirty-nine [*dharma*s or sections]. The characteristics of the precepts of these two groups [i.e., monks and nuns] are explained as usual.

Of the *skandhaka*s "Receiving the Precepts" (*Pravrajyā-skandhaka*), "Reciting the Precepts" (*Poṣadha-skandhaka*), "Retreat" (*Varṣā-skandhaka*), and the "End of the Retreat" (*Pravāraṇā-skandhaka*) individually explain the teaching as their names indicate.

The *skandhaka* "Leather Goods" (*Carma-skandhaka*) elucidates the use of leather goods, such as sandals one layer or many layers in thickness. It is also in this *skandhaka* that the rules for five persons receiving the precepts in an isolated spot, the number of times one may wash and bathe, receiving cloth for a period of ten days, etc., are taught.

The *skandhakas* "Robes" (*Cīvara-skandhaka*), "Medicine" (*Bhaiṣajya-skandhaka*), and "Kaṭhina-Robes" (*Kaṭhina-skandhaka*) each respectively explain their *dharmas*.

The teaching of the *skandhaka* "The Monks of Kośāmbī" (*Kośāmbaka-skandhaka*) takes its name from the country. The *bhikṣus* of that country quarrelled among themselves, and sought out one another's good and bad points with curses and slanders. One person possessing the qualities [of holiness] pointed out their faults in the proper (*dharmeṇa*) manner; and having put an end to their quarrelling they lived together in harmony. The thrice *karma-vacana* ritual regarding unseen transgressions, unconfessed transgressions, etc., is in this chapter.

In the *skandhaka* "The Monks in Campā" (*Campā-skandhaka*), the proper and the improper ways of carrying out the *karman* ritual are explained, and the ceremonies that should be performed are legislated.

A visiting *bhikṣu* carried out a *karma-vacana* on behalf of a senior *bhikṣu*. The Tathāgata admonished against this, and preached concerning the seven improper *karma-vacanas*, i.e., the "unlawful," the "small congregation," "harmony," etc. He also taught the four characteristics, "obtained," "satisfied," "not to be done," etc., and the seven improprieties, etc.

In the *skandhaka* "Censuring" (*Pāṇḍulohitaka-skandhaka*), the seven ways of putting down errors, such as scoldings, etc., and ways to subdue the seven types of obstinate, hard-to-convert persons are taught. The teaching is applied according to the Dharma so one can practice in peace.

In the *skandhaka* "Persons" (*Pudgala-skandhaka*) the *Saṅghāvaśeṣa* rules [any breaking of which necessitates a formal meeting of the Sangha], such as "the six nights," "dwelling separately," "the day in question," etc., are fully explained, as is confession to remove the results of karma and repentance to eliminate impropriety (*adharma*).

In the *skandhaka* "Hidden Faults" (*Pārivāṣika-skandhaka*) various types of characteristics are explained with reference to only one hidden fault. By this teaching the impurities of this transgression are removed and eliminated.

12b In the *skandhaka* "Suspending the *Prātimokṣa*" (*Poṣadhasthāpana-skandhaka*), the impropriety of concealing one's own faults and pointing out those of others is taught. If one points out another's transgression, [the indictment] must have five qualities. If a person does this properly, he may be allowed to point out the faults of others. In this *skandhaka,* all these actions are explained in full.

In the *skandhaka* "Schism" (*Saṅghabheda-skandhaka*), acts that disrupt the Sangha are explained.

In the *skandhaka* "Resolving Disputes" (*Adhikaraṇa-śamatha-skandhaka*), seven ways of resolving disputes are explained.

In the *Bhikṣuṇī Skandhaka* all the rituals—receiving the precepts, reciting the precepts, etc.—pertaining to the congregating of nuns are explained.

In the *skandhaka* "Dharma" (*Dharma-skandhaka*), the actions of the monks are explained—their actions, rituals, and rules of discipline. This *skandhaka* is minutely arranged, and all these rules of discipline are clearly revealed.

In the *skandhaka* "Dwellings" (*Śavana-āsana-skandhaka*), the conditions for religious practice are explained. Among all the various material aids [to the religious life], rooms and buildings are the most essential.

In the Miscellaneous *Skandhaka* (*Kṣudraka-skandhaka*), the conditions that serve as an aid to the religious life [are seen as] many and various. Although [the *skandhaka* is] confused and complicated, those that should be taught are broadly explained. After the Miscellaneous *Skandhaka* the characteristics of the major and minor precepts are explained in detail.

The major precepts are the precepts kept by the *bhikṣus* and *bhikṣuṇīs*; the minor precepts are those practiced by the other groups [of persons that constitute the Sangha]. The four rules of discipline, both mental and physical, appear conjoined with the thought [that produced them]; and when [held] steadfastly in our minds, they remove all obstructions from our minds. [Thus does the *Vinaya Piṭaka*] broadly teach us to carry out such actions.

Both compilations [of the text of the *Vinaya Piṭaka*], [the one] by the Assembly of the Five Hundred and [the one] by the Assembly of the Seven Hundred, were [made] for the purpose of maintaining the Dharmas thus transmitted and not scattering them, and of recording them correctly and transmitting them to distant generations.

The section of the Vinaya "Putting Down" is about the previously mentioned text on precepts (i.e., the *Prātimokṣa*), concerning which Upāli raises questions and resolves his doubts. Each of the various sections on the various precepts sets up its own categories and examples in a very thorough question and answer form, but they gradually become more abbreviated until they come to the precept against baseless slander in the *saṅghāvaśeṣa* section. Then although [this catechismal form] may be said to be common to the eight types of offenses, it becomes even more abbreviated and is no longer taught.

The *Vinaya Piṭaka* section "Increasing by One" (*Ekottarika*) proceeds from the one to the many in explaining all of the teaching. It unifies and includes all the principles of the great teachings of the Vinaya in a continuous sequence of numbered *dharma*s, no *dharma* being omitted, in order that the characteristics of its transmission and its propagation may be manifested.

The numeral one is taken as basic, and one is added to it; thus [this section] is called "Increasing by One." The practice of increasing by one is common throughout the whole of this text.

Although the *dharma*s are numerous, the numerical categories are not necessarily totally exhausted. Thus from one to twenty-two, seven categories—fourteen, fifteen, sixteen, eighteen, nineteen, twenty, and twenty-one—are not discussed, so that fourteen "Increasing by One" [sections] among numerical categories are actually discussed. This section has as an example the "Increasing by One" *Āgama* (i.e., the *Ekottarika-āgama*).

The literature and the principles of the thirty-seven sections of the Fourfold [Dharmaguptaka] Vinaya Piṭaka are in the order given above; their characteristics are included as given here.

If we speak in general [of the contents of the *Vinaya Piṭaka*] with respect to a classification of its principles [they are divided into the headings of] the five chapters and the seven groups.

Whether it be in observing the precepts or in serving as a model of conduct, in upholding the prohibitions or in carrying out the injunctions, in committing error or in putting an end to error, the practices taught and their most basic, general nature may be explained as comprising four types of actions. In general they are called "keeping [those precepts that admonish against] committing [errors]."

Legislating the broad and supplementing the abbreviated; compiling the precepts and [their] periodic recitation; prohibiting and allowing; allowing and hindering; the environment and one's thoughts: these five chapter headings, which are the classifications of all the principles of the *skandhaka*s, are the classifications of the principles of the *Vinaya Piṭaka.*

12c All the characteristics of the items of the teachings, and all the classifications of principles in the Three Major Works of the master Tao-hsüan, are numberless and cannot be fully narrated here.

Thirty-second Question

What are the characteristics of the cutting off [of hindrances] and the results that a follower of the Vinaya tradition obtains once he has generated the mind of Enlightenment and approached the path [of the religious life]?

Answer: All sentient beings have the Buddha nature, but it is obscured by thoughts of error and so cannot be revealed. With one's original Enlightenment as an internal cause, and with a friend in the teaching as an external condition, the mind of Enlightenment is generated and the Way [of the religious life] is practiced. The great thought of Enlightenment is the marvellous cause of Buddhahood, and the practice of the three learnings leads to progressive advancement in religious practice.

The learning of the precepts is none other than the perfect production of the threefold pure precepts. The learnings of meditation and wisdom are none other than perfect insight into consciousness only. When the teaching of consciousness only is practiced, the mind of insight becomes stilled and clear. When mental thoughts are calmed, both thoughts and ideas are totally cut off. They do not exist either here or there; this is called the learning of meditation.

And when this mind of insight is brightly illumined, all things are reflected in it. This is called the learning of wisdom.

The learning of the precepts is limitless and contains the learnings of meditation and wisdom. All actions are the learning of meditation. All actions are the learning of wisdom. Each one of them contains the wisdom of the precepts and of meditation on the precepts.

They naturally permeate all things; there is nothing that is not perfectly contained in them. If one practices [the religious life] as given here, one will progress in accord with the stages of the bodhisattva. The hindrances are cut off, and Truth is realized. When this practice is completed, one becomes a Buddha.

Thirty-third Question

How many stages will the Mahayana bodhisattva pass through in undertaking all of the various actions and in attaining Buddhahood?

Answer: The venerable master Tao-hsüan set up four stages, which are based upon the *She-ta-ch'eng-lun,* and which include the stages of cause and effect. These four stages are first, the stage of understanding; second, the stage of insight; third, the stage of meditation; and fourth, the stage of the Ultimate.

The master Tao-hsüan also set up fifty-two stages that completely embrace all the stages of both cause and effect for bodhisattvas. This is also based completely upon the teaching of the *She-ta-ch'eng-lun.* In his *Kuei-ching-i,* Tao-hsüan says:

> A saint is not made a saint by himself; ultimately he relies upon instruction and is thus gradually illumined. A common person is not necessarily [always] common; he too depends upon explanations and comes to understanding.
>
> Know then that whether [one is] dull or wise, profound or shallow, in the stages of the wise and the bold, depending upon the extent of one's understanding and practice, one attains differences of intelligence or stupidity.
>
> Hence in the *She-ta-ch'eng-lun* it says, "Nondiscriminatory wisdom is none other than the bodhisattvas; bodhisattvas are none other than nondiscriminatory wisdom. [As for] the stages of the bodhisattvas, there are fifty-odd grades presented."
>
> Know then that the purport of this passage is that [within] nondiscriminatory wisdom there are from thought to thought [differences of] intelligence and stupidity.

13a The so-called fifty stages of the bodhisattvas are the ten stages of faith, the ten abodes, the ten practices, the ten transferences of merit, and the ten realms. The other stages are two, namely the Stage Almost Equal to Enlightenment and the Stage of Marvellous Enlightenment.

In Tao-hsüan's *Ching-hsin-kuan* (Meditation upon the Pure Mind) it says, "The forty-two stages—the three [stages of the] wise, the ten realms, the stage of the undefiled, and the Stage of Marvellous Enlightenment—are the truth of the tradition of emptiness."

The stage of the undefiled is the Stage Almost Equal to Enlightenment. In the *Ying-lo-ching,* the Stage Almost Equal to Enlightenment is called the "realm of the undefiled," thus establishing this term.

In the *Ching-hsin-kuan,* before [it speaks of] the three wise stages, it speaks of the "rising up of a pure mind of faith in the Mahayana." This is the ten stages of faith.

Thirty-fourth Question

The four stages of the *She-ta-ch'eng-lun* and the fifty-two stages are mutually contradictory in both their major and minor features. How are their characteristics reconciled?

Answer: The fifty-two stages are included within the four stages.

The forty mental stages are embraced within the stage of understanding. They are the ten stages of faith, the ten abodes, the ten practices, and the ten transferences of merit.

The whole stage of the first realm is embraced within the stage of insight. This may be called the mind of entering, as the mind of entering is the Way of insight. The stage of meditation is from the second to the seventh realm. [This may be called] the diamond-like mind. The stage of the Ultimate includes the eighth realm up to Buddhahood; or this is simply Buddhahood.

However, in the *She-ta-ch'eng-lun,* the stages of the Cloud of the Dharma and Marvellous Enlightenment are held to constitute the Ultimate. The tenth realm is the perfection of cause. The realm of Marvellous Enlightenment is the perfection of the result, whereas the Stage Almost Equal to Enlightenment is the perfection of the cause.

[Attaining] the forty mental stages within the stage of understanding requires the first *asaṃkhyeya*[-*kalpa*]; the first realm to the seventh realm require the second *asaṃkhyeya*[-*kalpa*]; and the eighth realm to the Stage Almost Equal to Enlightenment require the third *asaṃkhyeya*[-*kalpa*]. By fulfilling [the tasks of] these three *asaṃkhyeya*[-*kalpa*]s, one attains Ultimate Enlightenment.

Thirty-fifth Question

What acts does the bodhisattva perform within these various stages in order to perfect the two benefits [i.e., enlightening oneself and others]?

Answer: The practitioner of the One Vehicle of this perfect teaching of consciousness only, after he has generated the mind of Enlightenment, directs himself toward all practices and practices all of the above four stages. In the marvellous insight of consciousness only, both principle and phenomena are carried out; they are perfectly interfused.

The six *pāramitās*, the four *vastus* by which the bodhisattva embraces all sentient beings, the two truths, the two emptinesses, the three natures, the three non-natures, the three emptinesses, and the four immeasurable hearts [of love, sympathy, joy, and equanimity]—all these are perfectly possessed in their fullness and pervade everywhere. Such characteristics as these are the general practice [of all of the stages].

In the stage of understanding, the four roots of good are the [following] practices: the four investigations, within which one understands the emptiness of the object of cognition, and the four types of wisdom that accord with reality, within which one understands the emptiness of consciousness.

In the ten stages of faith, one practices the five roots—faith, etc.—non-retrogression, the transference of one's merit to others, and the protection of the Dharma, the precepts, and the vows. In each of these ten stages of faith, one practices the ten practices—faith, etc.—as well as all the practices of the six *pāramitās*. When all these various practices are fully completed, and when the ten stages of faith are perfected, one initially enters into the stage of non-regression. The ten stages of faith are the stages of the common person.

From the stage of the first abode onward there are the stages of the inner common person. These ten abodes are in general called the stages of cultivating meditation. In the ten abodes, one under-
13b stands all the teachings of the Buddhas, and one dwells in the wisdom of these expedient doctrines. The marvellous practice of *prajñā* is very subtle and very profound.

In the first abode, the path of the eighty-four thousand higher virtues is practiced. In the second abode, the eighty thousand teachings of the four meditations are practiced. In the third abode, one cultivates all the ten *āyatana*s [stages of consciousness generated through the interaction of the sense organs and their environments]. In the fourth abode, one cultivates the eight superior [meditations on one's surroundings]. In the fifth abode, one practices the eight Enlightenments of great persons [i.e., *śrāvaka*s, *pratyekabuddha*s, and bodhisattvas]. In the sixth abode, one practices the eight [meditations aimed at] liberation. In the seventh abode, one practices the six [*pāramitā*s by which fellow devotees may reside together in] harmony and respect. In the eighth abode, one cultivates the three paths of emptiness. In the ninth abode, one cultivates the Four Noble Truths. In the tenth abode, one cultivates the six meditations.

In the ten practices, one cultivates the ten higher virtues as follows, on the basis of the teaching of the *Pen-yeh-ying-lo-ching:* in the first practice, one cultivates the four correct exertions; in the second practice, one develops the four divine supports [of meditation]; in the third practice, one develops the five sense faculties; in the fourth practice, one cultivates the five divisions of the Body of the Dharma; in the fifth practice, one practices the Noble Eightfold Path; in the sixth practice, one cultivates the seven [parts of] Enlightenment; in the seventh practice, one practices the five roots of good; in the eighth practice, one develops the four unhindered understandings; in the ninth practice, one develops insight into twelvefold dependent causation in the three periods of time; and in the tenth practice, one meditates upon the three treasures of bodhisattvas.

In the ten transferences of merit, one first meditates on the three truths; second, [one meditates] on the five divine powers; third, [one meditates] on the four indestructible purities; fourth, one meditates on the three characteristics of production, remaining, and decline; fifth, one meditates on the elements of the five *skandhas*; sixth, [one meditates] on the twelve *āyatanas*; seventh, [one meditates] on the eighteen *dhātus*; eighth, one meditates on the nongeneration and nondestruction of cause and effect; ninth, one meditates on the nonsubstantiality of the two truths; and tenth, one cultivates the meditation on the highest principle of the truth of the middle path.

From the first realm onward, there are the stages of partial holiness. All the various stages from [the first] realm onward are in their natures broad and profound, and it is with reference to the teachings of the five vehicles that the shallownesses or the depths of the various realms are revealed.

The first, second, and third realms have characteristics in common with the worldly [vehicle, i.e., the vehicle of men and *devas*]. In the first realm, one practices the virtue of charity. In the second realm, one practices the ten roots of good. In the third realm, one cultivates meditation; the four *dhyānas* and the eight *samādhis* are cultivated and attained in this realm.

In the fourth, fifth, and sixth realms one resides provisionally in the two vehicles [of *śrāvakas* and *pratyekabuddhas*]. In the fourth realm, one develops the thirty-seven aids to Enlightenment. In the fifth realm, the Four Noble Truths are seen to reveal the ten truths. In the sixth realm, the twelvefold causal arising is fully cultivated, and the practice of insight into the ten teachings is perfectly cultivated by the three insights.

In the seventh realm, all the constituent parts of Enlightenment are developed. This is the transworldly teaching of the Mahayana. The three vehicles [i.e., of *śrāvakas*, *pratyekabuddhas*, and bodhisattvas] are all transworldly Dharmas.

From the eighth realm onwards, one resides in the Dharma of the One Vehicle. This is the trans-transworldly Dharma without active function.

Up to and including the fourth realm, there is separate insight into the Absolute and the relative. From the fifth realm onward, there is insight into the essential unity of the Absolute and the relative.

The sixth realm is the stage possessing characteristics and active functioning. The seventh realm is the practice of active functioning without characteristics. The eighth realm is without active functioning [and is the realm in which] the threefold worldly spheres are accomplished freely and at will, with no obstruction whatsoever.

In the ninth realm, one has the forty skills in speech and can freely preach the Dharma for the conversion of others; one's expedient means are inexhaustible.

The tenth stage is the Ultimate: an inexhaustible body is enjoyed, a great rain cloud [of the Dharma] is given, and all are saved. All the various practices within the stages of practice and cultivation are perfectly completed.

After the stage of the diamond-like mind, Buddhahood appears; and until the end of endless time, both the person and his works are perfected.

Thirty-sixth Question

With what bodies does one follow this path to Buddhahood?

Answer: There are two types of bodies that are the basis of this practice.

First are the bodies that have differences and gradations and are subject to birth and death. These are the results received in the four types of birth in the six realms of rebirth within the three
13c spheres. The hindrances of illusions constitute their condition and impure karma their cause. Such bodies are the results that are experienced [by the practitioner]. There are limitations to their life spans; and because of retribution there are gradations [i.e., differences] in [bodily] shapes. Upon dying here [in one place], they are born there [in another place]. In bodily features, they are gross and inferior. In general, these bodies are called bodies subject to differences and gradations.

Second are the bodies of transformation [which are yet subject to] birth and death. These are the results received outside the three spheres. Subtle and marvellously superior, these retribution bodies are inconceivable. The hindrances of knowledge constitute their conditions, since they exist in the sphere of the two benefits [i.e., enlightening oneself and others]. Pure karma constitutes their causes, and they truly create a delicate recompense. Both the cause and the result [of these bodies] are subject to various shapes. In a fine and delicate manner these bodies are produced and extinguished. These bodies undergo transformations in accordance with one's will. In general, such bodies are called those subject only to mental transformations.

Before the [ten] realms, one receives a body having differences and gradations. From the first realm onward, one receives a body subject to transformations that changes as one wills. Up to the stage of the diamond-like mind, one has a body subject to transformations; but with the first thought of Buddhahood, the body subject to transformations is cast off.

Buddhahood is unique to itself. It dwells high beyond any boundary and mystically transcends the two types of death. Being without hindrance, it is perfect freedom.

Thirty-seventh Question

Within the various stages of the bodhisattvas of the perfect teaching, what are the characteristics of [the hindrances] that are cut off, and how does one cut them off?

Answer: There are two types of hindrances that are cut off, and the path to their cutting off is that of undefiled wisdom, etc. The two hindrances are first, the hindrance of illusions, greed, hatred, ignorance, etc., which arise at the same time, torment both body and mind, and thus hinder Nirvana; second, the hindrance of knowledge, which hinders the two realms of phenomena and principle, which should be known; by causing [these two realms] not to be attained, it hinders Enlightenment.

Within the hindrances of illusions, there are four abiding realms; these abiding realms of views and desires are delusions of discrimination. Arising simultaneously, they are divided into three, thus corresponding to the three spheres [of desire, of form, and of nonform].

Should we fully discuss their various characteristics, there are in general one hundred twenty-eight types of fundamental illusions and various divisions and grades of subordinate illusions that are outflows [from the fundamental ones]. In general it is said that there are ten fundamental [illusions]: greed, hatred, ignorance, pride, doubt, erroneous views regarding the body, extreme views, false views, attachment to erroneous views, and attachment to erroneous precepts. These ten are all present in the arising of discrimination. These six, greed, hatred, ignorance, pride, erroneous views regarding the body, and extreme views, may all arise spontaneously.

There are one hundred twelve separate illusions arising from erroneous discrimination, as they are errors with regard to the principles of the Four Noble Truths in the three spheres.

The Four Noble Truths in the sphere of desire possess all of these ten. In the Truths in the two higher spheres, each [has all ten] with the exception of the illusion of hatred [i.e., each has nine illusions].

There is a total of seventy-two types [in the higher spheres], which, together with the previous [ten in the sphere of desire], make one hundred twelve [illusions].

In the sphere of desire, there are six illusions that are produced spontaneously. In the spheres of form and nonform [the illusion of] hatred is lacking—two fives [give a total of] ten, which, together with the previous [six in the sphere of desire], make sixteen.

Hence there are together one hundred twenty-eight illusions to be eliminated in the stages of insight and meditation.

In the case of the teachings of the principles as evolved [for the capacities of all sentient beings, i.e., truth], there are a total of ninety-eight hindrances of illusions, which are completely identical with the [enumerations as given in the Hinayana] Abhidharma.

The *Yü-ch'ieh-lun* and others are the teachings of the principle of the [Absolute] Truth of the Mahayana. Thus there are one hundred twenty illusions [mentioned in that text].

There are twenty subordinate illusions: anger, resentment, concealment, vexation, pretense, flattery, parsimony, jealousy, con-
14a ceit, violence, disbelief, laxity, negligence, torpor, agitation, nonhumility, nontimidity, forgetfulness, distraction, and evil [or incorrect] knowledge. [The above twenty are from the *Commentary on the Hundred Dharmas,* etc.] [Also, there are] perverse desires and perverse understanding. [These are added in the *Yü-ch'ieh-lun.*] This makes a total of two hundred thirty subordinate illusions.

In each of the Four Noble Truths in the sphere of desire there are twenty-two, since anger, resentment, etc. [as above] are all present; thus there are a total of eighty-eight.

In the Four Noble Truths of the sphere of form, each Truth has eliminated nine, i.e., anger, resentment, concealment, vexation, parsimony, jealousy, violence, nonhumility, and nontimidity. The remaining thirteen are present in each of these Four Noble Truths, making a total of fifty-two.

In the Four Noble Truths of the sphere of nonform, each truth has eliminated eleven; nine are those that are eliminated in the sphere of form, and two more, pretense and flattery, are eliminated. The remaining eleven are present in each of the Four Noble Truths, which together comprise forty-four.

Within the Four Noble Truths in all three spheres, there are a total of one hundred eighty-four subordinate illusions.

Twenty-two illusions are eliminated in the stage of meditation in the sphere of desire. With the exception of the nine [illusions], such as anger, etc., there remain thirteen [illusions] to be eliminated in the stage of meditation in the sphere of form.

With the further exception of flattery and pretense, there remain eleven [illusions] to be eliminated in the stage of meditation in the sphere of nonform. The delusions eliminated in the stage of meditation within the three spheres form a total of forty-six. Combined with the previous one hundred eighty-four illusions eliminated in the stage of insight, there are a total of two hundred thirty subordinate illusions.

Further, combined with the one hundred twenty-eight basic [illusions], there are a total of three hundred fifty-eight hindering illusions. These are all of the illusions.

The karma that [the illusions] generate and the results that one experiences from them are all taken to constitute the nature of the hindering illusions.

The hindrances of knowledge, in their nature, in their characteristics, and in their quantity, are similar to the hindrances of illusions. The only difference is that these hindrances of knowledge hinder the two elements of Enlightenment and Nirvana.

The fundamental illusions and the subordinate illusions are likewise similar [to one another] in their characteristics.

However, the hindrances of the illusions are gross; hence they are of great quantity. They are those hindrances that are cut off by the two vehicles [i.e., of the *śrāvaka*s and *pratyekabuddha*s]. As they are only of an evil or of a morally neutral nature, it is by means of numbers that they may appear gross.

These hindrances of knowledge are minute and not of great quantity. These are cut off only by bodhisattvas. Also, these are embraced by a morally neutral retributing [consciousness]. Hence they are not revealed by means of numbers.

Although one may be deluded with respect to both principles and particulars [i.e., by phenomena], it is only [delusion] with respect to knowledge [that which is to be known for deliverance] that is in general called "ignorance."

In addition to the four abiding realms, this one hindrance [i.e., of knowledge] is added. Thus these are called the five abiding realms.

However, there are three types of each of these two hindrances [i.e., of illusions and of knowledge]: its present manifestations, its seeds, and its remaining impregnations. In the [category of the illusions to be eliminated in the stages of] insight and of meditation, each has its present manifestations, its seeds, and its impregnations. In general they may be subsumed under two: the illusions themselves and their impregnations. Their effects and their seeds together are called "the illusion itself."

In the ten stages of faith, the ten evil acts are thwarted. One does not fall into any of the evil realms of rebirth. Hence these are called the stages leading to good realms of rebirth. Although this is not the primary subduing of the illusions, these are the expedients of such primary subduing [of the illusions]. They only partially resemble such primary subduing in their thwarting of the illusions.

In the stages of the ten abodes, there is the subduing of the present manifestations of the illusions of discrimination that have arisen due to perverse teachers. In the stages of the ten practices, perverse doctrine [is subdued]. In the ten transferences of merit, delusions of perverse thoughts are subdued. This is a gradual subduing and is common to the two types of hindrances. After the ten transferences of merit, one practices the four roots of good. At this time, all the various discriminations previously held
14b are quickly subdued. In the stage of the four roots of good, the

spontaneously arisen passions, etc., are gradually subdued. These are the delusions that are associated with the six consciousnesses.

However, as for the two types of hindrances within the eight levels of consciousness, in the storehouse consciousness there is nothing that corresponds to the two hindrances; in the mind [*manas*] consciousness, there are four delusions—greed, ignorance, pride, and [the idea of] self. However, these are spontaneous, and there is no differentiation among them. In the sixth consciousness, consciousness corresponds to delusion and is eliminated in the stages of insight and meditation.

In the five consciousnesses, there are only the three illusions of greed, hatred, and ignorance. These, however, arise spontaneously and do not hinder the mind consciousness. Rather, they lead this consciousness and give rise to delusions to be eliminated in the stage of insight.

The two hindrances are also common to the mind consciousness, or else they only give rise to the hindrances of illusion. The delusions that are in conjunction with the mind consciousness are of a morally neutral nature and yet still hinder [the path to holiness]. In the sixth consciousness, spontaneously arisen erroneous views regarding the body and extreme views have the nature of still hindering [the path to holiness]; all the rest are morally evil. The delusions produced by the five consciousnesses are also morally evil.

In the two upper spheres [of form and of nonform], all the illusions have the nature of [only] still hindering [the path to holiness], because they are to be subdued by *samādhi*. [Hence they are not morally evil.]

The above concludes a description of the characteristics of the practice of subduing and cutting off in the stage of understanding. The characteristics of that which is cut off and that to which one is enlightened in the stage of the Way of insight is as follows: in the uninterrupted mind in the stage of the highest worldly Dharma [i.e., in the last moment in the practice of the last of the four roots of good], one enters the stage of the Way of insight. The hindrances are cut off and principle is realized.

In the Liang dynasty translation of the *She-ta-ch'eng-lun,* it says that when one enters into the stage of insight one realizes and attains basic nondiscriminating wisdom as well as acquired wisdom. One cuts off and destroys illusions, one realizes the Truth, and one attains an understanding of all the elements of phenomena.

According to the *Tsa-chi-lun,* the *Ch'eng-wei-shih-lun,* and other texts, the cutting off of illusions and the Enlightenment of this basic wisdom is called the true Way of insight, because at this time there is an actual cutting off and an actual Enlightenment. The meditation of wisdom after this [above experience] is called the similar Way of insight, because it resembles the [above true] cutting off and Enlightenment.

In the true Way of insight, when undefiled wisdom arises, the seeds of the two discriminative hindrances are quickly cut off. This is called the "uninterrupted mind" and is the first undefiled thought of the stage of the Way of insight.

Next, in the Way of liberation, one is enlightened to the principles of the two types of emptiness. Next is the Way of superior advancement. Although this stage has a duration of three instants, they are together one thought, and hence this stage is called the "true Way of insight in one thought."

Next one enters "the similar Way of insight," which has a total of three thoughts or sixteen thoughts, which gradually progress [from one stage to another]. In the "similar Way of insight" of the three thoughts, the two hindrances each form two grades, higher and lower.

First, meditation on the emptiness of self cuts off the higher, grosser grades of the discriminative hindrances of illusion. Next, meditation on the emptiness of the *dharma*s cuts off the higher, grosser grade of the discriminative hindrance of knowledge. Later, entering into both emptinesses, one cuts off the seeds of each of the lower [more subtle] grades of the two hindrances. Next, one enters into the sixteen thoughts, of which there are two types: the first is the sixteen thoughts both objectively and subjectively grasped; the second is the sixteen thoughts of the eight [i.e., two Four Noble] Truths in the upper [spheres of form and nonform] and in the lower [sphere of desire], which gradually progress [from one stage to another].

The "similar Way of insight" of the three thoughts are provisionally established truths, but the characteristics of the sixteen thoughts are truths absolutely established.

The two types of the Way of insight are the thoughts that enter into the first [of the ten] realms.

The stage of meditation is made up of those stages that follow the thought that dwells in the first [of the ten] realms.

In the ten realms in the Way of meditation, there are ten hindrances. In each of the realms, one hindrance is cut off. In each realm Ultimate Reality is realized. The Enlightenment of these ten realms is none other than the ten Ultimate Realities.

However, in each of the stages of the ten realms, there are the three thoughts. In each of the three thoughts in each realm, there
14c are hindrances that are cut off and principles that are realized.

When in the scriptures it speaks of the ten hindrances and the ten Ultimate Realities, this refers only to the cutting off and the Enlightenment of the mind that enters each one of these stages. For this reason, the initial hindrance having the nature of common persons is spoken of with respect to the delusions of discrimination; and its cutting off and its Enlightenment are thus explained in these terms.

The cutting off and the Enlightenment following the mind that abides in the stage of the first realm is truly the cutting off and the Enlightenment that apply to the Way of meditation.

The characteristics of the cutting off and the Enlightenment of the stage of the Ultimate are the three thoughts of the tenth realm, which is, however, further divided and therefore here refers to its last mind [the mind that departs from these stages]. This is called the Stage Almost Equal to Enlightenment.

The last thought in the Stage Almost Equal to Enlightenment—the stage of diamond-like mind—cuts off the last hindrance to Buddhahood. These ten hindrances are most subtle and minute and thus hinder the stage of the realm of the Buddha. This diamond-like mind is the uninterrupted path; the next instant of mind is the path of liberation, the first thought of Buddhahood.

Now what we mean by Ultimate is the great, unhindered activity of the mind from the result of this first thought of Buddhahood until the end of unending time.

There is nothing that is not totally completed—the three bodies, the four qualities, the four wisdoms—all are perfect. This is none other than the characteristic of the fourth stage, the stage of the Ultimate. In this stage of the Ultimate there are two recompenses, the material worlds, and bodies and minds. The bodies and minds are the three bodies of a Buddha—the Dharma Body, the Recompense Body, and the Transformation Body.

The material worlds are the characteristics of either the four lands or the two lands. The four lands referred to are exclusively Pure Lands. The Land of Tranquility and Light is the abode of the Dharma Body; and this is called the Land of the Dharma Nature. The Land of True Recompense is the abode of the Body of Self-enjoyment; the Pure Land of Phenomena is the abode of the Body of the Enjoyment of Others. The Pure Land of Transformations is none other than the abode of the Transformation Body.

There are also in outline essentially two lands. First is the Land of Recompense, which is primarily the Recompense Body but which also embraces the Dharma Body. Second is the Land of Transformation, the abode of the Transformation Body that is common to both the pure and the impure lands.

In this way, Buddhahood, the bodies and minds and the material world, one's own Enlightenment, and the conversion of others continue eternally as great, inexhaustible activity that permeates all the cosmos.

This is none other than the Great Vehicle of the bodhisattvas, the great, the highest result, the Ultimate attained by those who practice the Vinaya tradition.

Thirty-eighth Question

The Buddha legislated the precepts and the Vinaya for his disciples. The disciples received them, kept them, and spread them about.

From the time when the Buddha was in this world to the period after the death of the Buddha; from the time of the True Dharma to the era of the Latter [days of the] Imitation Dharma; from the length and breadth of India to China and her surrounding regions; from China and her surrounding regions to present-day Japan; from ancient times to the present, [the precepts and the Vinayas] have been transmitted in turn. Being handed down [from one generation to the next], they have been disseminated. What are the features [of this transmission]?

1. India

Answer: The Buddha, attaining Enlightenment, preached the Dharma for all sentient beings. For forty-nine years, as the occasion demanded it, he legislated the precepts. All his great disciples mastered the Tripiṭaka and transmitted both the Mahayana and the Hinayana. There was nothing they did not thoroughly understand.

However, in the transmission [of the Vinaya] there were some who were especially good [at certain aspects of the teaching]. The Venerable Upāli and the Venerable Gavāṃpati were renowned far and near for their keeping of the Vinaya and for their explanation of the Vinaya.

Gavāṃpati died [early], letting loose a torrent of water from the heavens. Upāli, thus residing alone, greatly spread the Vinaya Piṭaka.

The Venerable Kāśyapa assembled the vast Tripiṭaka and, holding this up as a standard, upheld the Buddha's Dharma. For
15a this reason, the Tathāgata entrusted all of the Tripiṭaka to

Kāśyapa, bidding him to propagate it widely. Kāśyapa entrusted the Vinaya Piṭaka to Upāli; Upāli, accepting this charge, transmitted it to later generations.

There are two explanations concerning this wide [i.e., later] transmission by Upāli, namely, the two transmissions, the one of the Mahāsāṅghika Vinaya and the one of the *Shan-chien-lun,* in which the names of the persons concerned are entirely different.

The transmission in the Mahāsāṅghika Vinaya is in the thirty-second volume of that Vinaya [text]. After the Venerable Upāli, there is Daśabala. Next is Sutidaśa. Next is Gīta. Next is Indriyapāla. Next is Dharma [?]. Next is [?]. Next is Mukta. Next is Pālin. Next is Mahāna. [These are ten.] Next is Makuta. Next is Kośala. Next is Gopāla. Next is Supāla. Next is Pālajīva. Next is Sada. Next is Yaśa. Next is Putila. Next is Vibaka. Next is Dharmagupta. [These are ten.] Next is Dinaka. Next is Dharmasena. Next is Buddhin. Next is Saṅghadeva. Next is Dharmajaya. Next is Puṣyabhadra. Next is Mārgabala.

The above, starting first with the Venerable Upāli and ending with the Venerable Mārgabala, total altogether twenty-seven persons who in turn received [the Vinaya], maintained it, protected it, and widely spread it about.

Although that Vinaya text enumerates twenty-seven persons, it does not clarify how many years elapsed after the death of the Buddha. The twentieth master is named Dharmagupta, [who is] exactly the same as the master of the Fourfold [Dharmaguptaka] Vinaya.

But this Mahāsāṅghika Vinaya is a basic [i.e., an early] text, while the master of the Fourfold Dharmaguptaka Vinaya [dates from] a period one hundred years [after the death of the Buddha].

Among the twenty divisions [in the later Sangha] there is a Dharmagupta division, the master of which took the Dharma name of the earlier individual and maintained the basic Mahāsāṅghika [doctrinal position].

This was during the period three hundred eighty years [after the death of the Buddha]. What objection can there be to this? Although this is a private opinion, it has been widely propagated.

The [teachers named in the] Vinaya transmission in the *Shan-chien-lun* are, first, Upāli. Next is Dāsaka. Next is Sonaka. Next is Siggava. Next is Moggaliputta Tissa. Next is Mahinda. Next is Ariṭṭha. Next is Tissadatta. Next is Kālasumana. Next is Dīgha[suma]na. [These are ten.] Next is Sumana. Next is Kāla-su[ma]na. Next is Dhammagupta. [These are thirteen]. Next is Tissa. Next is Deva. Next is Sumana. Next is Cūḷamāga. Next is Dhammapāli[ta]. Next is Khema. Next is Upatissa. [The above are twenty.] Next is [?]. Next is Abhaya. Next is Deva. Next is Śiva.

From Upāli to Śiva there were twenty-four persons who in turn transmitted the Vinaya. As in the case of the above twenty-seven persons in the Mahāsāṅghika text, all are great, venerable arhats who transmitted the Vinaya Piṭaka in an unbroken succession.

In the *Shan-chien-lun,* the various teachers are enumerated; but a chronology is not specifically pointed out. However, in this *Shan-chien-lun,* it says, "At that time, after all the various worthies had arrived in Siṅha-dvīpa [Ceylon], Mahinda was made the elder.
15b At this time, when the Buddha-Dharma was transmitted to Siṅha-dvīpa, it was two hundred thirty-six years after the Nirvana of the Buddha."

Mahinda was the sixth [teacher] in the transmission of the Vinaya. It was at that time that he transmitted the Buddha-Dharma [to Ceylon].

As for Dharmagupta, who was the thirteenth teacher [in the above Vinaya transmission], the Vinaya master Ting-pin of Sung-yüeh judged that "this Dharmagupta is none other than that master of the Fourfold Vinaya."

To speak now in greater detail, the Vinaya master Dharmagupta appeared one hundred years after the death of the Tathāgata. The *Shan-chien-lun* says that the sixth teacher Mahinda appeared some two-hundred-odd years [after the death of the Buddha]. Therefore how could [the Vinaya master Dharmagupta] correspond to the thirteenth [teacher]? But we can say that the Dharmagupta of the twenty divisions [of the Sangha], who here is called Fa-tsang, Fa-mi, Fa-hu, Fa-sheng, and also Fa-tsang [*sic*], [appeared] three hundred eighty years [after the death of the

Buddha]. This chronological division corresponds to the sense of the *Shan-chien-lun*.

In the opinion of the Sung-yüeh master [Ting-pin], his name [i.e., the name of the thirteenth master in the above *Shan-chien-lun*] is the same as that of the master of the Fourfold Vinaya. Hence the later Dharmagupta is called the author of this Vinaya. What objection is there to this? This *Shan-chien-lun* was composed seven hundred years [after the death of the Buddha]. The twenty-fourth master, the arhat Śiva, appeared during this period.

Since the facts may be said to be thus, the master Yüan-chao says that the later Dharmagupta division [of the Sangha] took the former's name, as in the example of Dharmatara.

The Venerable Kāśyapa is Mahākāśyapa, who received the charge of the Buddha in person and who transmitted the Buddha-Dharma, saving all sentient beings.

When Kāśyapa was about to pass into [final] meditation, he entrusted the Dharma to Ānanda. When Ānanda was approaching death, he entrusted the Dharma to Madhyāntika. When Madhyāntika was approaching death, he entrusted the Dharma to Śāṇavāsa. (Even though he also received [the Dharma] from Ānanda, according to the explanations of the transmission from teacher to pupil of the Sarvāstivādins, the transmission was thus.) When Śāṇavāsa was about to die, he entrusted the Dharma to Upagupta.

This transmission is called the "vertical five masters," those masters who succeeded one another in different generations. They each spent twenty years in propagating the Buddha-Dharma. [They spent] longer or shorter [periods of time in propagating the Buddha-Dharma]; we give here their average [number of years of activity].

By the time of Upagupta, one hundred years had already elapsed. All of the above teachers propagated the Tripiṭaka.

Now in considering the further transmission of the Vinaya, Upagupta had five disciples, namely Dharmagupta, Sarvatha, Mahīśāsaka, Kāśyapīya, and Vātsīputrīya. There were five arhats of the Tripiṭaka and the five Piṭakas, etc., but we shall now consider them solely with reference to the further transmission of their Vinayas.

These five masters were called the "horizontal five teachers," five teachers who were contemporaneous. They transmitted the lamp [of the Dharma] simultaneously, and each transmitted [his interpretation] to succeeding generations.

It was also some one-hundred-odd years after the death of the Buddha that because of the five items of Mahādeva, the multitude of the followers of the Buddha-Dharma split, forming two groups, namely the Mahāsāṅghikas [i.e., those who followed the Great Assembly, or the Majority], and the Sthaviravādins [i.e, those who followed the Elders].

Two-hundred-odd years [after the death of the Buddha], the Mahāsāṅghikas gradually divided, forming eight other groups. From three-hundred-odd years to four hundred [years after the death of the Buddha], the Sthaviravādins divided, producing ten other groups. Together with the two original groups, these consti-
15c tute twenty groups in all. There is also [an enumeration of] twelve groups, of five hundred groups, etc.

Each of these various groups had its own Vinaya Piṭaka; but although there were some twenty groups, only five of these Vinayas which belong to the Sthaviravādins have been transmitted to posterity, namely, the Sarvāstivādins, the Vātsīputrīyas, the Mahīśāsakas, the Dharmaguptakas, and the Kāśyapīyas.

These five took the names of the five groups [that appeared] during the period one hundred years [after the death of the Buddha]; hence they have the same names. This is the origin of these various names. However, various teachers have differing opinions about this.

The Dharma of the Vinaya in India, of the twenty groups, etc., was greatly propagated in their respective countries. It flourished over a [wide] area and over time, and the lineages were transmitted [in such profusion that] it is difficult to discuss or to know them [in detail].

2. China

Concerning the transmission of the Vinaya into China—when the times were appropriate and conditions fitting, it was transmitted without error. In the past, [it was not until] the tenth year of Yung-ping (A.D. 67), in the reign of the Emperor Ming of the Later Han dynasty, that Kāśyapa-mātaṅga came to China and first transmitted the Buddha-Dharma. Although the principles were then first established, the Dharma of the precepts was not yet transmitted.

From the tenth year of Yung-ping (A.D. 67), *ting-mao,* to the first year of Chia-ping (A.D. 249), *chi-ssu,* of the Ts'ao-Wei dynasty, there elapsed a total of one hundred eighty-three years in which the Dharma of the Vinaya was not propagated. During this interval various Tripiṭaka masters gradually came to China and translated Mahayana and Hinayana scriptures.

However, for seventy-one years after the death of Kāśyapa-mātaṅga [in the eighteenth year of Yung-ping (A.D. 75)] and after the Emperor Chang, the third sovereign of the Later Han dynasty, ascended the throne, no Indian monks came, and China was without any *śramaṇa*s.

After the first year of Chien-ho (A.D. 147), in the reign of the Emperor Huan, the eleventh sovereign of this dynasty, *śramaṇa*s gradually came and transmitted and translated the Buddha-Dharma, namely, Chih-lou chia-ch'an (Lokakṣema), An Shih-kao, Chu Fo-shuo, An-hsüan, Chih-yao, Yen Fo-t'iao, K'ang Meng-hsiang, Chu Ta-li, T'an-kuo, and others. Although monks came, there was no receiving of the precepts [i.e., there were no ordination ceremonies].

In the third year of Huang-ch'u (A.D. 222), in the reign of the first sovereign of the Wei dynasty, the emperor Wen, Dharmakāla first came to the empire of the Wei. However, the various conditions were not yet complete, and he spent twenty-eight years in vain.

Finally, in the second year of Chia-ping (A.D. 250), an ordination of ten persons was performed. Thus it was during the rule of the Wei dynasty that this radiant pearl was first obtained. This was the first transmission of an ordination of the great Sangha. The first transmission of an ordination of *bhikṣuṇīs* was in the tenth year of Yuan-chia (A.D. 433) of the Liu-Sung dynasty, 1199 years after the death of the Tathāgata.

Ever since the ordination ceremony of the great Sangha was first transmitted into China, masters and their disciples have succeeded one upon another, and there has been no interruption of the ordination ceremony in China.

In the Chia-ping era (249–254), Dharmakāla [i.e., Fa-shih] translated the *prātimokṣa* of the Mahāsāṅghikas, and the Tripiṭaka master T'an-t'i translated the *karma-vacana* [ritual] of the Fourfold Vinaya of the Dharmaguptakas. These two works were first translated in Lo-yang, and this was the first transmission of a text of the Vinaya.

In understanding the nature of the precepts, one necessarily depended upon this *karma-vacana* ritual; and this *karma-vacana* ritual was carried out according to the Dharmaguptaka texts.

For this reason, China's first ordination ceremony was done by the precepts of the Dharmaguptakas; but in the application of the rules of training, the Mahāsāṅghika Vinaya was revered.

Although the practice of the precepts and the *prātimokṣa* text were transmitted to China, a complete text of the Vinaya Piṭaka had not yet been transmitted.

16a From the second year of Chia-ping (250) to the fifth year of Hung-shih (403) of the Yao-Ch'in dynasty, there elapsed a total of one hundred fifty-four years.

In the following year (404) Puṇyatara first translated the Sarvāstivāda Vinaya. Dharmaruci and Vimalākṣa continued in succession to translate this text. The complete Sarvāstivāda Vinaya, in sixty-one volumes, passed through three translators in all, until the whole corpus was completed.

Next, in the twelfth year of Hung-shih (410), Buddhayaśas—called in China Chüeh-ming, "Glory of Enlightenment"—translated the Fourfold [Dharmaguptaka] Vinaya, initially in forty-five volumes but later in sixty volumes.

In the fourteenth year of Yi-hsi (418), in the reign of the Emperor An of the Eastern Chin dynasty, the Tripiṭaka master Buddhabhadra translated the Mahāsāṅghika Vinaya in forty volumes.

In the first year of Ching-ping (423), during the Liu-Sung dynasty, Buddhajīva translated the Fivefold [Mahīśāsaka] Vinaya in thirty volumes.

Among these four Vinayas, the Mahāsāṅghika Vinaya is basic [i.e., the earliest text], and the other three are its offshoots. Of the five Vinaya texts [now extant], three texts had then been transmitted.

Of the Kāśyapīya text, only the *Prātimokṣa* in one volume was transmitted; this is the *Chieh-t'o chieh ching.* This was translated in the first year of Wu-ting (543) of the Eastern Wei dynasty. This corresponds to the ninth year of Ta-t'ung of the Liang dynasty, and to the fourth year of the reign of the Japanese Emperor Kinmei. Its complete Vinaya has never yet been transmitted to China.

The precepts and the Vinaya of the Vātsīputrīyas have not yet been transmitted to China.

There are also Vinaya commentaries explaining the main Vinaya texts: the *Sutra on the Origin of the Vinaya,* the *Sarvāstivāda-Vinaya-Mātṛkā,* and the *Sarvāstivāda-Vinaya-bhāṣya* (these above three all pertain to the Sarvāstivāda Vinaya); the *Shan-chien-lun,* which explains the Fourfold [Dharmaguptaka] Vinaya; the *Lü-erh-shih-erh Miao-liao-lun,* which explains the Vinaya of the Sāmmatīyas; and the *P'i-nai-yeh-lü.*

The four Vinayas were transmitted and propagated subsequent to their translations.

The Sarvāstivāda Vinaya was the most frequently lectured upon. Next [in popularity] was the Fourfold [Dharmaguptaka Vinaya]. Lectures upon the Mahāsāṅghika Vinaya and upon the Fivefold [Mahīśāsaka Vinaya] gradually declined [in popularity].

Although all these Vinayas were widely spread about, in later ages the only Vinaya to be popular was the Fourfold Vinaya.

Some sixty-odd years after the translation of the Fourfold, in the reign of the sixth sovereign of the Yuan-Wei dynasty, the

Emperor Hsiao-wen, there was the Vinaya master Fa-ts'ung of Pei-t'ai, who had originally studied the Mahāsāṅghika Vinaya and had penetrated to a thorough understanding of it. However, upon investigating the first ordination in China, he discovered that a Dharmaguptaka Vinaya had been used as its text. He thereupon ceased his lectures on the Mahāsāṅghika Vinaya and began to propagate the Fourfold.

Now both the receiving [of the precepts, i.e., the ceremony] and the following [of the precepts, i.e., their subsequent practice] tallied one with the other, and all such matters were based upon one authority.

But this is oral tradition and has never been recorded.

After Tao-fu, commentaries were made, and texts were commented upon.

The Fourfold Vinaya tradition sets up nine patriarchs: first, the master of the Vinaya, the elder Dharmagupta; second, the elder Dharmakāla, the first patriarch in China; third, the Vinaya master Fa-ts'ung, who was the first founding patriarch; fourth, the Vinaya master Tao-fu, who wrote commentaries and established principles, and who answered questions and determined [orthodoxy]; fifth, the Vinaya master Hui-kuang; sixth, the Vinaya master Tao-yün; seventh, the Vinaya master Tao-chao; eighth, the Vinaya master Chih-shou; ninth, the Vinaya master of Chung-nan-shan, Tao-hsüan.

The Ta-chih Vinaya master Yüan-chao set up this above enumeration and made it definitive.

After the time of Hui-kuang, there were also essays and commentaries written. Although commentaries on the Fourfold Vinaya Piṭaka have been numerous, the works of three masters have been praised through the world. These are first, the *Abbrevi-*
16b *ated Commentary* by Kuang-t'ung, in four volumes; second, the *Expanded Commentary* by Chih-shou, in twenty volumes; and third, the *Medium Length Commentary* by Fa-li, in ten volumes. These are called the Three Essential Commentaries, and persons everywhere study and use them.

In former times, there were two illustrious disciples of Tao-yün, namely, Hung-tsun and Tao-hung. The succession continued as follows: Hung-tsun, Hung-yüan, Fa-li, and Tao-ch'eng.

In Tao-ch'eng's school there were Man-i and Huai-su. Each one set up his own group of disciples that continued and expanded in later generations.

The succession of masters continued as follows: Tao-chao, Chih-shou, and the Chung-nan-shan master Tao-hsüan. This school flourished in later generations.

Due to the differences in interpretation the Fourfold Vinaya divided into three schools: the Hsiang-pu school, the Nan-shan school, and the Tung-t'a school. The scholars of these three schools argued and debated with one another without ceasing.

After the Yung-heng era (682–83), the *New Commentary* of the Tung-t'a master Huai-su flourished throughout the world.

The Vinaya master Fa-shen received the precepts from Tao-ch'eng. He also studied the Vinaya under Huai-su [the Tung-t'a Vinaya master] and faithfully lectured on his *New Commentary.* Fa-shen's students were many. The "three worthies," I-sung, Ju-ching, and Ch'eng-ch'u all studied the *New Commentary* and propagated this school; so the Vinaya of the Tung-t'a master Huai-su was spread to later generations.

The Vinaya master Man-i of Hsi-t'a propagated the Hsiang-pu school of the Vinaya. His followers were many, and each glorified the ideas of this school. They were the Vinaya master I, the Vinaya master Shun, the Vinaya master Kang, the Vinaya master Wen-hui, the Vinaya master Ssu-hui, the Vinaya master Fa-tsang [the *Hua-yen* master Hsiang-hsiang], the Vinaya master Yüan, the Vinaya master Wei, the Vinaya master Heng, the Vinaya master Yüan-chih, the Vinaya master Ch'üan-hsiu, the Vinaya master Hui-ying, the Vinaya master Ta-liang, the Vinaya master Ch'a, the Vinaya master Chao-yin, and others.

The Vinaya master Ting-pin was a disciple of Man-i.

Huai-su defeated the sixteen major principles of Fa-li. Ting-pin wrote the *Record of the Destruction of Erroneously Held Views,* salvaging the major principles of Fa-li and destroying the erroneous thoughts of Huai-su.

The two Japanese monks Yōei and Fushō went to T'ang dynasty China in search of the Vinaya. In the twenty-first year of K'ai-yüan (733) [which corresponds to the fifth year of Tempyō in Japan], they requested that the Vinaya master Ting-pin serve as *upādhyāya* and transmit the precepts to them.

Man-i transmitted the Dharma to Ta-liang, and Ta-liang transmitted it to T'an-i. Master T'an-i lectured on the Fourfold Vinaya thirty-five times. T'an-i died in the sixth year of Ta-li (771), *hsin-hai,* at the age of eighty. The disciples of T'an-i continued and flourished.

The *T'ien-t'ai* patriarch Chan-jan of Ching-hsi and [the *Hua-yen* patriarch] Ch'eng-kuan of Ch'ing-liang both studied the Vinaya under T'an-i.

T'an-i propagated both the Hsiang-pu and the Nan-shan schools of the Vinaya Dharma. He wrote the *Record of Presenting Orthodoxy* (*Fa-cheng-chi*) in reference to [i.e., as a commentary on] the *Hsing-shih-ch'ao* of Tao-hsüan. In this way the Hsiang-pu school was propagated.

There were two outstanding disciples of the Vinaya master Chih-shou who propagated the Vinaya. They have from olden times been termed [the founders of] the Ch'ao school and the Yao school. They are the Vinaya master Hsüan-hui, who wrote the *Pi-ni t'ao-yao,* and the Vinaya master of Chung-nan-shan, Tao-hsüan, who wrote the *Hsing-shih-ch'ao.* Therefore, the *T'ao-yao* belongs to the Nan-shan Vinaya school. The Nan-shan Vinaya school was transmitted to many later generations.

The master of Chung-nan-shan, Tao-hsüan, was the ninth of nine patriarchs, but he is now established as the great master and first grand patriarch.

16c The grand patriarch's personal name was Tao-hsüan. His natural capacities were outstanding, and his understanding was pure and penetrating. In the eleventh year of Ta-yeh (615), when he was fully twenty years old [this corresponds to the twenty-third year of the reign of the thirty-fourth Japanese sovereign, the

Empress Suiko], Tao-hsüan received full ordination from the Vinaya master Chih-shou. In the Wu-te era (618–626) of the great T'ang dynasty, he attended twenty complete lectures on the Vinaya given by Chih-shou.

He understood both scriptures and commentaries and widely studied the Mahayana and the Hinayana. He embraced Buddhist and non-Buddhist subjects and penetrated both sacred and secular learning. His conduct was more lofty than the firmament, and his virtue was deeper than the ocean. He illumined the five Vinayas like the rays of the sun, and his glory shown upon nine generations [of emperors].

Tao-hsüan composed the *Hsing-shih-ch'ao* in three volumes, dazzling both the past and the present. He composed two works of commentaries and thus [distinguished] the right from the wrong. In his *Ni-ch'ao* and his *Seng-ch'ao,* both monks and nuns received salvation. He marvellously penetrated the profound depths and was enlightened to all principles. His spiritual authority was superior to that of one thousand ancients; his abiding in and his keeping of [the precepts] superseded ten thousand generations.

His literary works were many and varied, totaling in all some two-hundred-odd volumes, such as *Praises, Collections, Meditations, Principles, Biographies, Records, Commentaries,* and *Essays.* They were widely propagated. When Hsüan-tsang was translating scriptures, Tao-hsüan assisted at the Translation Bureau. The Indian monks termed him "the bodhisattva of the East."

The Vinaya master Chih-shou decided the points of similarity between the five Vinayas and initiated the propagation of this teaching, yet its particulars were not yet widely disseminated. However, in the era when the great master of Chung-nan-shan, Tao-hsüan, kept [the precepts], scholarship advanced throughout the empire, and this school flourished in all corners.

The tradition of the Dharmaguptaka precepts, being dependent upon the right conditions, was now truly begun. This was due to the controlling power of the great master and lord of the Vinaya, Tao-hsüan.

The Vinaya regulations elucidated by Tao-hsüan came exclusively from the Fourfold [Dharmaguptaka Vinaya]. For commentaries, he relied upon the two traditions of the *Ch'eng-shih-lun* and the *She-ta-ch'eng-lun*. For scriptures, he depended upon the *Lotus* and the *Parinirvāṇa* scriptures. In his doctrinal classification, he established his teaching according to the three insights.

In general, he raised the wide net of the eight schools; but he specifically abided in the highest rank of only one school. Truly there was a reason for his embracing and propagating the True Dharma.

In the second year of Kan-feng (667), on the third day of the tenth month [this corresponds to the sixth year, *hinoto-u,* of the reign of the thirty-ninth Japanese sovereign, the Emperor Tenchi], sitting up properly, he died. Tao-hsüan was seventy-two years of age and was in the Sangha for fifty-two years.

There were many disciples of the great master of Chung-nan-shan, Tao-hsüan. Chiin of Silla was the first to write a commentary on the *Hsing-shih-ch'ao,* and the Vinaya master Ta-tz'u also compiled such a commentary.

The Vinaya master Hung-ching caused the *T'ien-t'ai* to flourish greatly; he kept the precepts as well as saved sentient beings. He was a disciple of the master of Chung-nan-shan, Tao-hsüan, who had reordained him; and it was he who was the *upādhyāya* who gave Chien-chen full ordination. Hung-ching wrote the *Vinaya Notes on the Hsing-shih-ch'ao* (*Lü-ch'ao-chi*) and lectured on the Vinaya over one hundred times.

The Vinaya master Huai-su initially studied the *Hsing-shih-ch'ao* of Tao-hsüan and also studied the Hsiang-pu school. He too was a reordained disciple of the master Tao-hsüan. The Vinaya masters Tao-an, Jung-chi, and others were disciples of the master Tao-hsüan.

Among Tao-hsüan's disciples, the Vinaya master Chou-hsiu was the second patriarch. The third patriarch was the Vinaya master Tao-heng of Su-chou. He composed a ten volume work, the *Records* (*Chi*), as an explanation of the *Hsing-shih-ch'ao.* The fourth patriarch was the Vinaya master Hsing-kung of Hui-chao-ssu

Monastery in Yang-chou, who composed the *Records in Accord with Orthodoxy* (*Hsun-ch'eng-chi*) as an explanation of the *Hsing-shih-ch'ao.* The fifth patriarch was the Vinaya master Hui-cheng. The sixth patriarch was the Fa-pao master Hsüan-yang of Ching-
17a chao. He wrote the *Record of the Revelation of Orthodoxy* (*Hsien-cheng-chi*) as an explanation of the *Hsing-shih-ch'ao.*

The seventh patriarch was the Vinaya master Yüan-piao of Yueh-chou, who composed the *Record of the Principles of the Hsing-shih-ch'ao,* the *Ch'ao-i-chi,* in five volumes. The eighth patriarch was the Vinaya master Shou-yen, who received the Dharma from Yüan-piao and who intensively studied this tradition's doctrines. The ninth patriarch was the Vinaya master Yüan-chieh of K'ang-chou. The tenth patriarch was the Vinaya master Fa-jung. The eleventh patriarch was the Vinaya master Ch'u-heng of K'ang-chou [also called Ch'u-yün], who wrote the *Records of Collecting That Which Had Been Overlooked* (*She-i-chi*) in three volumes. The twelfth patriarch was the Vinaya master Tse-wu of K'ang-chou, of the Sung dynasty. He wrote the *Records of a Garden of Principles* (*I-yüan-chi*) in seven volumes. The thirteenth patriarch was the Vinaya master Yün-k'an of T'ai-chou, of the Sung dynasty [also called Chen-wu], who received the Dharma from Ts'e-wu and who widely propagated the Vinaya tradition's literary works. He was born in the second year of Ching-teh (1005) in the reign of the third sovereign of the great Sung dynasty, the Emperor Chen-tsung [this corresponds to the second year of Kanwa, *kinoto-mi,* in the reign of the Emperor Ichijō of Japan]. Yün-k'an composed commentaries on all of the ten works of the master Tao-hsüan. Hence he was commonly called the "lord of the commentaries on the ten books" (*shih-pen-chi-chu*). He composed the *Hui-cheng-chi* as a commentary on the *Hsing-shih-ch'ao.* He composed the *Fan-yun-chi* as a commentary on the *Chieh-shu.* He composed the *Chen-yüan-chi* as a commentary on the *Yeh-shu.* He composed the *Fu-yao-chi* as a commentary on the *I-ch'ao.* He composed the *T'ung-yen-chi* as a commentary on the *Chiao-chieh-lu-i.* He composed the *Fa-shen-ch'ao* as a commentary on the *Ching-hsin-chieh-kuan.* And he also composed other works. These works flourished during the Sung dynasty [to such an extent that] the Nan-shan school was called the "Hui-cheng school."

The fourteenth patriarch was the Vinaya master Tse-ch'i. The fifteenth patriarch was the Ta-chin Vinaya master Yüan-chao of K'ang-chou. He penetrated both Buddhist and non-Buddhist learning and embraced both the Mahayana and the Hinayana. He was enlightened to the *T'ien-t'ai* tradition and spread the Pure Land teachings. He composed commentaries on all of the three major works of the Nan-shan school. On the *Hsing-shih-ch'ao* he composed the *Tzu-chih-chi.* On the *Chieh-shu* he composed the *Hsing-tsung-chi.* On the *Yeh-shu* he composed the *Chi-yüan-chi.* He also composed other works.

The master Yüan-chao was born in the eighth year of Ching-li (1048) in the reign of the fourth sovereign of the great Sung dynasty, the Emperor Jen-tsung. [This corresponds to the third year of Eishō, in the reign of the Emperor Go-Reizen of Japan.] He died on September 1, in the sixth year of Cheng-ho (1116), *ping-shen,* in the reign of the eighth sovereign of the Sung dynasty, the Emperor Hui-tsung. [This corresponds to the fourth year of Eikyū in the reign of the Emperor Toba of Japan.] [Yüan-chao was over sixty-nine years of age.]

From the year of his death to the present, which is the fourth year of Kagen (1306), *hinoe-uma* in Japan, one hundred ninety-one years have already elapsed.

The sixteenth patriarch was the Vinaya master Chih-chiao of the K'ai-yüan ching-yuan. [Some regard Tao-piao as the sixteenth patriarch.] The lineage of Shinjō adopts the Vinaya master Chih-chiao, while the lineage of Shunjō adopts Tao-piao.

The seventeenth patriarch was the Vinaya master Chun-i of Tung-t'ang. The eighteenth patriarch was the Vinaya master Fa-ch'eng of Chu-hsi. The nineteenth patriarch was the Vinaya master Fa-chiu of Shi-ku, who received the Dharma from Fa-ch'eng. He absorbed the teachings into himself and practiced them to perfection. One of his disciples was the Vinaya master Liao-hung of Ju-an, who was as a divine star of his age. Liao-hung received the Vinaya teachings from Fa-ch'eng and thoroughly penetrated this tradition's teachings. The Japanese monk Shunjō crossed the seas to Sung dynasty China, became one of his disciples, and extensively studied the Vinaya Piṭaka. After several years passed, Shunjō returned home and spread this teaching. The Vinaya master Shou-i was a disciple of Liao-hung of Ju-an. He thoroughly studied the precepts and the Vinaya and greatly established these principles.

17b The twentieth patriarch was the Vinaya master Miao-lien of Shang-weng. He studied the precepts and the Vinaya with the Vinaya master Fa-chiu, and he debated this tradition's principles with the master Shou-i. In the third year of Ching-ting (1262), *jen-hsu,* in the reign of the fourteenth sovereign of the great Sung dynasty, the Emperor Li-tsung [this corresponds to the second year of Kōchō, *mizunoe-inu* in the reign of the eighty-ninth emperor of Japan], on the third of January, Miao-lien died in the Chi-lo-an, at over eighty-one years of age.

The twenty-first patriarch was the Vinaya master Hsing-chu of Shi-lin. He received the teaching from the master Miao-lien and thus upheld the Vinaya Piṭaka.

From the master of Chu-hsi [i.e., the eighteenth patriarch Fa-ch'eng], all four patriarchs resided in Kuang-fu Vinaya Monastery of Ch'ao-hsin, where they upheld this transmitted Dharma, and where they held the doctrine in the Imitation Period.

The Japanese Vinaya master Shinjō went to the China of the great Sung dynasty, where he studied with the master Miao-lien, from whom he received the precepts and whom he questioned regarding the Vinaya. Shinjō also studied with the master Hsing-chü, from whom he studied the Vinaya and by whom he had his questions resolved. Shinjō was in China for three years during the period of the Shōgen (1259–60) and Kōchō (1261–64) eras.

After the time of the patriarch Hsing-chü, the Vinaya tradition in the great Sung Empire continued and spread in unbroken succession down to the present time.

We thus end the description, related above, of the transmission of the teachings of the Vinaya in China from ancient times on.

3. Japan

Regarding the propagation of the precepts and the Vinaya in Japan: the things to be said about its origins and its history are many. From its early foundations, from small beginnings, it became manifestly great.

In the thirteenth year (552), *mizunoe-saru,* of the reign of the thirteenth Japanese sovereign, the Kinmei Emperor, Ama-no-kuni Oshi-hiraki Hinoniwa, who was Prince Shiki-shima-no-Kanasashi-no-miya, the teachings of the venerable Śākyamuni first entered this land.

One thousand sixteen years after the death of the Tathāgata, Indian Buddhism first entered China in the tenth year of Yung-ping (A.D. 67), in the reign of the Emperor Ming of the Later Han dynasty.

Three hundred years later, Chinese Buddhism was transmitted to Paekche. One hundred years after that, Paekche Buddhism was first transmitted to Japan. This was the transmission in the *mizunoe-saru* year (552) of the Hironiwa Emperor (Kinmei). Buddhism was gradually introduced, but the Dharma of the precepts had not yet been initiated.

In the fifth year of the reign of the Emperor Bidatsu (576), *hinoe-saru,* Vinaya masters, meditation masters, Mantra masters, *bhikṣuṇīs*, and others came from Paekche bringing scriptures and commentaries. From this time onwards, monks gradually came to Japan.

In the first year of the reign of the Emperor Sujun (588) a monk from Paekche arrived; and [Soga no] Umako-sukune requested from that monk the Dharma [i.e., the ceremony] of receiving the precepts. Although such was the situation, all parties were not in harmony, and so it was not possible to carry out an orthodox (*nyohō*) ceremony of transmitting the precepts.

There was a group of three nuns in Japan who were born in Japan and who were the first to have left the householders' life. The first was called Zenshin-ni [originally the wife of Kimatsu]; the second was called Zenzō-ni [originally the wife of Tose]; and the

third was called Ezen-ni [originally the wife of Ishi]. These three nuns had the intention of receiving the precepts and thus desired to go to Paekche. Because of this intention, they had asked [a monk] if they might receive the precepts. The monk replied that because the two [validly ordained] Sanghas did not exist, the
17c ceremony of receiving the *bhikṣuṇī* precepts could not be carried out.

Because of this, the three nuns crossed over to Paekche in the year *tsuchinoe-saru* (588). In that year, they received the ten precepts (*daśa-śīla*) and the six rules of training [for postulants, *śīkṣamāṇya-dharma*].

The following year (589), *tsuchinoto-tori,* in March they received full ordination. The following year (590), *kanoe-inu,* they returned to Japan and resided in the Sakurai-dera. They later resided in the Kaijō-ji, which is the present Toyoura-dera.

In the year (588), *tsuchinoe-saru,* six monks were sent from Paekche. They were the Vinaya master Yŏngjo, the Dharma master Hyech'ong, the Dharma master Yŏngwi, the Dharma master Hyehun, the Dharma master Tosŏng, and the Dharma master Yŏnggye. These six monks were lodged in temporarily constructed monastic lodgings in Mukuhara village, [within a] temporarily [constructed] boundary (*sīma?*). Later this temple was splendidly decorated and its construction completed; this was the origin of Gangō-ji Monastery.

Such were the origins of monks and nuns in Japan. After this, monks and nuns gradually increased and filled the land.

However, the various conditions were incomplete, and there was no performing of the [orthodox ceremony of] receiving the [full] precepts. The monks that came to Japan from other countries were *bhikṣus* from [other] countries; but they were unable to transmit the full ordination in this country.

Nevertheless, later monks studied and practiced the various traditions of Buddhism. They understood meditation and wisdom and very thoroughly investigated the scriptures and commentaries. They relied upon the teachings of the *Chan-ch'a-ching,* the *P'u-sa ti ch'ih-ching,* and others. Some received the threefold precepts from other monks, and some obtained auspicious signs and performed the ceremony for receiving the precepts by one's self-vow. These are both rituals for the general receiving of all the threefold bodhisattva precepts.

The Dharma master Chikei is said to have been the first to have performed these ceremonies in the Yuima-dō; thus the basis for this practice is quite clear. It was in such a ceremony that the bodhisattva Gyōgi received full ordination from the Dharma master Tokukō.

In the eighth year of Tempyō (736), *hinoe-ne,* the Vinaya master Tao-hsüan came from T'ang China to Japan. Yet the number of validly ordained monks was insufficient, and he could not perform any ordinations.

From the *mizunoe-saru* year (552) of the Emperor Kinmei to the fifth year of Tempyō-shōhō (753), *mizunoto-mi,* in the reign of the forty-sixth sovereign of Japan, the Empress Kōken, she who was Princess Takaya-no-hime [this corresponds to the twelfth year of T'ien-pao in the reign of the sixth sovereign of the great T'ang dynasty, the Emperor Hsüan-tsung], two hundred two years had already elapsed. In that interval, the precepts and the Vinaya had not been transmitted.

In the fifth year of Tempyō (733), *mizunoto-tori,* in the reign of the forty-fifth Japanese sovereign, the Emperor Shōmu, who was Prince Shirushi-no-kuni Oshi-hiraki Toyo-Sakura-hiko [this corresponds to the twenty-first year of K'ai-yüan of the great T'ang dynasty], there was an imperial decree that both of the venerable meditation masters Yōei and Fushō of Kōfuku-ji Monastery should go to T'ang China for study.

Both these masters went to T'ang China and invited a *śramaṇa* of Ta-fu-kuang-ssu Monastery of the Eastern Capital (Lo-yang), the Vinaya master Tao-hsüan, to be the first to go to Japan. They proposed that he become the teacher to transmit the precepts there.

Both Yōei and Fushō remained in T'ang China to study.

In the eighth year of Tempyō (736), *hinoe-ne,* [this corresponds to the twenty-fourth year of K'ai-yüan of the T'ang dynasty], the

master Tao-hsüan, at the age of thirty-five, accompanied the ship of the assistant ambassador Nakatomi no Ason Nashiro and came to Japan. The master Tao-hsüan had penetrated the profound teachings of the Vinaya, the *Hua-yen,* the *T'ien-t'ai,* and the Northern school of Ch'an and had thoroughly mastered these
18a traditions. Although he did not carry out an ordination ceremony, he lectured on the Vinaya and opened the eyes of the multitudes.

When, in olden times, the master Tao-hsüan's *Hsing-shih-ch'ao* was initially introduced to this country, there was no one to lecture on it. The meditation master Tao-jung was the first to lecture on it. After Tao-hsüan arrived in Japan, it was lectured on and discussed in many places.

It was Rōben who first performed the *poṣadha,* (i.e., the twice monthly recitation of the *prātimokṣa*) in the Kinshō-ji, as he was told to do in a miraculous dream. He asked the master Tao-jung to preach on the *Fan-wang-chieh-ching* [in accordance with the dream]. This was the first *poṣadha* in Japan.

After this, the master Tao-jung would lecture on the *Hsing-shih-ch'ao* in the Kensakudō. The master Chikei likewise lectured on the *Hsing-shih-ch'ao* in many different places.

When Tao-hsüan came to Japan, he would always lecture on the *Hsing-shih-ch'ao.* He resided in the Dai'an-ji, and in the Tō-in of this monastery he would lecture on Tao-hsüan's *Hsing-shih-ch'ao* and discuss the various works of Tao-hsüan.

He had many disciples, and those that could explain the Vinaya were numerous. The Vinaya master Zenshun of the Dai'an-ji, who had a reputation for explaining the Vinaya, and others were Tao-hsüan's disciples.

While they were in T'ang China, Yōei and Fushō studied the various teachings for ten years. In the first year of T'ien-pao (742), *jen-wu* [this corresponds to the fourteenth year of Tempyō in Japan], they visited the Ta-ming-ssu in Yang-chou. There they did homage to the great *upādhyāya* Chien-chen. They told him in detail of their purpose in coming and requested that he cross eastward across the sea and spread the precepts and the Vinaya to Japan.

The *upādhyāya* thereupon agreed; his disciple Hsiang-yen was the first to agree to accompany him. Eventually there were twenty-one persons, Tao-hsing, Shen-hsiang, and others, who, being of the same mind, vowed to accompany him. With various other monks and laymen, there was a total of over eighty persons. After they had completed the necessary arrangements, they had a ship constructed and provided with supplies.

In crossing the seas, they encountered a variety of difficulties. Adverse currents and turbulent waves caused them to return to China each time they attempted to cross the seas. Four times they built a ship, and five times they put out to sea. For twelve years, they experienced hardships without number. Thirty-six monks and laymen died; among them were Yōei, Hsiang-yen, and others. Those who turned back were two hundred eighty persons.

It was only the *upādhyāya* Chien-chen, Fushō, and Ssu-ch'a who, though anticipating death, never thought of turning back.

The first time they set out was in the second year of T'ien-pao (743), *kuei-wei,* and the sixth and last time was in the twelfth year of T'ien-pao (753), *kuei-ssu,* [this corresponds to the fifth year of Tempyō-shōhō in Japan].

On the fifth of the eleventh month, they boarded their ship and departed from T'ang China. The disciples who accompanied Chien-chen were fourteen: the monk Fa-chin of Po-t'a-ssu Monastery, Yang-chou; the monk T'an-ching of Ch'ao-kung-ssu Monastery, Ch'üan-chou; the monk Ssu-ch'a of K'ai-yüan-ssu Monastery, T'ai-chou; the monk I-ching of Hsing-yün-ssu Monastery, Yang-chou; the monk Fa-tsai of Ling-yao-ssu Monastery, Ch'u-chou; the monk Fa-ch'eng of K'ai-yüan-ssu Monastery, Teng-chou, and others; the nun Chih-shou of T'ung-shan-ssu Monastery, T'ou-chou, and three others; the layman Fan Hsien-t'ung of Yang-chou; the Parthian Pao-tsui Ju-pao; Chün Fa-tao from K'un-lun; and Shan T'ing from Champā. In all, twenty-four persons set out upon the
18b sea for Japan. Finally, in the fifth year of Tempyō-shōhō (753), *mizunoto-mi,* on the twentieth of the twelfth month, they reached Japan.

In the sixth year (754), *kinoe-uma,* of the reign of the sixth sovereign of the T'ang, the Emperor Hsüan-tsung [this corresponds to the thirteenth year of T'ien-pao], on the fourth of the second month, they entered the capital [Nara]. They were escorted to Tōdai-ji Monastery and resided there. The deep joy and delight of the Emperor were without limit.

In the giving of the precepts and in the transmission of the Vinaya, everything was entrusted to the *upādhyāya* Chien-chen.

In the fourth month of that year (754), Chien-chen first had an ordination platform constructed in front of the Hall of Vairocana [at the Tōdai-ji].

First the emperor ascended the ordination platform and received the bodhisattva precepts; next the empress and the crown prince also ascended the ordination platform and received the precepts. And then Ch'eng-hsiu and others, some four-hundred-forty-odd persons, received the precepts.

Also eighty-odd fully ordained monks discarded their old precepts and received the precepts given by the *upādhyāya* Chien-chen. These were Ryōfuku, Kenkei, Shichu, Zenkō, Dōen, Byōtoku, Ningi, Zensha, Gyōsen, Gyōnin, and others.

Later, to the west of the Great Buddha Hall, the Chapel of the Ordination Platform was constructed independently [of any other buildings]. The earth of the ordination platform upon which the emperor had received the precepts was used in its construction.

In the third year of Tempyō-hōji (759), *tsuchinoto-i,* the great *upādhyāya* had Tōshōdai-ji Monastery constructed. It was presented with an official title, which was recorded and officially placed at the proper spot in the temple.

The Vinaya master Zenshun of the Dai'an-ji was asked to lecture on Fa-li's *Vinaya Commentary* (*Lü-shu*), on Tao-hsüan's *Hsing-shih-ch'ao,* and on other texts.

When the "sea-crossing *upādhyāya*" (Chien-chen) arrived in Japan, the master Ssu-ch'a acceded to the request of Ningi and others of the Dai'an-ji and lectured for four or five years at the

Tō-in [i.e., the Eastern Chapel] of that monastery on Fa-li's *Commentary* and on the *Records for Protecting the Nation* (*Chen-kuo-chi*) [Ting-pin's *Records of Ornamenting the Tradition* (*Shih-tsung-chi*)]. Later Ningi, Chūe, and others lectured in various different monasteries on Fa-li's *Commentary* and other texts.

The great *upādhyāya* had studied exclusively the two schools of Fa-li and Nan-shan. For that reason, when Chien-chen came to Japan, he greatly propagated these two schools.

When the master Chien-chen was eighteen years of age, he received the bodhisattva precepts from the Vinaya master Tao-an. At the age of twenty-one he received full ordination from the Vinaya master Hung-ching. He had studied the *Hsing-shih-ch'ao* and other texts with the Vinaya master Jung-chi.

Chien-chen had studied with the five eminent teachers I-wei, Yüan-chih, Kmsu, Hyech'aek, and Ta-liang, and he had studied Fa-li's *Vinaya Commentary* (*Lü-shu*). These five masters were direct disciples of the Vinaya master Man-i.

The great *upādhyāya* likewise penetrated into the *T'ien-t'ai* tradition's insight into the *Lotus Sutra*. He embraced the five vehicles and thoroughly understood the Tripiṭakas. He investigated both Buddhist and non-Buddhist teachings, and he embodied both the Mahayana and the Hinayana. He was miraculous in defense of the Dharma, and his spiritual manifestations converted and led many. Lecturing on the scriptures, the Vinayas, and the commentaries, he exhorted and led laymen. The echo of his fame reverberated far in the four directions, and his virtue flowed into eight vast regions. The nine provinces [i.e., the whole country] revered him as the *upādhyāya* from whom one receives the precepts.

He lectured on the Vinaya and its commentaries forty times. He lectured and expounded upon the *Hsing-shih-ch'ao* a total of seventy times. He lectured upon the major and minor precepts and the *karma-vacana* ritual ten times apiece.

In all, he ordained over forty thousand persons, of whom thirty-five persons especially stood out among the multitude. Each one built up one area and propagated the teachings of the Imitation Period.

There were three ordination platforms consecrated in Japan:
18c first, the ordination platform of the Tōdai-ji; second, the ordination platform of the Kanzeon-ji in the West; and third, the ordination platform of the Yakushi-ji in the East. In all three the imperial will was respected, and they carried out ordination ceremonies [as they were directed].

At the ordination platform of the Tōdai-ji, ten persons officiated at the ordination ceremonies according to the manner of a central country (*madhyama-deśa*). At the two provincial ordination platforms, five persons officiated at the ordination ceremonies according to the manner of a peripheral country.

An ordination platform was also constructed at the Tōshōdai-ji so that on both the east and the west sides of the capital, the precepts were handed down without interruption.

After Chien-chen's arrival in Japan, a total of ten years elapsed. For the first five years he resided at the Kaidan-in of the Tōdai-ji; the Tōzen'in was his actual permanent residence. For the last five years, he resided at the Tōshōdai-ji.

Of the disciples who constantly accompanied him, those who are known to later generations were the venerable masters Jen-kan, Fa-chin, T'an-ching, Fa-ke, Ssu-ch'a, I-ching, Chih-wei, Fa-tsai, Fa-ch'eng, Ling-yao, and Huai-ch'ien. These eleven persons received full ordination in T'ang China.

Ju-pao *shōsōzu* (minor bishop), the Vinaya master Hui-yün, the venerable masters Hui-liang, Hui-ta, Hui-ch'ang, and Hui-hsi—these six persons were natives of China but received full ordination in Japan.

The *śramaṇa* Tao-ch'in was also a native of China.

These seventeen [*sic*] persons accompanied Chien-chen from China to Japan. They were always with him and aided their master in his teaching and in his converting.

In the seventh year of Tempyō-hōji (763), *mizunoto-u* [this corresponds to the first year of Kuang-te, *kuei-mao,* in the reign of the eighth sovereign of the T'ang, the Emperor Tai-tsung], on the sixth day of the fifth month, sitting upright, the great *upādhyāya* Chien-chen died at the age of over seventy-seven. The master

Chien-chen had propagated both the Nan-shan and the Hsiang-pu schools [of the Vinaya tradition].

According to the Nan-shan lineage the master Tao-hsüan was the first patriarch, Hung-ching was the second patriarch, Chien-chen was the third patriarch, and Fa-chin and Ju-pao were both the fourth patriarchs.

According to the Hsiang-pu school, the first patriarch was Fa-li, the second patriarch was Tao-ch'eng, the third patriarch was Man-i, the fourth patriarch was Ta-liang, and the fifth patriarch was Chien-chen.

As Chien-chen was the first to transmit the Vinaya teachings to the East beyond the sea [i.e., to Japan], he, the great *upādhyāya,* is considered to be the first patriarch in Japan.

The *upādhyāya*'s disciple Fa-chin *daisōzu* (great bishop) was at his ease with the five literary corpora [of Vinaya texts] and had thoroughly read the four *Āgamas*. He had carefully studied the teachings and the meditational practice of the *T'ien-t'ai,* and he widely taught the Piṭaka of the bodhisattva precepts.

In the transmission of the precepts in Japan, the master Chien-chen was the first patriarch, Fa-chin *daisōzu* (great bishop) of the Tōdai-ji was the second *upādhyāya,* Ju-pao *shōsōzu* (minor bishop) of the Yakushi-ji was the third *upādhyāya,* Shōzen *risshi* (Vinaya master) of the Gangō-ji was the fourth *upādhyāya,* and Buan *zō-sōjō* (posthumous archbishop) of the Tōshōdai-ji was the fifth *upādhyāya.* In this way, the Vinaya masters of all seven major temples filled the office of *upādhyāya* in turn according to their seniority in the Sangha.

The ordination ceremony has been maintained and the Vinaya tradition upheld without interruption for many generations, up to the present day, to the one hundred seventh *upādhyāya,* the venerable master Zōshin of Kōfuku-ji Monastery.

19a The ordination ceremony at the Tōdai-ji has been maintained for many generations, as shown above. This is likewise the case with the transmission of the precepts at the Kanzeon-ji.

The Yakushi-ji ordinations were interrupted in medieval times and have not since been performed.

The *upādhyāya* Chien-chen bequeathed the Tōzen'in to Fa-chin. It is his disciples who have transmitted its succession generation upon generation.

When the *upādhyāya* was nearing his death, he bequeathed the Tōshōdai-ji to Fa-tsai, I-ching, and Ju-pao. These three masters, being of like resolve, combined their strength and caused this temple to flourish and to propagate the Vinaya teachings.

Each one had his own school of disciples, which grew and prospered while propagating and adhering [to the Vinaya teachings].

Speaking generally, there were ten-odd disciples of the *upādhyāya*. Each one had his own school of disciples that has lasted for generation upon generation without interruption.

The great *upādhyāya* was the first patriarch. The next was the venerable master Fa-tsai, the next was the master Shinkei, the fourth was the master Kaishō, the fifth was the master Jukō, the sixth was the master Zōshi, the seventh was the master Anchin, and the eighth was the master Kikan. From the time of the great *upādhyāya* [died 763] to the Ninna era (885–89), this tradition's lineage has continued for eight generations as given above.

In addition however, the great *upādhyāya* was succeeded by Ju-pao *shōsōzu* (minor bishop). The next was Buan *zō-sōjō,* the next was the Vinaya master Dōjō, the next was the venerable master Ninkai, and the next was the master Shinkū. In this way, this tradition's lineage succeeded for six generations without interruption. Concerning the traditions of the other disciples, we must now abbreviate the rest for fear of being prolix. After the Ninna period (885–89), the disciples in the lineage of the Tōshōdai-ji were very many; however, we shall not record them

In a later era, Jippan *shōnin* of Naka-no-kawa entered the Tōshōdai-ji and received the precepts. A great number of masters received the precepts. Although their names are not known, their Dharma lineages continued to later generations. After Jippan, a succession of persons continued his Dharma lineage without interruption.

The Vinaya flourished in the Tōshōdai-ji. After receiving the precepts, monks from the various other temples would reside in this temple for five or six years and study the Vinaya intensively; but in later generations, this practice declined.

Right after the time of Buan and Dōjō, both the study and the practice of the Vinaya never slackened. But two-hundred-odd years afterwards, the practice [of the precepts] gradually became lax, even though scholastic achievements continued from generation to generation without interruption.

In the reign of the seventy-fourth sovereign, the Emperor Toba [reigned 1107–22], there was an outstanding genius of Kōfuku-ji Monastery, the venerable master Jippan of Naka-no-kawa. According to the request of the master Kinzei of the Kōfuku-ji, Jippan read the Vinaya Piṭaka and studied the teachings concerning the precepts. He composed the *Rituals of the Ordination Platform* (*Kaidanshiki*) and revived the teaching of the Vinaya. The revival of the teaching of the precepts was the achievement of the master Jippan.

Jippan *shōnin* had gone to the Tōshōdai-ji and met an old monk (*ippan rōtoku*) who transmitted to him the *prātimokṣa* text of the Fourfold [Dharmaguptaka Vinaya]. Thereupon Jippan later read the *Ta-ch'ao* [i.e., Tao-hsüan's *Hsing-shih-ch'ao*] and thoroughly studied the Dharmaguptaka Vinaya and K'uei-chi's *Chapter Dealing with Vijñapti- and Avijñapti-Rūpa* [i.e., the *Piao wu-piao chang*]. He clarified the nature of the precepts as
19b they relate to the three vehicles. He was well versed in the *Pŏngang-gyŏng kojŏk-ki,* the commentaries of all the masters, and the precepts of both the Mahayana and the Hinayana. His fame in elucidating the Vinaya spread throughout the world.

Eighty-odd years later, in the reign of the eighty-third sovereign, the Emperor Tsuchimikado, there was a wise monk of Kōfuku-ji Monastery, Jōkyō *shōnin.* Jōkyō received the Dharma from Kakuken; Kakuken had received it from Zōshun; and Zōshun had received it from Jippan. In this manner, the succession was successively intertwined. Jōkyō's understanding penetrated to the two knowledges, his learning encompassed the Tripiṭaka, his virtue filled the cosmos, and his majesty moved both the visible and the invisible [worlds]. Again and again he propagated the precepts, and he led and converted many.

At that time, two scholars, Kainyo and Kakushin, took Jōkyō as their master and studied the Mahayana and Hinayana precepts under him.

The venerable master Kakushin was resolved to revive [the Vinaya tradition] and so he had the Jōki'in built to serve as a house of study.

Kainyo *shōnin* produced as students many learned persons: Ensei, Kakujō, Keison, Kakuchō, Zenkan, Ren'i, Renkaku, and others. If anyone desired to study with Kainyo, they resided in the Jōki'in, where they heard lectures and studied the various Vinayas of both the Mahayana and the Hinayana.

In the second year of Katei (1236), *hinoe-saru,* in the reign of the eighty-sixth sovereign, the Emperor Shijō, there were four very eminent scholars, Ensei, Yūgen, Kakujō, and Eison, who deeply lamented that although there was scholastic understanding, the practice of the precepts was lacking.

Therefore relying upon the teachings of the scriptures and commentaries, and according to the rituals for receiving all of the threefold precepts, these four worthies, being of one accord, prayed for auspicious signs that they might receive the precepts by self-vow and so practice the precepts. When the auspicious signs had been accomplished, these four individually took the precepts by self-vows within the Great Buddha Hall [of the Tōdai-ji]. This was on the second and the fourth day of the ninth month [1236].

After this, the venerable master Ensei resided in the Fukū'in. He later moved to Kyoto, where he lectured on the Vinaya Piṭaka.

Kakujō *shōnin* resided initially in the Shō'in of the Kōfuku-ji for seven or eight years. He later moved to the Tōshōdai-ji, where he lived for six years.

Eison *shōnin* resided in the Saidai-ji, where he lectured on the Vinaya and transmitted the precepts. He revived both the revealed and the secret teachings.

In the *hinoe-saru* year (1236), Eison had received all of the threefold precepts. Ten years later, in the second year of Kangen (1244), *kinoe-tatsu,* in the middle of the ninth month, in the Iehara-dera in Izumi Province, Eison performed for the first time the separate receiving of [the first of the threefold] bodhisattva precepts.

The venerable master Eison of Saidai-ji Monastery had initially attended Ensei's lecture of the *Hsing-shih-ch'ao* [the first part of the first volume]. Later he read by himself the major literary corpus of Tao-hsüan and studied these works minutely and thoroughly. Under the venerable master Kakujō, he heard lectures on the *Chapter Dealing with Vijñapti- and Avijñapti-Rūpa* and other works. He attended lectures on the *Pŏngang-gyŏng Kojŏk-ki* under Kainyo and Kakuchō.

Kainyo had studied under Jōkyō *shōnin* and had studied the *Pŏngang-gyŏng Kojŏk-ki,* the *Chapter Dealing with Vijñapti- and Avijñapti-Rūpa,* and other works.

Kakujō had studied under Kainyo and had attended his lectures on the *Chapter Dealing with Vijñapti- and Avijñapti-Rūpa,* the *Pŏngang-gyŏng Kojŏk-ki,* and other works.

Kakujō *shōnin* resided in the Tōshōdai-ji, where he revived the ancient [Vinaya] heritage of the great *upādhyāya,* Chien-chen. He once lectured on the three major Vinaya works of the master
19c Tao-hsüan from beginning to end. He would lecture on all the other minor works on the Mahayana and Hinayana precepts whenever it was appropriate.

People came from the four quarters to receive the precepts and to hear lectures on the Vinaya. In later times, various worthies, good teachers having the Buddha's eyes of wisdom, the Zenjō-*taikō* of the Hōshō-ji, whose name (*imina*) was Gyōe; Ryōben, the Hoin *gon-daisōzu* (great bishop of lower rank); Jōken *gon-risshi* (Vinaya master of lower rank) [who changed his *gō* (name) to Shinkū]; the *ācārya* Jōkei; the *śramaṇa* Daijōshin; Nyūa; Jakue; Keiun; Shōshū; Zenna [who received the precepts twice]; Enshō; Shōgen; Jizai; and others penetrated according to their abilities and, whenever the opportunity presented itself, propagated the three learnings, the two Piṭakas, the revealed and the secret teachings, the Yogācāra and the Madhyamaka, the teachings of converting and of legislating, the Buddhist and non-Buddhist teachings, or the two aspects of teaching and insights [in the *Tendai* tradition]. Truly, these monks were as the male and female phoenixes of Śākyamuni's teachings and as dragons and elephants for Buddhism. Each converted his own area and yet served as a model to the world. All had studied the great threefold bodhisattva precepts under the *upādhyāya* Kakujō.

Among their number, the venerable master Shōgen succeeded in the footsteps of the *upādhyāya* Kakujō and resided in the Tōshōdai-ji. After Shōgen, his disciple Shinshō resided as abbot in the same monastery. There were many scholar monks among Shōgen's disciples who constructed monasteries or chapels and who propagated his teachings. The controlling virtue of the master Shōgen surpassed that of the multitude. He resided in the Tōshōdai-ji for forty-four years, spreading both the revealed and the secret teachings and lecturing without ceasing.

In the fifth year of Shōō (1292), *mizunoe-tatsu,* on the fourth day of the eighth month, Shōgen died. He was seventy-three years of age.

Shinshō served as abbot of the Tōshōdai-ji for thirteen years. He lectured continuously and gave the precepts to a multitude of persons. In the second year of Kagen (1304), *kinoe-tatsu,* on the first day of the second month, Shinshō died. He was sixty-nine years of age.

Next the venerable master Jinsan resided as abbot in the monastery [i.e., the Tōshōdai-ji] giving the precepts and transmitting the Dharma. He was revered by everyone. In the fourth year of Kagen (1306), *hinoe-uma,* on the fifteenth day of the second month, Jinsan died. He was seventy-nine years of age.

The venerable master Enshō was among Shōgen's disciples. He had studied the Vinaya Piṭaka and, further, understood the various traditions [of Buddhism]. He resided in the Tōshōdai-ji and lectured without ceasing.

There was also the venerable master Dōgyō, who was a disciple personally ordained by Shōgen. His virtue and leadership were known afar. He resided in the Hōkongō'in in Kyoto. When Shinshō was nearing his death, he had Dōgyō reside in the Tōshōdai-ji; but Dōgyō handed [the office of abbot] over to Jinsan and returned to Kyoto.

The *upādhyāya* Enshō popularized the ordination platform and propagated the Vinaya. He lectured without tiring. Numerous were his disciples who upheld the teachings of the [Vinaya] tradition.

The *upādhyāya* Zenne was an outstanding teacher of the Vinaya. He constructed temples in his area and produced pupils of genius.

The venerable master Keiun was a firm and principled Dharma teacher. He revived the sacred heritage [of Chien-chen] and illumined the glory of the virtue of transmitting the precepts.

Shinkū *shōnin* caused Kannon'in [Kibata] to prosper and propagated both the revealed and the secret teachings.

Shōshu *shōnin* revived the Shingon'in, and practiced and propagated both the revealed and the secret teachings.

20a The venerable master Shōnen was a disciple of Shōshu. He received the secret teachings from the master Shōshu and received the precepts from Shōgen. He studied the Madhyamaka and stood out from the multitude.

The venerable master Mitsugon studied the *Tendai* and the secret teachings. He revived Yakushi-ji Monastery in Shimotsuke. He was a disciple personally ordained by Ryōben *shōnin.*

The *upādhyāya* Kakujō died early. In the first year of Kenchō (1249), on the nineteenth day of the fifth month, he died. He was fifty-seven years of age. He had lived fourteen years after he had received the precepts by self-vow.

The disciples of the *upādhyāya* Eison of the Saidai-ji were very numerous: they were Ninshō *shōnin,* Kennin, Zenson, Kōen, Jakuson, Raigen, Eishin, Shinkū, Sōji, Shōyu, Genki, and others. They were all pillars and beams of the Dharma, standards and guides of Buddhism. Whenever it was appropriate, they mastered and preached on the principles of the Tripiṭakas of the Mahayana and of the Hinayana, on the revealed and secret teachings, on the two teachings of converting and legislating, on the Yogācāra and the Madhyamaka, and on the Buddhist and non-Buddhist teachings. Penetrating deeply into these teachings, each converted people in his one area and served as a model of the Dharma. Truly these were as great generals in propagating [the Dharma]; they were elders of the Enlightenment and salvation [of all creatures].

Ninshō *shōnin* travelled in the eastern provinces, greatly spreading the Vinaya. Many were his disciples who brightened the glory of the teachings. Of those many disciples of Ninshō who spread the Dharma, some were [teachers] of the revealed teachings and some were [teachers] of the secret teachings. They were proficient both in wisdom and in eloquence. They filled the eastern provinces, each establishing his teachings.

The virtue of the *upādhyāya* Eison covered all creatures. His majesty moved both the invisible and the visible worlds. He met with nine sacred sovereigns, and he was the State Teacher (*kokushi*) to five emperors. His spreading of the precepts filled the world; his teaching of the secret Piṭaka transversed all the corners of the universe. In his studies of the Tripiṭaka, he continually investigated the Mahayana and the Hinayana. Wise monks were produced [under his tutelage], and their monasteries filled the various provinces. In the third year of Shōō (1290), *kanoe-tora,* on the twenty-fifth day of the eighth month, he died. He was ninety years of age. His posthumous title was Bodhisattva Promoter of Righteousness (*Kōshō-bosatsu*).

The venerable master Raigen resided in Sanson-ji Monastery in the province of Hitachi and propagated the Dharma of the Vinaya.

The venerable master Eishin resided in Gokuraku-ji Monastery after the master Ninsho. There he caused the two truths to flourish and practiced both the revealed and the secret teachings.

After the master Eison, the venerable master Shinkū resided in the Saidai-ji, where he transmitted the precepts and lectured on the Vinaya. Many looked to his virtue. Masters and pupils flourished through the years. Many men of wisdom were produced who aided in the converting work of the Dharma.

Sōji *shōnin* was the same type of person as the Bodhisattva Promoter of Righteousness [i.e., Eison]. He was superior in learning and in understanding, and he was unique in his traversing of the path of the Vinaya.

The venerable master Kōson was both broad and deep [in his understanding of] the sea-like Vinaya. He would lecture upon it day after day. Many were the wise and virtuous persons produced by him. He resided in the Kairyūō-ji, and his name was spread far and near.

The venerable master Shin'en surpassed the multitude in his learning and in his understanding. He was proficient both in principles and in their discussion. He resided in the Hannya-ji, and his fame flew far and near. He stood out from the crowd in wisdom and in virtue, and both these qualities caused the garden of the Vinaya to bloom.

These were all disciples personally ordained by the *upādhyāya* Eison.

The venerable master Shōyu was a disciple personally or-
20b dained by the master Eison. He was formerly a pillar of the three mysteries [i.e., the secret teachings]. He joined the school of Eison and transmitted what his master had propagated. After [the death of] the master Eison, his tradition was transmitted in many places, far and near.

Relying largely upon the Yoga [i.e., the *Hossō* tradition], those persons to whom Eison had transmitted this Dharma flourished greatly. They may be said to have excelled their teachers in the same way that ice outshines water and indigo outshines blue.

The venerable master Seishin travelled in the east [i.e., in the Kantō plains area]. Establishing himself in one location, he widely propagated the Dharma of the Vinaya.

The venerable master Jūzen was a disciple who had obtained the precepts from the master Eison. He had received instruction in the Vinaya from Zenne *shōnin,* who in turn was formerly a pupil of Enshō *shōnin.* In his learning of the Vinaya, Jūzen excelled the multitude. He stood apart from the crowd in the secret teachings. He penetrated freely into the *Sanron* [i.e., the Madhyamaka] and was unique throughout the land.

This revival of the Vinaya tradition filled the whole land. It was truly due to the strength of the great vow of marvellous means of the two worthies Kakujō and Eison.

In the reign of the eighty-second sovereign, the Emperor Go-Toba, in the Kenkyū era (1190–98), there was a *śramaṇa,* a native of Kyūshū, whose personal name was Shunjō. His will was centered in studying, and he thought only of the precepts and the Vinaya. He came to the southern capital [Nara] in order to search out the Dharma of the Vinaya. At that time, there was a venerable master whose name in religion was Rengō, and Shunjō studied the precepts and the Vinaya under him. But not being able to obtain [the full particulars concerning] the positive and the negative precepts, Shunjō looked to a different, distant land. In the first year of Shōji (1199), *tsuchinoto-hitsuji,* in the reign of the Emperor Tsuchimikado, at the age of thirty-four, Shunjō crossed the seas and went to Sung China. This corresponds to the fifth year of Ch'ing-yüan of the thirteenth sovereign of the great Sung dynasty, the Emperor Ning-tsung.

Initially Shunjō met the Dharma master Tsung-yin of Pei-feng, with whom he studied the *T'ien-t'ai* tradition. Later he received instruction in the Nan-shan Vinaya school under the Vinaya master Liao-hung of Ju-an. He studied most diligently. In these two traditions, there was nothing he omitted.

He studied the Dharma in China for thirteen years. He returned home in the first year of Kenryaku (1211), *kanoto-hitsuji,* in the reign of the Emperor Juntoku. Subsequently he erected the Sen'yū-ritsu-ji in the Higashi-yama section of the northern metropolis [i.e., Kyoto].

He widely propagated the precepts and the Vinaya and lectured extensively upon the traditions of the *T'ien-t'ai.* For seventeen years he propagated the Vinaya in Japan. He never ceased in either his lecturing or his giving of the precepts. His lectures flourished greatly.

Fukaki-hōshi [literally, The Dharma Master Who Could Not Be Abandoned, i.e., Shunjō] was the first patriarch of the revived Vinaya propagation in the northern metropolis.

In the third year of Karoku (1227), *hinoto-i* [which was the first year of the new Antei era], on the eighth day of the third month, Shunjō died. He was some sixty-two years old.

The virtue of this Dharma master swayed both countries, and his authority moved ten thousand generations.

In the Vinaya area of the Sen'yū-ji, the precepts and the Vinaya were greatly practiced. Lectures have not ceased even up to the present time but have greatly flourished. One of Shunjō's disciples was the *ācārya* Jōshun, who lectured much on the precepts and the Vinaya and who greatly influenced the trend of his time. All the various venerable masters of later ages, such as Chikyō, Dōgen, Jōin, and others, were disciples of the master Jōshun.

In the spring of the third year of Karoku (1227), *hinoto-tori,* the *ācārya* Jōshun came to Kairyūō-ji Monastery in the southern capital [Nara] where he lectured on the Vinaya texts of the Hinayana and other works. The multitude were pressed shoulder to shoulder; thus did they assemble to hear these lectures. Eison, Zenne, Genshun, and others all heard his lectures.

20c After Jōshun, the venerable master Chikyō was the abbot of Sen'yū-ji. There he propagated the Vinaya. The master Chikyō had crossed the seas and gone to Sung China. There he heard lectures on the Vinaya and imbibed the tradition.

The venerable master Ninkū imbibed the tradition from Chikyō. Afterwards he moved to the Kaidan-in [of the Tōdai-ji]. There he became Enshō's disciple, received full ordination, and studied the precepts and the Vinaya. The two teachings of receiving all the threefold precepts and of separately receiving only the precept that embraces all the rules of discipline were fully transmitted to him. Ninkū also studied with Eison *shōnin,* from whom he received full ordination for a second time.

After the master Chikyō, the venerable master Shiin resided as abbot in Sen'yū-ji Monastery, where he lectured on the Vinaya and propagated its teachings. He personally received the precepts from the founder [of Sen'yū-ji Monastery] Fukaki-hōshi [i.e., Shunjō]. Later he studied the Vinaya with Jōshun.

The venerable master Jōin received the Dharma from Jōshun and in addition studied with Chikyō. He resided in the Kaikō-ritsu-ji, where he greatly propagated the Dharma of the Vinaya in the

Imitation Dharma Period. His converting influence flowed to the eastern provinces, and he served as a model for distant generations.

The venerable master Shinshō formerly studied with Enshō *shōnin,* from whom he received the precepts and heard lectures on the Vinaya. He also studied with Jōin *shōnin,* from whom he heard lectures on the major commentarial works on the Vinaya. Ninkū also heard these lectures given by Jōin on the Vinaya.

Shinshō went to Sung China and met Miao-lien and Hsing-chü, with whom he studied the Vinaya and through whom his doubts were settled. After his return to Japan, he propagated the Vinaya at the Kaidan-in [of the Tōdai-ji]. Later he moved to the Sen'yū-ji, where he studied with Shiin, with whom he studied the Vinaya and by whom his doubts were settled.

There was one venerable master, Genshun, who was originally from the southern capital [Nara] but who later received the teachings from Chikyō. Diligent and persevering, he penetrated the tradition of the precepts. Establishing himself in one location, he greatly propagated the Dharma of the Way.

After Shiin, Gangyō *shōnin* resided in the Sen'yū-ji. After him, the monastery and its chapels were entrusted to the venerable master Kakua.

Kakua had studied with the two masters, Chikyō and Jōin, with whom he had studied the Vinaya Piṭaka. His virtues were greatly manifested by his propagation of both the revealed and the secret teachings. Kakua then entrusted the monastery and its chapels to his disciple, the venerable master Chigen. The master Chigen managed the monastery, propagated the tradition, and lectured on the Vinaya.

In this way, the Dharma of the Vinaya was revived. In both the southern and northern capitals [i.e., Nara and Kyoto], in the five *ki* and the seven *dō* [i.e., all Japan], it was widely diffused according to conditions. As conditions were opportune, [the Vinaya revival] spread about. In space it was as universal as here presented. In time it can thus be plumbed.

Being the merit by which the Buddha-Dharma abides for a long time, the Vinaya is truly ever new. An auspicious sign augering the peace of the nation, this tradition is indeed great. In protecting the Dharma, it is unfathomable. In saving all creatures, it is inexhaustible. The merit of the precepts and the Vinaya is apparent in all phenomena. The power of *śīla* is clearly obvious.

The essentials of the Vinaya tradition are in outline thus.

Glossary

Abhidharma(s): commentaries on the Buddha's teachings. Cf. Tripiṭaka.

Absolute Truth. *See* two truths.

ācārya: a teacher.

Āgama: a collection of early Buddhist scriptures.

ālaya-vijñāna ("storehouse consciousness"): the latent, seminal consciousness that supports karmically defiled awareness.

Ānanda: a disciple of the Buddha, a specialist in sutras.

arhat: a Hinayana (q.v.) saint who has completely destroyed his evil passions and attained emancipation from cycles of birth and death (q.v.). Cf. four fruits; Hinayana.

asaṃkhyeya-kalpa: an uncountable aeon.

avijñapti-rūpa: an unmanifest form; a nonactive element.

āyatana ("entrance"): a sense organ and the sense data that enter it to be discriminated.

bhikṣu: a monk. Cf. seven groups of persons.

bhikṣuṇī: a nun. Cf. seven groups of persons.

bīja ("seed"): the inner habit-energies that lie in the *ālaya-vijñāna* (q.v.).

birth and death (samsara): the endless cycle of death and rebirth that traps ordinary, unenlightened beings in this defiled world.

bodhi. See Enlightenment.

bodhisattva: one who aspires to the attainment of Buddhahood.

Body of Recompense. *See* three bodies of the Buddha.

Buddha: an awakened person, an enlightened one. Cf. Three Refuges.

Buddha-Dharma. *See* Dharma.

Buddha nature: the basic enlightened nature of sentient beings, which is chronically obscured by their ignorance. The complete unfolding of the Buddha nature is Enlightenment itself.

causation: the complex holistic combination of causes and conditions that brings into being all phenomena and events in this world. *See also* emptiness; karma.

Conventional Truth. *See* two truths.

Dharma: Law, truth; Buddhist teachings, the Buddha's doctrine. Cf. Three Refuges.

dharma: a thing, element.

Dharma Body. *See* three bodies of the Buddha.

Dharmaguptaka: an early Buddhist school; the Vinaya (q.v.) recension of this school.

dhyāna: meditation.

diamond-like mind: the indestructible mind of the bodhisattva, which is compared to a diamond.

eighteen *dhātus*: the six sense organs, the six objects of the senses (sounds, smells, etc.), and the six consciousnesses (q.v.) associated with the six sense organs.

eight Enlightenments of great persons: the eight spiritual qualities leading to Buddhahood, which are attained by superior practitioners such as bodhisattvas, *pratyekabuddhas* (q.v.), and *śrāvakas* (q.v.)—(1) little desire, (2) contentment, (3) detachment, (4) effort, (5) right mindfulness, (6) right meditation, (7) right wisdom, and (8) not engaging in idle discussions.

eight levels of consciousness: (1) eye-consciousness, (2) ear-consciousness, (3) nose-consciousness, (4) tongue-consciousness, (5) body-consciousness, (6) *mano*-consciousness (the mental sense or intellect), (7) *manas* (ego consciousness), and (8) *ālaya-vijñāna* (q.v.).

eight precepts: (1) not to kill, (2) not to steal, (3) not to engage in sexual acts, (4) not to lie, and (5) not to drink liquor, (6) not to use high or broad beds, (7) not to put perfumes or oils on the body nor to sing or dance, and (8) to eat only at designated times. Cf. five precepts; six rules; ten precepts; *upavasatha.*

emptiness/nonsubstantiality (*śūnyatā*): the doctrine that all phenomena exist only in dependence on a complex web of causes and conditions and go on existing only as long as those causes and conditions prevail. Nothing, therefore, has "true," independent, permanent existence. *See also* causation; two emptinesses.

Enlightenment (*bodhi*): a state in which one is awakened to the true nature of things. *See also* two truths; two emptinesses.

expedient means (*upāya*): the skillful methods that a Buddha or bodhisattva uses to teach sentient beings and bring them to Enlightenment.

Fan-wang-ching: a Mahayana text elucidating the major and minor precepts.

fifty-two stages [of bodhisattvahood]: (1) the ten stages of faith; (2) the ten abodes; (3) the ten practices; (4) the ten transferences of merit; (5) the ten realms; (6) the Stage Almost Equal to Enlightenment, i.e., the fifty-first stage; and (7) the Stage of Marvellous Enlightenment, i.e., the fifty-second stage.

five faculties: (1) faith, which destroys doubt, (2) effort, which destroys laziness, (3) mindfulness, which destroys falsity, (4) meditation (q.v.), which destroys confusion, and (5) wisdom (q.v.), which destroys all delusions.

Fivefold Vinaya: the Vinaya (q.v.) of the Mahīśāsakas.

five precepts: (1) not to kill, (2) not to steal, (3) not to engage in sexual misconduct, (4) not to lie, and (5) not to drink liquor; the precepts for lay people. Cf. eight precepts; six rules; ten precepts.

five *skandhas* ("aggregates"): the five aggregates that make up sentient beings—(1) form (*rūpa*), (2) sensation (*vedanā*), (3) conception (*saṃjñā*), (4) volition (*saṃskāra*), and (5) consciousness (*vijñāna*).

forty-eight minor precepts: the minor precepts listed in the *Fan-wang-ching* (q.v.), against actions such as drinking alcohol, slighting one's master, and eating meat and the five pungent roots.

forty-four minor precepts: the minor bodhisattva precepts listed in the *Yü-ch'ieh-lun* (q.v.).

Fourfold Vinaya: the Vinaya (q.v.) of the Dharmaguptakas.

four fruits: the four stages on the Hinayana (q.v.) path—(1) stream-enterer (*srotāpanna,* one who has entered the stream of the undefiled noble path), (2) once-returner (*sakṛdāgāmin,* one who will return to the world only once more before full realization of arhatship), (3) nonreturner (*anāgāmin,* one who will never again be reborn in this world), and (4) arhat (q.v.).

four immeasurable hearts: the hearts of kindness, pity, joy, and equanimity.

four major precepts (for monks and nuns): (1) not to kill, (2) not to steal, (3) not to engage in sexual acts, and (4) not to lie.

Four Noble Truths: (1) life is suffering, (2) defilements are the cause of suffering, (3) all suffering can be ended, and (4) the way to end suffering is the Noble Eightfold Path (q.v.).

four qualities: the four excellent qualities of Nirvana—(1) eternally abiding, (2) blissful, (3) capable of manifesting itself and doing anything at will, and (4) free of defilements.

four teachings: (1) the teachings of *śrāvakas* (q.v.), (2) the teachings of *pratyekabuddhas* (q.v.), (3) the Mahayana (q.v.) teachings of bodhisattvas, and (4) the final perfect teaching of the One Vehicle (q.v.).

four types of birth: (1) from the womb, (2) from an egg, (3) from moisture, and (4) by metamorphosis (such as birth in one of the heavens).

four universal vows: the four vows undertaken by all bodhisattvas in their quest to bring Enlightenment to all sentient beings who are suffering in birth and death (q.v.)—(1) the vow to save all sentient beings, (2) the vow to cut off all defilements or passions, (3) the vow to study all teachings, and (4) the vow to attain Buddhahood.

four wisdoms: (1) the great, perfect, mirror-like wisdom (*ādarśa-jñāna*), (2) the wisdom that sees that all things are the same in nature (*samatā-jñāna*), (3) the wisdom of marvellous insight (*pratyavekṣaṇā-jñāna*), and (4) the wisdom that accomplishes the work that is to be done (*kṛtyānuṣṭhāna-jñāna*).

grand master of Nan-Shan: Tao-hsüan.

Hinayana ("Lesser Vehicle"): a derogatory term applied by Mahayanists to various schools of Buddhism that exalt as their ideal the arhat (q.v.). Cf. Mahayana.

hindrance of illusions. *See* two types of hindrance.

hindrance of knowledge. *See* two types of hindrance.

Hua-yen: a school based on the *Avataṃsaka-sūtra* (Chin. *Hua-yen-ching*/Jp. *Kegon-gyō*) which particularly emphasizes interdependence.

Imitation Dharma Period: the second period after the Buddha's death (usually said to begin after one thousand years and to last for a thousand years), during which Buddhist teachings and practice still exist but Enlightenment is no longer possible. It is followed by the third period, the Final Dharma, during which only the teachings exist.

jñeya-āvaraṇa. See two types of hindrance.

Kaidan-in: a building in the Tōdai-ji that housed one of the first ordination platforms in Japan.

kalpa: an aeon.

karma: action (morally good, evil, or neutral). The word also implies that all of our actions have multifaceted consequences. *See also* causation.

karman: a ceremony in which a person vows to observe the precepts or confesses his transgressions against the Vinaya (q.v.).

karma-vacana ceremony: an ordination ceremony in which someone is formally accepted into the Sangha of monks or nuns and the person publicly receives precepts. On this occasion the preceptor states once, "Please give permission for the ordination of this monk." Then he declares three times, "If you consent, please show it by silence. If you oppose it, please explain the reason."

Kāśyapa: one of the chief disciples of the Buddha. He specialized in the Vinaya (q.v.).

kleśa-āvaraṇa. See two types of hindrance.

kṣaṇa: a moment.

Madhyamaka: the "middle path" (q.v.) school of Buddhism, founded by Nāgārjuna (ca. 150–250) and his followers. Its tenets are mainly based upon the *Prajñā-pāramitā-sūtra*s, which stress the teaching of emptiness (q.v.).

Mahāsāṅghika: one of the eighteen schools of early Buddhism, considered by most scholars to be the precursor of the Mahayana (q.v.).

Mahayana ("Great Vehicle"): teachings on the attainment of Enlightenment or Buddhahood; the seeker of Enlightenment is the bodhisattva (q.v.). Cf. Hinayana.

Maitreya: the future Buddha.

manas. *See* eight levels of consciousness.

meditation (*samādhi*): a state of serene contemplation or concentration; one of the six *pāramitās* (q.v.), one of the three learnings (q.v.).

middle path: the truth of nonduality that Śākyamuni taught; the truth of neither existence nor nonexistence. Cf. Madhyamaka.

Nan-shan master. *See* Grand Master of Nan-Shan.

New School of Translation: the translations of Buddhist texts into Chinese that were done by Hsüan-tsang (A.D. 600–64) and later translators.

Nirvana: the final goal of Buddhists; the extinction of all passions and desires; the state of liberation.

Noble Eightfold Path: (1) right view, (2) right thought, (3) right speech, (4) right action, (5) right livelihood, (6) right effort, (7) right mindfulness, and (8) right meditation.

nonsubstantiality. *See* emptiness/nonsubstantiality.

Old School of Translation: translations of Buddhist texts into Chinese that were done before Hsüan-tsang (A.D. 600–64).

One Vehicle (*ekayāna*): also called the Buddhayāna (Buddha Vehicle); the Mahayana (q.v.) doctrine that contains the final and complete Dharma of the Buddha and not merely a part, or a preliminary stage, as in the Hinayana (q.v.). It is often identified with the teaching of the *Lotus Sutra*.

ordination ceremony. See *karma-vacana*.

pārājika: an offense against the monastic rules so grave as to require expulsion of a monk or a nun from the Sangha (q.v.).

pāramitā ("perfection"): the term denoting the central practices that a bodhisattva performs in order to attain Buddhahood. Cf. six *pāramitās*; ten *pāramitās*.

passions: desire, aversion, delusion, and other attachments that hinder the pursuit of Enlightenment. Cf. three poisons; two types of hindrance.

perfect teaching. *See* perfect tradition.

perfect tradition: the teaching of the One Vehicle (q.v.), which is taught in the *Lotus Sutra*.

prajñā. *See* wisdom.

prajñā-pāramitā ("perfection of wisdom"). *See* six *pāramitās*; ten *pāramitās*.

prātimokṣa: monastic discipline; a text outlining the rules of behavior for monks and nuns.

pratyekabuddha ("solitary buddha"): one who attains Nirvana by contemplating the law of dependent origination without the help of a teacher. Cf. four teachings.

Pure Land teaching: the Buddhist doctrine that is based on faith in the Buddha Amitābha.

Risshū: Vinaya (q.v.) tradition.

samādhi. See meditation.

saṃvara: a rule of discipline.

Sangha: the community of Buddhists, especially of monks and nuns. Cf. Three Refuges.

seven groups of persons: (1) *bhikṣu*s (monks), (2) *bhikṣuṇī*s (nuns), (3) *śikṣamāṇā*s, female neophytes from age 18 to age 20, who study the six rules (q.v.), (4) *śrāmaṇera*s, male novices who have taken vows to obey the ten precepts (q.v.), (5) *śrāmaṇerikā*s, female novices who have taken vows to obey the ten precepts, (6) *upāsaka*s, laymen, and (7) *upāsikā*s, laywomen.

seven holy gifts: the seven virtuous practices enjoined for obtaining rebirth in heaven—(1) faith, (2) discipline, (3) modesty, (4) shame, (5) learning, (6) generosity, and (7) wisdom.

seven parts of Enlightenment: (1) mindfulness, (2) insightful study of the Dharma, (3) effort, (4) joy, (5) ease of mind and body, (6) meditation (q.v.), and (7) equanimity.

shōnin: a title given to an eminent monk.

śikṣamāṇā: a female neophyte. *See also* seven groups of persons.

śīla: discipline or morality.

six consciousnesses: the first six of the eight levels of consciousnesses (q.v.).

six *pāramitā*s ("perfections"): the six aspects of practice that a bodhisattva performs in order to attain Buddhahood—(1) generosity, (2) discipline, (3) patience, (4) effort, (5) meditation (q.v.), and (6) wisdom (q.v.). Cf. ten *pāramitā*s.

six realms of rebirth: (1) the realm of gods, (2) the realm of fighting spirits, (3) the realm of humans, (4) the realm of animals, (5) the realm of hungry ghosts, and (6) hell.

six rules: the six precepts given to female neophytes (*śikṣamāṇā*s)—(1) not to touch a man's body with a lustful mind, (2) not to steal, (3) not to kill, (4) not to lie, (5) to eat only at designated times, and (6) not to drink liquor. Cf. eight precepts; five precepts; seven groups of persons; ten precepts.

sōjō: the first grade in the Buddhist hierarchy; an archbishop.

śramaṇa: a holy person who has renounced the world; a forest-dwelling ascetic; a monk.

śrāmaṇera: a male novice. *See also* seven groups of persons.

śrāmaṇerikā: a female novice. *See also* seven groups of persons.

śrāvaka ("hearer"): originally, a disciple of the Buddha; later, a Hinayana (q.v.) follower who contemplates the Four Noble Truths (q.v.) to attain Nirvana. Cf. four teachings.

Stage Almost Equal to Enlightenment: the fifty-first of the fifty-two stages [of bodhisattvahood] (q.v.).

storehouse consciousness. See *ālaya-vijñāna.*

Sutra(s): the Buddha's sermons. Cf. Tripiṭaka.

Tathāgata: an epithet of the Buddha.

ten abodes: the second ten stages in the fifty-two stages [of bodhisattvahood] (q.v.).

Tendai: the Japanese Buddhist school founded by Saichō in 805, which contains elements of esoteric Buddhism, Zen, and the *Ritsu* (Vinaya) school. Based on the Chinese T'ien-t'ai school.

ten inexhaustible stores: ten "stores" or categories with reference to which the Dharma is preached by all Buddhas of the past, present, and future—(1) faith, (2) discipline, (3) modesty, (4) shame, (5) learning, (6) generosity, (7) wisdom (q.v.), (8) right thinking, (9) steadfastness, and (10) eloquence.

ten *pāramitā*s ("perfections"): the ten aspects of practice that a bodhisattva performs in order to attain Buddhahood—(1) generosity, (2) discipline, (3) patience, (4) effort, (5) meditation (q.v.), (6) wisdom (q.v.), (7) expedient means, (8) vow, (9) power, and (10) knowledge. Cf. six *pāramitā*s.

ten practices: the third group of ten stages in the fifty-two stages [of bodhisattvahood] (q.v.).

ten precepts: (1) not to kill, (2) not to steal, (3) not to engage in sexual misconduct, (4) not to lie, (5) not to drink liquor, (6) not to put perfumes or oils on the body, (7) not to sing or dance, (8) not to use high or broad beds, (9) to eat only at designated times, and (10) not to grasp gold, silver, or jewels. Cf. eight precepts; five precepts; six rules.

ten realms: the fifth group of ten stages in the fifty-two stages [of bodhisattvahood] (q.v.).

ten reasons for the Buddha's appearance: (1) to reveal the three bodies of the Buddha (q.v.), (2) to cause sentient beings to realize the three causes of the Buddha nature (q.v.), (3) to cause sentient beings to produce the three minds, (4) to cause sentient beings to realize the great outstanding qualities of the nature, characteristics, and function of the Absolute, (5) to cause sentient beings to engage in the three types of marvelous practice, (6) to cause sentient beings to fulfill the three transferences of merit, (7) to cause sentient beings to be enlightened in part to the three bodies of the Buddha (q.v.), (8) to cause sentient beings to attain the Buddhahood of the perfect three bodies, (9) to cause sentient beings to experience the qualities of the Dharma Body, and (10) to cause sentient beings to cut off and remove the three hindrances.

ten stages of faith: the first group of ten stages in the fifty-two stages [of bodhisattvahood] (q.v.).

ten transferences of merit: the fourth group of ten stages in the fifty-two stages [of bodhisattvahood] (q.v.) *See also* transference of merit.

thirty-seven aids to Enlightenment: the four mindfulnesses, the four right efforts, the four bases of miraculous powers, the five faculties (q.v.), the five powers, the seven parts of Enlightenment (q.v.), and the Noble Eightfold Path (q.v.).

thirty-two major marks: the major signs adorning the body of a Buddha or universal monarch, such as golden skin, blue eyes, and a long broad tongue.

three bodies of the Buddha: the Dharma Body, the Enjoyment (or Recompense) Body, and the Transformation Body.

threefold pure precepts: (1) the precepts that cut off all evil, (2) the precept that embraces all good *dharmas* (q.v.), and (3) the precept that embraces all sentient beings. Cf. two precepts.

three insights: (1) realization that the self is nonsubstantial, (2) realization that all phenomena are nonsubstantial, and (3) realization that in ultimate reality only consciousness exists.

Three Jewels: the Buddha, the Dharma, and the Sangha (q.v.). Cf. Three Refuges.

three learnings: the three learnings that the practitioner practices in order to attain the fruits of arhatship—discipline (*śīla*), meditation (*samādhi*), and wisdom (*prajñā*).

three natures: the three modes of existence according to the *Hossō* or Yogācāra (q.v.) doctrine: (1) the illusory or imaginary (*parikalpita*) nature of existence, (2) the dependent (*paratantra*) nature of existence, i.e., originating from causes and conditions, and (3) the true or perfect (*parinispanna*) nature of existence. Since the three natures do not have a self nature (or substantiality) and are empty, they are also called the three non-natures.

three non-natures: *See* three natures.

three Piṭakas: *See* three natures.

three poisons: desire, aversion, and delusion, which hinder the pursuit of Enlightenment. Cf. passions; two types of hindrance.

Three Refuges: the Buddha, the Dharma, and the Sangha (q.v.). So called because one becomes a Buddhist upon "taking refuge" in them.

three traditions: the Hinayana (q.v.), the Mahayana (q.v.), and the perfect teaching (q.v.).

transference of merit: according to Mahayana (q.v.) doctrine, it is possible to transfer the merit attained through religious practice to other sentient beings, so as to benefit them.

Transformation Body: *See* three bodies of the Buddha.

Tripiṭaka ("three baskets"): the three categories of the Buddhist canon—(1) the Sutra(s), the Buddha's sermons, (2) the Vinaya(s), rules of conduct for monks and nuns, and (3) the Abhidharma(s), commentaries on the Buddha's teachings.

two emptinesses: (1) emptiness of the self (or soul) and (2) emptiness of *dharma*s (q.v.). *See also* emptiness.

two precepts: (1) the precept that embraces all good *dharma*s and (2) the precept that embraces all sentient beings. Cf. threefold pure precepts.

two truths: (1) Absolute Truth, the transcendent truth that is beyond conceptualization and (2) Conventional Truth, the truth that can be put into words.

two types of hindrance: (1) the hindrance of illusions, passions, or defilements (*kleśa-āvaraṇa*)—evil passions that hinder the practice of the Buddhist path and the realization of Nirvana and (2) the hindrance of knowledge or intellectualization (*jñeya-āvaraṇa*)—a mental function that obscures the correct knowledge of objects and thus obstructs the realization of Enlightenment.

upādhyāya: a teacher.

upāsaka: layman. Cf. seven groups of persons.

upāsikā: laywoman. Cf. seven groups of persons.

upavasatha: the eight precepts (q.v.) of abstinence which laymen and laywomen take occasionally for limited periods. Cf. five precepts; six rules; ten precepts.

uposatha: fortnightly recitation of the *prātimokṣa* (q.v.) by monks and nuns.

Vairocana or (Mahāvairocana): the principal Buddha in the *Avataṃsaka-sūtra*.

vijñapti: a representation, a manifestation.

vijñapti-rūpa: an active element.

Vinaya(s): rules of conduct for monks and nuns. Cf. Tripiṭaka.

wisdom (*prajñā*): enlightened understanding and insight into things-as-they-are, not mere worldly cleverness.

Ying-lo-pen-yeh-ching: a Mahayana text elucidating the bodhisattva precepts. Traditionally said to have been preached twenty-eight years after the Enlightenment of the Buddha.

Yogācāra: a Buddhist school, founded in the fourth century by Vasubandhu, which advocates the doctrine of "mind only."

Yü-ch'ieh-lun: a Mahayana text elucidating the bodhisattva precepts as well as the doctrine of Absolute Truth.

Index

BDK English Tripiṭaka 97-II

THE COLLECTED TEACHINGS OF THE TENDAI LOTUS SCHOOL

by

Gishin

Translated from the Japanese

(Taishō, Volume 74, Number 2366)

by

Paul L. Swanson

Numata Center
for Buddhist Translation and Research
1995

Contents

Part Two: The Practice of Contemplation

Translator's Introduction

The Collected Teachings of the Tendai Lotus School (Tendai Hokke-shū Gishū) is an introduction to the doctrine and practice of the Japanese Tendai school. It was compiled by Gishin (781–833), the monk who accompanied Saichō (767–822) to T'ang China as his interpreter, so that he might help to transmit the Chinese T'ien-t'ai tradition to Japan. He later succeeded Saichō as head of the Tendai establishment on Mt. Hiei. The content of this work consists, for the most part, of extracts from the writings of Chih-i (538–97), the founder of Chinese T'ien-t'ai Buddhism; and it concisely outlines the basic tenets of Tendai doctrine and practice. Except for the introduction and colophon, it takes the form of a catechism. It is divided into two major sections, on doctrine and on practice. The section on doctrine contains a discussion of the Four Teachings, the Five Flavors, the One Vehicle, the Ten Suchlikes, Twelvefold Conditioned Co-arising, and the Two Truths. The section on practice discusses the Four Samādhis and the Three Categories of Delusions.

The Collected Teachings of the Tendai Lotus School was compiled in response to an imperial request that each Buddhist school prepare a description and defense of its own doctrine for submission to the court. The resulting texts are often referred to as "The Six Sectarian Texts Compiled by Imperial Request in the Tenchō Era (824–34)." In addition to Gishin's compilation they include

(1) *Summary of the Great Teachings of the Mahāyāna Sanron* [*School*] (*Daijō sanron daigishō*), by Gen'ei (?–829–?), in four fascicles, for the Sanron School.

(2) *Meticulous Studies of the Mahāyāna Hossō* [*Teachings*] (*Daijō hossō kenjinshō*), by Gomyō (750–834), in five fascicles, for the Hossō School.

(3) *Treatise on Discerning the One Vehicle Doctrine of the Kegon School* (*Kegon-shū ichijō kaishinron*), by Fuki (?–830–?), in six fascicles, for the Kegon School.

(4) *Catechism on Essential Matters Concerning the Transmission of the Precepts* (*Kairitsu denrai shūshi mondōki*), by Buan (?–824–833–?), for the Ritsu School.

(5) *The Secret Maṇḍala and the Ten Stages of the Mind* (*Himitsu mandara jūjūshinron*), by Kūkai (774–835), in ten fascicles, for the Shingon School.

The exact date of compilation of this present work is uncertain. The *Tendai zasu ki,* an ecclesiastical history of the Tendai prelates, claims that Gishin compiled it in 823; but the closing verse in the *Collected Teachings* itself mentions the Tenchō era (824–34). It was probably submitted to the court in 830 along with the other five works.

The Collected Teachings of the Tendai Lotus School is the shortest of the works submitted to the court by the six Buddhist schools. It is in especially marked contrast to the lengthy *Ten Stages of the Mind,* Kūkai's *magnum opus.* Its content is limited to Tendai proper and does not discuss esoteric Buddhism, Zen, or precepts, the other three of the so-called "four pillars of Japanese Tendai." This was the cause of some controversy, since it ignored both esoteric Buddhism, which was in such great demand at the time, and the important issue of Hīnayāna vs. Mahāyāna precepts. Perhaps Gishin felt that a straightforward presentation of the unique features of Tendai proper, as presented in the writings of Chih-i, was most important. Thus the final incorporation of esoteric Buddhism into Japanese Tendai was left to later monks such as Ennin (794–864), Enchin (814–89), and Annen (841–?).

Gishin was born in 781 (some sources say 757 or 779) in Sagami province, just south of the present-day Tokyo area. He studied Hossō at Kōfuku-ji and Chinese at Tōdai-ji before joining Saichō on Mt. Hiei. In 804 he accompanied Saichō to T'ang China as his interpreter. Gishin shared Saichō's experiences in China, which included receiving the Mahāyāna precepts from the T'ien-t'ai monk Tao-sui and an esoteric initiation under Shun-hsiao. These experiences gave Gishin the status and authority needed to succeed Saichō as head of the Tendai establishment after the latter's death in 822.

This succession was not without controversy. In 812 Saichō was very ill and appointed his close disciples Taihan (778–858?) and Enchō (771–837) as his successors. At this time Gishin was not on Mt. Hiei, having gone to his home province of Sagami after his return from China in 805. Soon thereafter Saichō regained his health, Taihan switched his allegiance to Kūkai, and Gishin returned to Mt. Hiei. When Saichō was on his deathbed ten years later, he designated Gishin as his successor. Supporters of Enchō questioned this decision, but Saichō clearly indicated that Gishin was his final choice. This caused some unrest among members of the community on Mt. Hiei, some of whom considered Gishin an outsider; but Gishin's status as Saichō's fellow traveller and recipient of initiations in China could not be denied. Enchō's supporters finally had their way when Enchō was appointed head of the Tendai community after Gishin's death in 833. (Gishin's disciple and appointed successor Enshū left Mt. Hiei humiliated and debarred from office.) Meanwhile Gishin administered the founding of the Mahāyāna precepts platform on Mt. Hiei and was one of the first fourteen monks to receive the Bodhisattva precepts there in 823. He compiled *The Collected Teachings of the Tendai Lotus School* near the end of his life and passed away during the summer of 833.

Gishin's compilation was not utilized extensively on Mt. Hiei, perhaps owing to the success of the Enchō faction after Gishin's death and the popularity of esoteric Buddhism. It did exert considerable influence, however, in setting the pattern and defining the topics for the doctrinal debates that were an important part of a monk's life on Mt. Hiei. Its use as an introductory text to Tendai has been overshadowed in the past three hundred years by the popular *T'ien-t'ai ssu chiao i* of Chegwan (d. 971). However, whereas the *T'ien-t'ai ssu chiao i* emphasizes the T'ien-t'ai doctrinal classification scheme of the Five Periods and Eight

Teachings, Gishin's work offers more detail on basic Tendai philosophy and practice and is a more accurate reflection of Chih-i's original T'ien-t'ai system. Its true value as an introductory text and its influence on Japanese Tendai doctrine and practice are subjects in need of further research.

I have taken some liberties with the text to compensate for the lack of notes, and further details and explanations of terms can be found in the glossary. My translation aims to provide clear, readable English rather than a strict literal rendering. I have added some section headings to clarify the structure of the text. Also, much of the *Collected Teachings* consists of direct quotes from Chih-i's texts, such as the *Mo-ho chih-kuan* (Jp. *Makashikan*) and the *Fa-hua hsüan-i* (Jp. *Hokke gengi*). In cases where the quotations in the *Collected Teachings* differ from the original text of Chih-i, I have followed the readings of the original text of Chih-i.

The Collected Teachings of the Tendai Lotus School (*Tendai Hokkeshū Gishū*) in One Fascicle

263a Presented to the court by Gishin, of the rank "Great Dharma Master Who Transmits the Light," a monk affiliated with the Enryaku-ji on Mt. Hiei who went to T'ang China to learn the Buddha-dharma.

Preface

I humbly submit that true reality is without marks and not something known through discrimination. The nature of reality is beyond words. How can it be adequately grasped through conceptualization? Nevertheless the Great Hero [the Buddha] transmitted the truth by relying on forms and images in accordance with [the capabilities of] sentient beings. The noble Buddha was spiritually proficient and assumed subtle language in order to foster the Path. At the beginning in the Deer Park, his first words were the teaching of the Four Noble Truths, and so on until the perfect culmination in the teaching of the three points [of the Dharma Body, the *prajñā*-wisdom, and liberation before entering Nirvāṇa] at Kuśinagara. During this period his words flowed forth unceasingly, so that an elephant or horse could not carry [all the texts]. His various sermons were so abundant that the Dragon Palace could be filled without exhausting them. Surely a trap is used to catch rabbits, but after the rabbits are caught one forgets the trap. By means of a pointing finger one can find the moon; after one finds the moon the finger is ignored. The Dharma Body is established at sixteen feet tall for those who are attached to formal existence. The highest Path finds its ultimate expression in written texts for those who are caught up in verbal teachings. The one-sided emotional understanding of ordinary people is not the profound erudition of the Enlightened One.

Furthermore, when the sun is wrapped up in shadows, the moon succeeds it in giving forth light. Thus Śākyamuni Buddha "unleashed [the horse from] the carriage" [i.e., passed away into Nirvāṇa] and the Bodhisattvas propagated the Path. Thereafter Aśvaghoṣa and Nāgārjuna revived the declining Law [of the Buddha in India], and then Mo-t'eng and Fa-lang passed on the secret key [in China]. Thenceforth pure men of wisdom appeared one after the other, and men of eminent spiritual talents followed, so that they could not all be counted.

The two masters, Hui-ssu of Mt. Nan-yo and Chih-i of Mt. T'ien-t'ai, appeared in the eras of the Ch'en and the Sui. They had been on the sacred Vulture Peak in the distant past and heard the subtle teachings of the *Lotus Sutra* directly. Reborn in China, they propagated the teaching of the One Vehicle, entered a quiet state of concentration and settled their thoughts, aroused pure wisdom and understood the various potentials [of sentient beings], and once again revealed the Buddhist doctrines and perfected the way of contemplation. All people respected them and accepted from them the pure ambrosia [of the Buddha-dharma]. The four types of Buddhists [monks, nuns, laymen, and laywomen] paid them homage and thus partook of the quintessential taste of ghee. Thereafter the four major [delusions of sentient beings] were further reduced; and the three fields [of precepts, concentration, and wisdom] increasingly prospered.

During the great T'ang dynasty, the Dharma Master Chan-jan, following the standards of past sages and the thousand-year [tradition of Buddhism], was singularly astute. The restoration of the Path was truly due to this man. In his [*Chih-kuan*] *i-li* [Chan-jan] says, "The gist of the teachings of this Tendai school is to utilize the *Lotus Sutra* for its essential structure, the *Ta chih tu lun* for its instruction, the *Mahāparinirvāṇa Sūtra* for commentarial

support, and the *Pañcaviṃśati-sāhasrikā-prajñā-pāramitā Sūtra* for methods of contemplation; to quote all Sutras to increase faith; and to quote all treatises as aids to understanding. The contemplation of the mind is its warp and all doctrines its woof. The many
263b texts are thus woven together, and not in the same way as others." Thus from the beginning it was a fast boat [for crossing over] the waters of wisdom, and a diked road for the subtle vehicle [to cross to the other shore of enlightenment].

This compilation first presents the two main topics, Doctrine and Contemplation. Next, under these categories it lists all the essential points and outlines them. However, the doctrine is vast, so that shallow and ignorant people become lost. Mysterious reality is deep and profound, so that fools cannot measure it. It is like scooping up the ocean with a broken gourd or viewing the heavens with a tiny tube. Therefore I clumsily take up this great rope [of the vast Buddha-dharma] and feebly attempt to compose this work. At times the text is brief and the meaning hidden, at times [it is] short or long. If one tried to exhaust all the details, the result would be too complicated. As an incomplete presentation of the essentials of our school, it resembles a crude commentary. The attempts at summation often miss the mark, and the essential content is difficult to outline.

The reason that the Four Teachings and the Five Flavors stand at the beginning is that these are the fundamental doctrines of the original Buddha and the basis of this [Tendai] school's profound teaching. The other doctrines are numerous, but they depend on and proceed from these first two. This work consists of one fascicle and is called *The Collected Teachings of the Tendai Lotus School.*

The Emperor has grasped the essence and attained understanding of the one truth, so transformations increase and save all people. The jeweled mirror is hung and the golden wheel turned, so the dark clouds are dispelled, revealing the Buddha's light. Having studied the nine classical subjects, he has already mastered them; and having discerned the eight teachings [of all the Buddhist schools], he can select the best.

I, Gishin, am not very eloquent, and my wisdom is insufficient to inherit [the Tendai traditions, as water is] poured from one vessel to another. In vain I yearn for the true joy which comes from contributing to the good of others. In the end there is little that is worthy of praise. I humbly submit this introduction.

Part One

DOCTRINE

Chapter I

The Meaning of the Four Teachings

The ability to respond to the Buddha's teaching is not the same for all sentient beings; it depends on their aspirations and desires. The teachings of the Noble One rely on these transformational conditions and thus are different for each person. A Sutra says, "From the night the Buddha realized the Path until the night of his final Nirvāṇa, the doctrine that he preached was true and not vain wisdom." In reverently examining the gist of the teachings, it is [seen to be] profound and worthy of reliance; therefore it is summarized as the Four Teachings and classified into the categories of tentative and real.

Now I shall interpret the meaning briefly by clarifying [the Four Teachings] in four steps: first, by interpreting the terms; second, by quoting scripture; third, by explaining the content; and fourth, by a final summation.

A. Interpretation of Terms

Question: What are the names of the Four Teachings?

Answer: (1) The Tripiṭaka Teaching, (2) the Shared Teaching, (3) the Distinct Teaching, and (4) the Perfect Teaching.

Q: Why are all four called "Teaching"?

A: "Teaching" contains the meaning of elucidating reality and
263c transforming beings; therefore they are called teachings.

Q: We agree that teachings are used for elucidating reality, but what do you mean by "transforming beings"?

A: "Transforming beings" refers to transforming and converting the minds of beings.

Q: How many meanings are there to "transformation and conversion"?

A: There are three meanings.

Q: What are these three meanings?

A: The first is the conversion of evil to good. The second is the conversion of delusion to understanding. The third is the conversion of the ordinary to the noble. Therefore it is said that beings are transformed.

Q: Why are they established as four Teachings, and not three or five?

A: The noble Buddha, in his sermon on the four unexplainables, used four methods of instruction, and according to conditions used four explanations. Therefore the Four Teachings were established. (The meaning of the four methods of instruction will be explained later.)

B. Scriptural Support

Q: Is there any evidence for these Four Teachings?

A: If all the Sutras are widely quoted, the supporting passages are abundant. Now I shall first establish the Four Teachings on the basis of one Sutra.

Q: Which passage of what Sutra?

A: The *Mahāparinirvāṇa Sūtra* says, "One does not perceive the Buddha-nature and attain the enlightenment of the Śrāvaka due to inferior wisdom and insight. One does not perceive the Buddha-nature and attain the enlightenment of the Pratyekabuddha due to middling wisdom and insight. One perceives the Buddha-nature but not completely and attains the enlightenment of the Bodhisattva due to superior wisdom and insight.

One perceives the Buddha-nature completely and attains the enlightenment of the Buddha due to the highest superior wisdom and insight."

Q: This is an illustration of the wisdom and insight of those of the four vehicles, not an illustration of the Four Teachings. How can this be called evidence?

A: The Four Teachings are teachings in which wisdom is explained.

Q: We agree that the Four Teachings should be so. What are the illustrative texts for each of the Tripiṭaka, Shared, Distinct, and Perfect Teachings individually?

A: The *Lotus Sutra* speaks of "Students of the Tripiṭaka who are attached to the inferior vehicle." The *Ta chih tu lun* says, "Kātyāyanīputra, with astute intelligence, clarified the meaning of the Tripiṭaka in the [*Abhidharma-jñānaprasthāna-śāstra,* the basis of the *Abhidharma-mahā-*]*vibhāṣa*[*-śāstra*]." The *Ch'eng shih lun* says, "I now desire to expound on the true meaning of the Tripiṭaka." These passages illustrate the Tripiṭaka Teaching. The *Pañcaviṃśati-sāhasrikā-prajñā-pāramitā Sūtra* says, "Those of the three vehicles sever passions in the same way by means of the Path that cannot be verbalized." The *Mahāsaṃnipāta Sūtra* says, "The three people sit on the single dias of liberation in the same way." The *Ta chih tu lun* says, "The three people are the same in severing passions and entering Nirvāṇa with and without remainder." These passages illustrate the Shared Teaching. The *Ta chih tu lun* clarifies the *prajñā*-wisdom that is unique to Bodhisattvas, and this is the explanation of that which is not shared by those of the two vehicles. The *Acintya Sūtra* is another example. These are illustrations of the Distinct Teaching. The *Lotus Sutra* says, "Pressing their palms together and with a respectful mind, they hoped to hear of the complete Path." The *Avataṃsaka Sūtra* says, "The perfectly complete Sutra." These illustrate the Perfect Teaching.

C. Explanation of the Content

Third, further explanation is divided into four parts, that is, the Four Teachings.

1. The Tripiṭaka Teaching

First, the clarification of the Tripiṭaka Teaching.

Question: What is the content of that called the Tripiṭaka Teaching?

Answer: This refers to the three stores [of the Buddha's teachings]: first, the collection of the Sutras; second, the collection of the *Vinaya;* and third, the collection of the *Abhidharma.*

264a *Q:* Are these terms, "Sutra" and so forth, Sanskrit, or are they Chinese?

A: They are Sanskrit.

Q: What are they in Chinese?

A: Sutra is sometimes translated and sometimes not. When it is translated, various people translate it in different ways. However, many use the translation "Dharma source." *Vinaya* is translated as "extinction." *Abhidharma* is translated as "incomparable Dharma."

Q: For what reason are the translations "Dharma source" and so forth used?

A: [A Sutra is] called a "Dharma source" because it is a source of verbal teachings concerning the world-transcending good Dharma. [In the *Vinaya*] the Buddha expounds on the intentional and spontaneous precepts and how to extinguish evil physical and verbal activity. Therefore it is translated as "extinction." [In the *Abhidharma*] the meaning of the Dharma is analyzed by the Noble One's wisdom, which is incomparable in this world. Therefore it is translated as "incomparable Dharma."

Q: Which Sutras and treatises are the "Dharma source" [in the Tripiṭaka Teaching]?

A: Here the fourfold *Āgama* is the Dharma source, the *Vinaya* of eighty recitations is the text for extinction [of passionate attachments], and the *Abhidharma* treatises are the "incomparable Dharma."

Q: Are these *Abhidharma* treatises taught directly by the Buddha or are they explanations by his disciples?

A: Whether they are analyses of the meaning of the Dharma by the Buddha himself or by the Buddha's disciples, they are all called *Abhidharma.*

Q: Of these two, whose explanation is indicated?

A: Indeed it indicates the Buddha's explanation.

Q: An exposition by the Buddha is called a Sutra and an exposition by a Bodhisattva is called a treatise. There are no treatises attributed to the Buddha during his life. How can there be an *Abhidharma* [attributed to the Buddha]?

A: From the standpoint of the Mahāyāna there are no collections of treatises attributed to the Buddha during his life. But from the standpoint of the Hīnayāna there are *Abhidharma* treatises [attributed to the Buddha].

Q: Supposing that there are Hīnayāna *Abhidharmas* [attributed to the Buddha]. These are expositions by Śāriputra and not by the Buddha.

A: These are expositions by Śāriputra that follow and repeat those of the Buddha.

Q: How can we know that the Buddha himself preached an *Abhidharma* treatise?

A: Because the *Hsiang-hsü-chieh-t'o ching* is also called an *Abhidharma* treatise.

Q: Why are these three Dharma collections all called "stores"?

A: They get this meaning by "containing."

Q: What Dharmas do they contain?

A: Some say that the text contains [the truth concerning] reality. Others say that reality contains the text. Therefore they are called "stores." Now I say that of these three Dharma [collections], each contains all verbal [truth concerning] reality; therefore they are called "stores."

Q: Do these three stores correspond to precepts, concentration, and wisdom?

A: They do correspond.

Q: How do they correspond?

A: The Sutras correspond to the concentration-store, the *Vinaya* corresponds to the precepts-store, and the *Abhidharma* corresponds to the wisdom-store.

Q: What is the basis of this correspondence?

A: The fourfold *Āgama* often clarify methods of cultivating the Dharma. The *Vinaya* correctly identifies how to keep the precepts according to the situation and the way to resist evil mental, physical, and verbal intentions. The *Abhidharma* is the analysis of the Dharma of undefiled wisdom.

264b *Q:* We agree that this correspondence is true. Why is their order different?

A: When one cultivates the Dharma, the collection of precepts has priority. When the teachings are preached, the collection of Sutras comes first. Now we are referring to the teachings, so the order is not the same.

Q: What reality does this Tripiṭaka Teaching clarify?

A: It clarifies the reality of the Four Noble Truths as the actual arising and perishing of conditioned co-arising.

Q: For whose sake is this taught?

A: It is taught as correct for those of the Hīnayāna and as marginal for instructing the Bodhisattvas.

Q: The Buddha first exposed [the doctrine of] the three vehicles within the Tripiṭaka Teaching. The Mahāyāna is the supreme teaching. Why is not the Mahāyāna presented as correct and the Hīnayāna as marginal?

A: At the Deer Park the Buddha first preached the sermon on the Four Noble Truths. Five men, Ājñāta-Kauṇḍinya and so forth, perceived the truth and realized the Path, and eighty thousand divine beings attained pure insight into the truth. However, since this was the attainment of the Hīnayāna Path, there was not yet any attainment of the Mahāyāna. So the Hīnayāna was taught as correct and the Mahāyāna as marginal.

Q: Who are the Hīnayānists, and who are the Mahāyānists?

A: The Śrāvakas and Pratyekabuddhas are the Hīnayānists. The Bodhisattvas are the Mahāyānists.

Q: Why are they called Śrāvakas, or "voice-hearers"?

A: They hear the Buddha's voice as he teaches; therefore they are called voice-hearers.

Q: There are many types of teachings taught by the Buddha's voice. Which verbal teaching do they hear?

A: They hear the exposition of the teaching of the principle of the Four Noble Truths as arising and perishing.

Q: Which delusions are severed by hearing this verbal teaching?

A: The delusions of false views and attitudes are severed.

Q: What is the meaning of "the delusions of false views and attitudes"?

A: This will be explained in detail in the section on severing delusions. [*See* Part Two, Chapter II.]

Q: How many stages does one pass through to attain the fruit of enlightenment by severing delusions?

A: One passes successively through four stages: (1) the lower level of ordinary people, (2) the higher level of ordinary people, (3) the partial attainment of sagacity, and (4) the ultimate stage of the sage.

Q: How many stages are there in the first, the lower level of ordinary people?

A: All together there are three stages: (1) the five meditations, (2) mindfulness concerning objects individually, and (3) mindfulness concerning objects in general.

Q: What are the five meditations?

A: They are: (1) to put the mind at rest by means of compassion, (2) to put the mind at rest by counting one's breaths, (3) to put the mind at rest by meditating on conditioned co-arising, (4) to put the mind at rest by meditating on impurities, and (5) to put the mind at rest by being mindful of the Buddha.

Q: How many obstacles are overcome by these five meditations?

A: Five obstacles are overcome. The meditation on compassion overcomes anger. The meditation of counting one's breaths overcomes distraction. The meditation on conditioned co-arising overcomes ignorance. The meditation on impurities overcomes covetousness. Being mindful of the Buddha overcomes obstacles to the Path.

Q: What are the characteristics and practices of mindfulness concerning objects individually?

A: Five obstacles have already been removed, and the wisdom of contemplation has been clarified considerably. Next one should perform the contemplation that involves mindfulness concerning four objects in order to destroy the four warped views.

Q: What is mindfulness concerning four objects and four warped views?

A: Mindfulness concerning four objects refers to that concerning the body, sensation, mind, and dharmas. The four warped views are those of permanence, pleasure, selfhood, and purity.

Q: What is the purpose of contemplation that involves mindfulness of these four objects?

A: To contemplate the impurity of the body, the lack of pleasure
264c in sensations, the transiency of the mind, and the non-substantiality of dharmas.

Q: Why are the warped views identified as those of permanence, pleasure, selfhood, and purity?

A: It is because ordinary people cling to permanence, pleasure, selfhood, and purity with regard to the impure and so forth.

Q: Are the four objects of which one is mindful and the five aggregates the same or different?

A: The terms are different but the meaning is the same.

Q: What do you mean [when you say] that their meaning is the same?

A: The body corresponds to the aggregate of form. Sensations correspond to the aggregate of sensation. The mind corresponds to the aggregate of consciousness. Dharmas correspond to the two aggregates of conceptions and volitional activities.

Q: Are there different capabilities for cultivating mindfulness of these four objects?

A: Those who have the capability for seeking liberation through wisdom cultivate only insight into the specific nature of each of the four objects of which one is mindful and thus destroy attachment to the four individual warped views [of permanence, pleasure, selfhood, and purity]. Those who have the capability for seeking liberation through both [wisdom and contemplation] cultivate insight into the common characteristics of the four aspects of which one is mindful and thus destroy the warped views concerning phenomena and reality. Those who have the capability for seeking liberation cultivate all three kinds of mindfulness concerning the four objects, that is, [(1) to be mindful of each] individually, [(2) to be mindful of their] common characteristics, and [(3) to be mindful of all their characteristics] simultaneously; and thus they destroy the four warped views concerning all phenomena, reality, words, and so forth.

Q: What are the practices of mindfulness concerning the common features of the four objects?

A: One has already destroyed the four warped views through the wisdom gained from mindfulness concerning the objects [of body, sensation, mind, and dharmas] individually. Now one destroys the four warped views generally through a profound and fine contemplative wisdom.

Q: How many kinds of mindfulness concerning the common features are there?

A: There are three distinct kinds: (1) general contemplation of the objects in general; (2) general contemplation of the objects individually; and (3) individual contemplation of the objects in general.

Q: It is as you say with regard to the lower level of ordinary people. How about the higher level of ordinary people?

A: There are four sub-levels of the higher level of ordinary people: (1) warming up, (2) the summit of concentration, (3) patience, and (4) Dharma supreme in the world.

Q: What is the meaning of the levels of warming up and so forth?

A: (1) The level of warming up refers to arousing approximate understanding through mindfulness of the four objects individually and in general, and thus attaining insight into the sixteen truths [the four aspects of the Four Noble Truths] and the aura of the Buddha-dharma. It is like kindling a fire and arousing smoke. (2) The level of the summit of concentration refers to approximate understanding that is further increased to the attainment of the four supranormal concentrative states and a further clarification of the sixteen truths that is superior to the level of warming up. It is like climbing to the mountain summit and observing all directions with complete clarity. (3) The level of patience refers to the desire for patience through [contemplation of] the Four Truths. (4) The level of Dharma supreme in the world refers to the highest level of ordinary people attained in an instant from the highest level of patience.

Q: The higher levels of ordinary people are as explained. How many levels are included in the stage of partial sagehood?

A: There are four causal stages and three resultant stages.

Q: What are they each called?

A: (1) The causal stage of the *srotāpanna,* (2) the resultant stage of the *srotāpanna,* (3) the causal stage of the *sakṛdāgāmin,* (4) the resultant stage of the *sakṛdāgāmin,* (5) the causal stage of the *anāgāmin,* (6) the resultant stage of the *anāgāmin,* and (7) the causal stage of the Arhat.

Q: Are the terms *srotāpanna,* and so forth, Sanskrit or Chinese?
A: They are Sanskrit terms.

Q: What are their Chinese equivalents?
A: Srotāpanna is translated as "entering the stream." It is also translated as "stream-winner." "Entering" has the same meaning as "winning." It refers to one who has just entered the noble stream [of the Buddhist Path]. *Sakṛdāgāmin* means "once-returner." It refers to one who, after finishing this present life, is reborn in
265a heaven, from which he is once more reborn as a human being who will attain the stage of the *anāgāmin. Anāgāmin* means "non-returner." It refers to one who will never again return to this world of desires.

Q: The stages of partial sagehood are such. What is the stage of ultimate sagehood?
A: The stage of ultimate sagehood is the resultant stage of the Arhat.

Q: Is there a translation for the term Arhat?
A: There is no translation for this term, but it contains three meanings.

Q: What are these three meanings?
A: One who has killed the traitor [of passions]; one who has no more rebirths; and one who is worthy of homage.

Q: Of these four levels how many are labeled "the wise" and how many "the sagacious"?
A: The two levels of ordinary people are labeled "the wise" and the two levels of partial and ultimate sagehood are labeled "the sagacious."

Q: What do you mean by labeling these "the wise" and "the sagacious"?

A: "The wise" is close to "the sagacious," therefore it is called wise. One is able to conquer the delusions of wrong views and concepts by means of approximate understanding. One arouses true understanding by means of this approximate understanding, and therefore it is called "close to sagacity." Sagacity means "correct." One is called a sage because he correctly contemplates suffering [and thus severs the delusions of mistaken views], thus arousing true understanding [and severing the delusions of false attitudes], leaving behind the stage of the ordinary person to enter that of the sage, and perceiving reality with true wisdom.

Q: Next, is the term "Pratyekabuddha" Sanskrit or Chinese?

A: It is Sanskrit.

Q: What is it in Chinese?

A: This is translated [into Chinese] as "one who is awakened concerning conditions." This refers to one who lives during the time of a Buddha and, by hearing an exposition on Twelvefold Conditioned Co-arising, immediately awakens to Pratyekabuddhahood.

Q: How many varieties of Pratyekabuddhas are there?

A: There are two kinds. Those who appear during the time of the Buddha have already been mentioned. If they are to appear during a time when there is no Buddha in the world, they have an immediate spontaneous awakening to Pratyekabuddhahood while contemplating the scattering of flowers or the falling of leaves.

Q: What is their status with regard to the stages of ordinary people and sages?

A: The distinct stages of the ordinary person and the sage, and the meaning of the resultant enlightenment upon severing delusions, are all the same as the Śrāvaka. There are no differences, except that they overcome the habitual propensities of passions.

Q: Next, is the term "Bodhisattva" Sanskrit or Chinese?

A: It is Sanskrit. [In Chinese] the longer transliteration is *P'u-t'i-sa-ta,* but here we use the abbreviation *P'u-sa.*

Q: What is the meaning in Chinese?

A: Bodhi means "enlightenment," or "the mind that aspires for the Buddhist Path," and *sattva* means "a sentient being."

Q: What vows are made by a Bodhisattva?

A: He makes four great vows at the time of his first aspiration for enlightenment.

Q: What are these four great vows?

A: (1) To save all who are not yet saved, by the vow "Though there are unlimited sentient beings, I vow to save them." (2) To awaken those who do not yet understand, by the vow, "Though there are unlimited passions, I vow to sever them." (3) To soothe those who are not yet settled, by the vow, "Though there are inexhaustible doctrines, I vow to know them." (4) To lead to Nirvāṇa those who have not yet attained Nirvāṇa, by the vow "Though the Buddhist Path is supreme, I vow to fulfill it."

Q: Concerning these four great vows, what conditions allow one to arouse the aspiration for enlightenment?

A: One arouses the aspiration for enlightenment and vows to save all who have yet to be saved by contemplating the truth of
265b suffering. One arouses the aspiration for enlightenment and vows to lead to understanding those who do not yet understand by contemplating the truth concerning the causes of suffering. One arouses the aspiration for enlightenment and vows to sooth those who are not yet settled by contemplating the truth of the Buddhist Path. One arouses the aspiration for enlightenment and vows to lead to Nirvāṇa those who have not yet attained Nirvāṇa by contemplating the truth concerning the extinction of suffering.

Q: What practices should be cultivated after arousing the aspiration for enlightenment?

A: One should cultivate the practice of the Six Perfections.

Q: What are the Six Perfections?

A: They are (1) *dāna-pāramitā,* (2) *śīla-pāramitā,* (3) *kṣānti-pāramitā,* (4) *vīrya-pāramitā,* (5) *dhyāna-pāramitā,* and (6) *prajñā-pāramitā.*

Q: Are *dāna-pāramitā* and so forth Sanskrit or Chinese?
A: They are Sanskrit terms.

Q: What are the Chinese equivalents?
A: *Dāna* means "charity." *Pāramitā* means "to reach the other shore," to leave behind this shore of the cyclic world of birth and death and arrive at the other shore of Nirvāṇa. The term *śīla* refers to the precepts. *Kṣānti* means "patience." *Vīrya* means "diligence." *Dhyāna* means "putting an end to evil [delusions through meditation]." *Prajñā* means "wisdom."

Q: What obstacles are overcome through the Perfections of charity, and so forth?
A: Covetousness is overcome through the Perfection of charity. The breaking of precepts is overcome through [the keeping of] precepts. Anger is overcome through patience. Slothfulness is overcome through diligence. Distraction and confusion are overcome through meditation. Ignorance is overcome through wisdom.

Q: How long must one cultivate these Six Perfections?
A: One must pass through three incalculable aeons.

Q: What is the first incalculable aeon, and so forth?
A: The first incalculable aeon is from the time the Bodhisattva Śākya first met the [ancient] Buddha Śākyamuni until the time of the Buddha Khāṇuśikhin. The second incalculable aeon is from the time of the Buddha Śikhin to the time of the Buddha Dīpaṃkara. The third incalculable aeon is from the time of the Buddha Dīpaṃkara to the time of the Buddha Vipaśyin.

Q: How many Buddhas did this Bodhisattva pay homage to during these three incalculable aeons?
A: In the *Abhidharmakośabhāṣya* it says that, "During each of the incalculable aeons he paid homage to seventy thousand Buddhas, and in addition he paid homage to five, six, and seven thousand Buddhas."

Q: What is the meaning of this treatise passage?

A: The treatise gives the following interpretation: "During the first aeon he paid homage to seventy-five thousand Buddhas. During the second aeon he paid homage to seventy-six thousand Buddhas. During the third aeon he paid homage to seventy-seven thousand Buddhas."

Q: Do [the periods of] meeting [the ancient] Śākyamuni to that of the Buddha Vipaśyin belong to the beginning or completion of an aeon?

A: The verses of the *Koṣa* say, "At the completion of the three incalculable aeons he respectively met, in reverse order, the Buddhas Vipaśyin, Dīpaṃkara, and Ratnaśikhin, and then he first became Śākyamuni."

Q: What is the meaning of these verses?

A: The treatise explains them as follows. At the beginning of
265c the first incalculable aeon he met [the ancient] Śākyamuni. At the completion of the first incalculable aeon he met the Buddha Ratnaśikhin. At the completion of the second incalculable aeon he met the Buddha Dīpaṃkara. At the completion of the third aeon he met Vipaśyin.

Q: At what time did this Bodhisattva acquire the thirty-two major marks [of a Buddha]?

A: After one hundred aeons at the latest and after ninety-one aeons at the earliest.

Q: How do we know that it was acquired after the earliest possible span of ninety-one aeons?

A: The Buddha Puṣya saw Śākyamuni and perceived that he had matured his potential as a disciple and that it would be easy for him to advance to the other shore of enlightenment. Therefore he cast a ray of light from within his cave that illuminated a great distance. The Bodhisattva saw this light and sought its source. He arrived at the place where the Buddha Puṣya was and for seven days and nights single-mindedly contemplated the Buddha without blinking his eyes. His ascetic practices were more praiseworthy than those of Maitreya, so he attained Buddhahood nine aeons earlier.

Q: What is required to fulfill the causes of the thirty-two major marks [of a Buddha]?

A: A hundred good qualities are needed to fulfill each and every cause.

Q: What is one good quality?

A: There are many interpretations of "good quality," so it is difficult to determine its exact meaning. Some say that the mastery that the world ruler has over all the lands under heaven is one good quality. Some say that the mastery of Indra in the thirty-three heavens is one good quality. Some say that to heal the blindness of people in this universe is one good quality. Some say that the ability to preach the Dharma in a way that leads all people who break the precepts to forsake their immoral ways is a good quality. Some say that it is beyond analogizing and that only the Buddha can know it.

Q: In which continent, in what body, at what time, and under what conditions were the causes of these marks planted?

A: The causes for these marks were planted in the southern continent, in a male body, at the time of the appearance of a Buddha in this world, under the conditions of a Buddha-body.

Q: In cultivating the Six Perfections, is there a specific time when this practice is perfected?

A: There is a time of perfection when one has no obstacles in giving alms. For example, charity was perfected when King Sivi gave his body [to be eaten by a hawk] on behalf of a dove. The keeping of the precepts was perfected when King Sutasoma, though losing his throne, still wrote a verse praising the moral life and did not indulge in slander. Patience was perfected when the hermit Kṣānti bore no resentment as his limbs were severed by King Kali, and his body was restored. Diligence was perfected when Prince Mahātyāgavat entered the sea to search for a [wish-fulfilling] jewel for the sake of all the people. He finally obtained the jewel [from the hair of the Dragon King] to help the poor. However, the sea god hid the treasure while he was sleeping. When the Prince awoke he vowed to scoop out the entire ocean with his own body. Indra was moved by this sight and all the heavenly deities helped him until it was half done. Also, for seven days Śākyamuni stood on one foot and praised the Buddha Puṣya. Concentration was perfected when a bird built a nest in the hair of the hermit Śaṅkhācārya while he was in a concentrative state. He did not emerge from his concentrative state until the chicks could fly away. Wisdom was perfected when the Prime Minister Govinda divided the land of Jambudvīpa into seven parts, which put an end to the bitter fighting between [the seven] countries.

Q: During which incalculable aeon did this Bodhisattva come to know that he would attain Buddhahood?

266a *A:* From the first incalculable aeon he was constantly free from having a female body but did not yet know that he would attain Buddhahood. During the second incalculable aeon he came to know that he would attain Buddhahood, but he did not verbally say so. During the third incalculable aeon he both knew and said so.

Q: If so, at what stage did he fulfill Buddhahood?

A: He passed through the lower, middle, and higher stages of patience and that of the Dharma supreme in the world, and in the last moment he attained Buddhahood.

Q: What time is referred to by the terms "lower stage of patience," to "the last moment"?

A: The last one hundred aeons within the third incalculable aeon, to the fulfillment of the Six Perfections, are the lower stage of patience. Next one enters the highest stage of the Bodhisattva just prior to attaining Buddhahood, is born in the Tuṣita heaven, enters his mother's womb, leaves home, and conquers Māra. After scattering the forces of evil he sits peacefully and cultivates concentration. This is the middle stage of patience. In the next moment he enters the higher stage of patience. In the next moment he enters the stage of the Dharma supreme in the world. In the next moment he attains the fulfillment of Buddhahood.

Q: What were his practices at the time of the fulfillment of Buddhahood?

A: He aroused true nondefilement, attained the thirty-four enlightened mental states by severing the bonds [of craving], and fulfilled Hīnayāna Buddhahood. The saint of the Himalayas offered some soft grass and the Tathāgata accepted it, [sat on it,] and fulfilled supreme enlightenment. This fulfillment of the Path on a grass seat under a tree is that of the inferior body of transformation.

Q: Do you have evidence for the type of Bodhisattva that you discuss?

A: The *Ta chih tu lun* clarifies that Kātyāyanīputra established [the classification of] Bodhisattvas of the Six Perfections of the Tripiṭaka Teachings. This is the evidence.

Q: Why do those of the two vehicles sever their bonds in this life and quickly attain the fruit of the Path, but Bodhisattvas do not yet sever their bonds while traversing from their first aspiration to the stage of conquering evil and do not attain the fruit of the Path quickly?

A: Those of the two vehicles contemplate the Four Noble Truths and Twelvefold Conditioned Co-arising and thus grow weary of the cycle of birth and death, seek Nirvāṇa on their own, and prepare themselves for their own salvation. Therefore they sever their bonds first and attain the fruit [of the Path] in this life. The Bodhisattva has compassion and thus puts [the benefits of] others first and himself last. For three incalculable aeons he cultivates the Six Perfections; therefore he does not attain the fruit quickly.

Q: The object of contemplation is not the same for those of the Hīnayāna and the Mahāyāna. Is there a difference also in the wisdom that does the contemplating?

A: There are distinctions with regard to the time necessary for cultivating the causes [of enlightenment]. The Śrāvaka takes three lifetimes during sixty aeons, the Pratyekabuddha takes four lifetimes during one hundred aeons, and the Bodhisattva takes three incalculable aeons. Nevertheless they all utilize the wisdom of inferior salvation through the understanding of emptiness by analysis, analyzing [all things] into the five substantial aggregates [from which they are composed]. Thus they all conclude with the same one-sided truth. This is explained in detail in the commentary [the *Ssu chiao i* by Chih-i].

2. The Shared Teaching

Q: What is the meaning of that called "Shared"?
A: Shared means "the same."

Q: Why is it said to be the same?
A: It is called Shared because those of the three vehicles [Śrāvakas, Pratyekabuddhas, and Bodhisattvas] all accept the same [content].

Q: If those of the three vehicles accept the same, then is it Mahāyāna or Hīnayāna?
A: It is actually meant for the Bodhisattvas but also shared on the side with those of the two vehicles. Therefore it is introductory Mahāyāna.

Q: How many types are there of this Shared Teaching?
A: There are many meanings, which can be summarized in
266b eight parts: teaching, reality, wisdom, severance, practice, levels, causes, and results. All of these are shared by those of the three vehicles.

Q: For what reason do you say that these teachings, and so forth through results, are shared?
A: (1) The teachings are shared because those of the three vehicles accept the same teaching concerning the emptiness of that which is conditionally co-arisen. (2) Reality is shared because they share the same one-sided view concerning reality. (3) Wisdom is shared because they are the same in attaining the wisdom [of the emptiness] of all things [so that they are] skillful in saving

[sentient beings]. (4) Severance is shared because their severance of the delusions of this triple world is the same. (5) Practice is shared because the practice for [attaining] nondefilement is the same. (6) The levels [of attainment] are shared because the stages from "parched wisdom" to the stage of Buddhahood are all the same. (7) Causes are shared because the nine non-obstructions are the same. (8) Results are shared because the results of the nine liberations and two types of Nirvāṇa are the same.

Q: There are eight meanings to the term "Shared." Why is one singled out and called "Shared Teaching"?

A: Without the Shared Teaching one cannot know the shared [perception of] reality, and so forth, and one cannot attain the shared results.

Q: Those of the three vehicles all accept these teachings. Why is it not called "Common Teaching"?

A: If it were called "Common," it would include only the attainment of the closer [Hīnayāna] extreme of the two vehicles, and not the further extreme [of the Mahāyāna]. If we use the term "shared," then this is convenient for both, and it includes the near [Hīnayāna Tripiṭaka Teaching] and far [Mahāyāna Distinct and Perfect Teachings].

Q: What do you mean by saying "convenient for both"?

A: It shares both the Distinct and the Perfect [Teachings].

Q: How about the levels of stages in this Teaching?

A: Those of the three vehicles commonly practice the ten stages.

Q: What are the names of these ten stages?

A: (1) The stage of parched wisdom, (2) the stage of potential, (3) the stage of eight personalities, (4) the stage of insight, (5) the stage of thinner [delusions], (6) the stage of freedom from desires, (7) the stage of conclusion, (8) the stage of the Pratyekabuddha, (9) the stage of the Bodhisattva, and (10) the stage of the Buddha.

Q: Why are these called "the stage of parched wisdom" and so forth?

A: At the stage of parched wisdom, one has not yet attained the water of [insight into] reality at the levels of "warming up" and "[Identity in] Outer Appearance," but wisdom is profound and penetrating with regard to mindfulness of marks in general. Therefore it is called "parched wisdom." At the stage of potential one has attained the Dharma of "warming up" and the water of [insight into] reality, so the mind is moistened and advances to the levels of the "summit," "patience," and "Dharma supreme in the world" and thus attains insight into the undefiled nature [of reality]. At the two stages of "eight personalities" and "insight," one never emerges from the state of contemplation, and one severs the delusions of mistaken views, arouses true nondefilement, and perceives the truth concerning reality. At the stage of "thinner [delusions]," one destroys the essence of the first six classes of deluded attitudes in the realm of desire. Therefore it is called "thinner [delusions]." At the stage of "freedom from desires," one severs the nine classes [of deluded attitudes] so that one no longer returns to the realm of desire. At the stage of "conclusion," those of the three vehicles advance to sever seventy-two classes of deluded attitudes in the realms of form and formlessness and exhaustively attain the fruit of the Arhat. At the stage of the Pratyekabuddha, though one has severed the same delusions of mistaken views and attitudes [as the Arhat], one has solid merits and sharp faculties, so one is also able to remove habitual propensities. The Bodhisattva, beginning with the first aspiration, contemplates the Four Noble Truths as not arising, arouses the mind of enlightenment, arrives at the sixth and seventh stages, and then reenters conventional existence from [the insight of] emptiness and fulfills [the salvation of] sentient beings. At the stage of Buddhahood the capabilities of those of the three vehicles are brought to maturity and, sitting on the seat of enlightenment, one attains universal wisdom. This is called the stage of Buddhahood.

Q: Why is it said that these ten stages are practiced in common?

266c *A:* Because the three people [of the three vehicles] are the same in severing the delusions of mistaken views and attitudes.

Q: If they are the same in severing the delusions of mistaken views and attitudes, are there any differences between the method of contemplation and that of the Tripiṭaka Teaching?

A: There are differences in being skillful and clumsy, for they are not the same [in understanding emptiness] by analysis and essentially.

Q: What is the meaning of "being skillful and clumsy . . . by analysis and essentially"?

A: Those of the Shared Teaching are called skillful in perceiving the truth concerning the essential [emptiness] of the aggregates, and those of the Tripiṭaka Teaching are called clumsy because they approach the truth by breaking down and analyzing the aggregates [and thus realize their non-substantiality].

Q: What is the meaning of "entering conventional existence from emptiness" in the stage of the Bodhisattva?

A: Conventional existence refers to the realm of transformations. Emptiness refers to [the state of contemplation that consists of] insight into emptiness. [The Bodhisattvas] vow to reserve habitual propensities [of craving] in order to return and be reborn in this triple world. Utilizing the wisdom that comes from having cultivated all practices, indulging in supranormal powers, and purifying the Buddha-lands, they fulfill [the salvation of] sentient beings.

Q: How about the severance of delusions and the attainment of the fruit of enlightenment in the tenth stage?

A: One severs and removes any remaining propensities by utilizing the final state of single-mindedness in which there is a correspondence of wisdom and reality; therefore it is called Buddhahood. This is the supreme body of transformation, the perfection of the Path under the seven-jeweled tree on the seat with a heavenly robe.

Q: Do the people of the three vehicles traverse the ten stages from that of "parched wisdom"?

A: A Śrāvaka traverses the first to the seventh stage, a Pratyekabuddha the first to the eighth stage, and a Bodhisattva the first to the ninth stage.

Q: Is there scriptural evidence for these ten stages?
A: Yes, in the *Pañcaviṃśati-sāhasrikā-prajñā-pāramitā Sūtra.*

Q: How do these ten stages compare to the levels of attainment in the Tripiṭaka Teaching?
A: The stage of parched wisdom corresponds to the levels of the five meditations, mindfulness concerning objects individually, and mindfulness concerning objects in general. The stage of potential corresponds to the levels of warming up, the summit, patience, and Dharma supreme in the world. The stages of eight personalities and insight correspond to the level of the *srotāpanna.* The stage of thinner [delusions] corresponds to the level of the *sakṛdāgāmin.* The stage of freedom from desires corresponds to the level of the *anāgāmin.* The stage of conclusion corresponds to the level of Arhat.

Q: If one advances from here to the Distinct or Perfect Teaching, to what level does it correspond?
A: If one is enlightened concerning the Middle Path, one fulfills the first Stage of the Distinct Teaching or the first Abode of the Perfect Teaching.

3. The Distinct Teaching

Next I shall clarify the Distinct Teaching.

Q: Why is this called "Distinct"?
A: "Distinct" is a term meaning "not common."

Q: What is meant by "not common"?
A: This teaching is explained apart from those of the two vehicles, therefore it is called the Distinct Teaching. Also, its [interpretation of] teaching, reality, wisdom, severance, practice, levels, causes, and results are distinct from [those of] the previous two Teachings and distinct from the last teaching of perfect integration. Therefore it is called "Distinct."

Q: What principle [of reality] is clarified in this Teaching?

A: It clarifies the principle of the Four Noble Truths as immeasurable.

Q: For whom is it taught?

A: Only to transform Bodhisattvas, and not to lead those of the two vehicles across.

Q: Why is this called the Distinct Teaching and not the Uncommon Teaching?

A: The *Ta chih tu lun* clarifies the *prajñā*-wisdom that is unique to Bodhisattvas. When the *Vaipulya Sūtra*s and the *Pañcaviṃśati-sāhasrikā-prajñā-pāramitā Sūtra* were preached, the Śrāvakas and Pratyekabuddhas also heard it but the Bodhisattvas were distinctly transformed. Therefore the term "Distinct" is used.

Q: What levels of practice are clarified in this Teaching?

A: It broadly clarifies the levels of gradual practice that the Bodhisattvas cultivate over many aeons.

267a *Q:* What are these levels?

A: The Ten Levels of Faith, the Ten Levels of Abodes, the Ten Levels of Practice, the Ten Levels of Merit Transference, the Ten Stages, the Level of Preliminary Awakening, and the Level of [Supreme] Subtle Awakening.

Q: On what Sutras are these levels based?

A: They are based on the *Avataṃsaka Sūtra,* the *Ying lo ching,* the *Jen wang ching,* the *Suvarṇaprabhāsa Sūtra,* the *Sheng-t'ien-wang ching,* and the *Mahāparinirvāṇa Sūtra.*

Q: Are the levels contained in these Sutras all the same?

A: Each has some but not others. The *Avataṃsaka Sūtra* clarifies forty-one levels: the Ten Abodes, the Ten Levels of Practice, the Ten Levels of Merit Transference, the Ten Stages, and Subtle Awakening. The *Ying lo ching* clarifies fifty-two levels: it adds the Ten Levels of Faith and the Level of Preliminary Awakening. The *Jen wang ching* does not discuss the Level of Preliminary Awakening so it only clarifies fifty-one levels. The *Suvarṇaprabhāsa Sūtra* has only the Ten Stages and the fruit of Buddhahood. The *Sheng-t'ien-wang ching* has only the Ten Stages. The *Mahāparinirvāṇa Sūtra* clarifies the five practices and the ten virtuous qualities.

Q: Why are the levels in the Sutras not all the same?

A: How can there be a set explanation [of stages] if they are to benefit [sentient beings] in accordance with their capabilities?

Q: On which Sutra is your explanation based?

A: I shall clarify seven levels based on the *Ying lo ching,* as listed above.

Q: What are the names of the different levels?

A: The Ten Levels of Faith are (1) Faith, (2) Mindfulness, (3) Diligence, (4) Wisdom, (5) Concentration, (6) Non-retrogression, (7) Merit Transference, (8) Preservation of the Dharma, (9) Discipline, and (10) [Fulfillment of] Vow. The Ten Abodes are (1) Aspiration, (2) Maintenance, (3) Cultivation, (4) Noble Rebirth, (5) Completion of Expedients, (6) Rectification of the Mind, (7) Non-retrogression, (8) Childlike Goodness, (9) Dharma-prince, and (10) Anointment. The Ten Levels of Practice are [characterized as] (1) Joyful, (2) Beneficial, (3) Lacking in Hate, (4) Unexhausted, (5) Unconfused, (6) Attractive, (7) Unattached, (8) Honored, (9) Exemplary, and (10) True. The Ten Levels of Merit Transference are (1) Salvation of Sentient Beings, (2) Indestructibility, (3) Equality with All the Buddhas, (4) Universal Pervasion, (5) Inexhaustible Virtue, (6) Correspondence with All Solid Good Roots of Non-differentiation, (7) Awakening of Equality toward All Sentient Beings, (8) the Manifestation of Suchness, (9) Unrestrained and Unattached Liberation, and (10) the [Immeasurable] Dharma Realm. The Ten Stages are [characterized as] (1) Joyful, (2) Undefiled, (3) Clear, (4) Radiant Wisdom, (5) Difficult to Conquer, (6) Face to Face [with Reality], (7) Far-reaching, (8) Immovable, (9) Good, and (10) Dharma-cloud.

Q: What are the practices associated with these levels?

A: Ordinary people of the lower level are on the Ten Levels of Faith and utilize the contemplation of emptiness by analyzing

and breaking down phenomena. Ordinary people who are on an advanced level are on the levels of Abodes, Practice, and Merit Transference. On the level of Abodes the contemplation of things as essentially empty is utilized. These are the two methods of contemplating emptiness: by analysis and as essentially empty. The perfection of this contemplation of emptiness destroys the delusions of mistaken views and attitudes. On the Ten Levels of Practice the contemplation of conventional existence is perfected, and this destroys minute delusions. On the Ten Levels of Merit Transference one cultivates the contemplation of the Middle Path and overcomes ignorance. On the level of partial enlightenment, that is, from the first Stage to the Level of Preliminary Awakening,
267b one partially destroys ignorance and is partially enlightened concerning the Middle Path.

Q: What about the level of ultimate sagehood?

A: The level of ultimate sagehood alone is Subtle Awakening that destroys the delusion of ignorance and puts an end to the birth and death of inconceivable transformations. This is the attainment of the Path on the seven-jeweled seat by the body of recompense.

Q: All obstacles are included under the "obstacles of passions" and the "wisdom obstacle." Why do you add the "minute delusions"?

A: These two kinds of obstacles are found in the *Bodhisattvabhūmi*. The three kinds of delusions are enumerated on the basis of the *Pañcaviṃśati-sāhasrikā-prajñā-pāramitā Sūtra* and the *Ta chih tu lun*.

Q: What are the phenomenal appearances and reality of the three kinds of delusions enumerated here?

A: The delusions of mistaken views and attitudes correspond to the obstacle of passions. Now if one exposes the meaning of phenomenal appearances and reality with regard to the wisdom obstacle, the obstacle to wisdom concerning phenomenal appearances corresponds to "minute delusions," and the obstacle to wisdom concerning reality corresponds to the "delusion of ignorance."

4. The Perfect Teaching

Next I shall clarify the Perfect Teaching.

Q: Why is this called "Perfect"?

A: "Perfect" means "not one-sided." It is different from the two previous Teachings in that it is direct in its explanation of subtle reality. It is different from the graded and differentiated Teachings in that its teachings are perfectly integrated and unobstructed. Also, its teaching, reality, wisdom, severance, practice, levels, causes, and results are perfect; therefore it is called the Perfect Teaching.

Q: What do you mean by "direct in its explanation of subtle reality," and "perfectly integrated and unobstructed"?

A: [In the Perfect Teaching] from the beginning one contemplates true reality, and objects are perceived as identical with the Middle; [one sees] that there is not one color or odor that is not the Middle Path. One knows directly the true reality of the perfectly integrated threefold truth. From beginning to end, there is no Buddha-dharma that is not truly real.

Q: What reality is clarified in this Teaching?

A: It clarifies the truth of the Middle Path, which is beyond conceptual understanding.

Q: For whose sake is it explained?

A: It is explained for the sake of those with the sharpest faculties.

Q: What levels [of attainment] are clarified for these people?

A: It clarifies the levels of the Six Identities.

Q: What are these Six Identities?

A: (1) Identity in Reality, (2) Verbal Identity, (3) Identity in Contemplative Practice, (4) Identity in Outer Appearance, (5) Identity in Partial [Realization of the] Truth, and (6) Ultimate Identity.

Q: Why do you posit Six Identities?

A: They are six so that nothing is left out from beginning to end. They are identities because they are interpenetrating from beginning to end. Their reality is the same, therefore they are "identical." Their phenomenological appearances are different, therefore they are six. From first to last their reality is the same; from beginning to end nothing is left out.

Q: What is the meaning of the gradual succession of the Six Identities?

A: Sentient beings are inherently endowed with the reality of three virtuous qualities [of the Dharma Body, *prajñā*-wisdom, and liberation]. This is called "Identity in Reality." They come to know this by being taught. This is called "Verbal Identity." The cultivation [of practice] that results from coming to know this is called "Identity in Contemplative Practice." Through contemplation and calming the mind one begins to simulate one's true function. This is "Identity in Outer Appearance." When the three virtuous qualities are partially manifested and one attains the Buddha-dharma partially, this is "Identity in Partial [Realization of the] Truth." When both wisdom and severance are perfected and the three virtuous qualities completely manifested, this is "Ultimate Identity."

Q: How do these levels of the Six Identities correspond to the level of the five preliminary grades and the fifty-two [Bodhisattva] levels?

A: The first two levels of identities do not correspond to any levels. The Identity in Contemplative Practice corresponds to the five preliminary grades. The Identity in Outer Appearance corresponds to the Ten Levels of Faith. The Identity in Partial [Realization of] the Truth corresponds to the Ten Abodes, the Ten Levels of
267c Practice, the Ten Levels of Merit Transference, the Ten Stages, and the Level of Preliminary Awakening. Ultimate Identity corresponds to the Level of Subtle Awakening.

Q: How do the preparatory levels of ordinary people and sages compare with regard to these levels?

A: The five preliminary grades of conventional designation correspond to the lower level of ordinary people. The purification of the six senses corresponds to the higher level of ordinary people. The levels from the Ten Abodes to the Level of Preliminary Awakening correspond to the level of partial sagehood. The one Level of Subtle Awakening corresponds to the level of ultimate sagehood.

Q: What are the "five preliminary grades" and the "purification of the six senses"?

A: To be endowed with the ten mental attributes [of the Ten Levels of Faith] is the first preliminary grade of Joy because of being in Accordance [with the Truth]. To read and chant the Sutras is the second preliminary grade. To add then the preaching of the Dharma is the third preliminary grade. To add the practice of the Six Perfections is the fourth preliminary grade. To practice the Six Perfections correctly is the fifth preliminary grade. The purification of the six senses means to purify the organs of (1) sight, (2) sound, (3) scent, (4) taste, (5) touch, and (6) thought.

Q: What Sutra is the basis of this level of five preliminary grades?

A: It is based on the [seventeenth] chapter of the *Lotus Sutra,* "Discrimination of Virtuous Qualities."

Q: Why do you establish five preliminary grades distinct and beyond the Ten Levels of Faith?

A: This is merely to distinguish differences and similarities. By similarities is meant that these [five preliminary grades] are included within the first mental state of the Ten Levels of Faith. By differences is meant that it is divided into five grades. These are differentiated now in order to illustrate the lower levels of ordinary people.

Q: What delusions are severed on the level of "Outer Appearance," and what delusions are destroyed on the level of "Partial [Realization of] the Truth"?

A: On the level of "Outer Appearance" one first spontaneously removes the delusions of mistaken views and attitudes. It is as in melting steel to make a vessel; one first gets rid of the crude impurities. On the level of "Partial [Realization of] the Truth" one destroys all the minute ignorance remaining in the forty-one levels of the transworldly realm.

Q: How can we know that the delusions of mistaken views and attitudes are severed on the level of "Outer Appearance" and that ignorance is severed on the level of "Partial [Realization of] the Truth"?

A: The *Jen wang ching* says, "The ten Bodhisattvas of goodness [the Bodhisattvas on the Ten Levels of Faith in the Perfect Teaching] arouse the great mind [of aspiration for enlightenment] and eternally depart from this oceanlike triple realm, which is a cycle of suffering." Therefore it is said that the delusions of mistaken views and attitudes are severed on the Ten Levels of Faith, or [the level of "Identity in] Outer Appearance." The *Avataṃsaka Sūtra* says, "At the time of the first aspiration one has already fulfilled complete awakening and fully penetrates the nature of the true reality of all dharmas. The essence of any and all wisdom is not realized from being taught by others." The *Lotus Sutra* says, "The Buddha's knowledge and insight are exposed." It should be known clearly that ignorance is severed on the level of the first aspiration for enlightenment, which is the first Abode stage.

Q: What is meant by "ignorance is severed on the level of aspiration for enlightenment, which is the first Abode stage"?

A: When one enters the level of the first Abode, the severance of one is the severance of all, and the attainment of the one body of the Tathāgata is the [attainment of] immeasurable [transformational] bodies. [The Buddha] is able to scatter his body in a hundred Buddha realms, appear in the ten realms of existence, and manifest his body of visible form everywhere in accordance with the capabilities [of sentient beings] and to save [sentient beings].

Q: If one fulfills complete awakening on the level of the first Abode of "aspiration," why is it necessary to go through the remaining levels?

A: What is meant by "fulfillment of complete awakening" is to fulfill the partial attainment of complete awakening. [The level of] the first Abode of "aspiration" is not identical to the fulfillment of ultimate, complete awakening.

Q: How can we know this?
A: The meaning can be known by the analogy of the lamp.

Q: What is this analogy?
A: The analogy is this: if one places a burning lamp in a dark
268a room, that room is lit all over, and if two or three or forty-two lamps are added, the illumination increases accordingly. If this analogy is understood, one should know the meaning of "all fulfilled in the fulfillment of one," and not fail to understand the clear difference between the beginning and end, and between illumination and darkness.

Q: With regard to what do you establish that "all is fulfilled in the fulfillment of one, and all is severed in the severance of one"?
A: "Fulfillment" is established with regard to wisdom, and "destruction" is established with regard to delusions. Wisdom and severance are non-dual; the fulfillment [of wisdom] and the destruction [of delusion] are simultaneous. It should be understood as analogous to the fact that when light arises darkness is extinguished. The analogy of the lamps is from the *Ta chih tu lun.*

Q: How much time do Bodhisattvas of this teaching pass through to fulfill Buddhahood?
A: In one life they enter the first Abode of "aspiration for enlightenment."

Q: How can we know this?
A: The *Sutra of Innumerable Meanings* (*Wu-liang i ching*) says, "In this body one attains the patience [which comes from realizing the truth] of nonarising and the instantaneous destruction of all passions and the cycle of birth and death." The *Mahāparinirvāṇa Sūtra* says, "On the Himalayan mountains there is a grass called 'forbearance.' If a cow eats this it will experience the most exquisite flavor." You should understand this meaning.

Q: Should this attainment of Buddhahood in one lifetime be understood as the fruit of partial realization or as the ultimate fruit of enlightenment?

A: It is the fruit of partial realization and not the ultimate fruit of enlightenment.

Q: If so, this one should be called a Bodhisattva and not a Buddha.

A: One who seeks that which is above is a Bodhisattva; one who seeks that which is below is a Buddha.

Q: What is ultimate Buddhahood in the Perfect Teaching?

A: The self-wrought reward body of enjoyment of the Tathāgata Vairocana.

Q: How is this known?

A: In the *Mo-ho chih-kuan* it says, "If one contemplates Twelvefold Conditioned Co-arising and culminates the reality of the Middle Path, this refers to the Buddha Vairocana of the Perfect Teaching. When he is seated on the seat of enlightenment, it becomes the seat of emptiness." The *Saddharmapuṇḍarīkasūtra Upadeśa* says, "Secondly, manifesting the wisdom of the Buddha [as reward body] and completing the practices of the Ten Stages, one attains the enlightenment of eternal Nirvāṇa, because, as the *Lotus Sutra* says, 'Good sons, I have actually already attained Buddhahood immeasurable and unlimited hundreds and thousands and millions and billions of aeons ago.'" The *Sutra of Meditation of the Bodhisattva Universal Virtue* [*P'u hsien kuan ching*] says, "The Buddha Śākyamuni is called 'Vairocana Who Pervades All Places.' This Buddha's abode is called 'Eternal Tranquil Light.' It is a place that embodies the perfection of permanence; a place where the perfection of the selfhood is established; a place where the marks of Being are extinguished by the perfection of purity; a place where the marks of body and mind do not abide due to the perfection of pleasure."

D. Final Summation

Q: How are these Four Teachings classified with regard to this realm of the [triple] world and the transworldly realm?

A: The two Teachings of the Tripiṭaka and the Shared both correspond to this realm of the [triple] world. Both Distinct and Perfect Teachings correspond to the transworldly realm.

Q: How are they classified with regard to phenomenal appearances and reality?

A: The Tripiṭaka Teaching corresponds to the phenomenal appearances of this realm. The Shared Teaching corresponds to the reality of this realm. The Distinct Teaching corresponds to the phenomenal appearances of the transworldly realm, and the Perfect Teaching corresponds to the reality of the transworldly realm.

Q: How are they classified with regard to Hīnayāna and Mahāyāna?

268b *A:* The Tripiṭaka Teaching belongs to the Hīnayāna. The Shared Teaching is common to both the Mahāyāna and the Hīnayāna. The Distinct and Perfect Teachings are completely Mahāyāna.

Q: Also, how are they classified with regard to the tentative and the real?

A: The first three are tentative, and the last one is real.

Q: The true essence of all Four Teachings is one. Why are there Four Teachings?

A: Although basically they are one, perceptions are not the same depending on the capabilities of sentient beings. This is the reason why Four Teachings arose. In the *Lotus Sutra* it says, "Three are taught and distinguished concerning the one Buddha-vehicle." The meaning is the same here.

Chapter II

The Meaning of the Five Flavors

Reality itself is beyond verbalization, but one must use conventional language to encounter reality. The Path cannot be grasped through discussion, but stages [of attainment] can be discerned through the process of discussion. Therefore many explanations are conventionally presented for the sake of beings in this realm of suffering, and to teach [the truth for the sake of] the deaf and the blind. [The classification scheme of] the Five Periods is utilized to illumine the hidden minuteness of the tranquil light of inherent awakening. Therefore we list the five light and heavy flavors and clarify the progression of the teachings. This meaning is interpreted in three sections: Introduction, Scriptural Support, and Interpretation.

A. Introduction

Question: What are the names of the Five Flavors?

Answer: (1) The flavor of milk, (2) the flavor of cream, (3) the flavor of curds, (4) the flavor of butter, and (5) the flavor of ghee.

B. Scriptural Support

Q: What Sutra contains the text explaining the Five Flavors?

A: The *Mahāparinirvāṇa Sūtra.*

Q: What does the text say?

A: This Sutra says, "It is analogous to a cow giving milk. Cream emerges from the milk. Curds emerge from the cream. Butter emerges from the curds. Ghee emerges from the butter. The twelvefold scripture emerges from the Buddha. . . ." The Sutras emerge from the twelvefold scripture. The *Vaipulya* texts emerge from these Sutras. The *Prajñā-pāramitā Sūtra*s emerge from the *Vaipulya* texts. The *Mahāparinirvāṇa Sūtra* emerges from the *Prajñā-pāramitā Sūtra*s.

C. Interpretation

Q: What doctrines are being compared to these Five Flavors?
A: It is an analogy for the sequence of the Buddha's teachings.

Q: What is this sequence?
A: The *Avataṃsaka Sūtra* is analogous to the flavor of milk. The *Āgama*s are analogous to the flavor of cream. The *Vaipulya* texts are analogous to the flavor of curds. The *Prajñā-pāramitā Sūtra*s are analogous to the flavor of butter. The *Lotus* and *Mahāparinirvāṇa Sūtra*s are analogous to the flavor of ghee.

Q: Why is the *Avataṃsaka Sūtra* analogous to milk, and so forth to the *Lotus* and *Mahāparinirvāṇa Sūtra*s being analogous to ghee?
A: When the Buddha sat on the seat of enlightenment and first perfected complete awakening, he expounded purely on the Mahāyāna for the sake of the Bodhisattvas. This was like the sun, which upon rising first illumines the tall mountains. Milk is the beginning of all the flavors. It is analogous to the direct teachings [of the Buddha immediately after his enlightenment] being the core of all the teachings. Also, the analogy of the flavor of milk has two other meanings. First, it is the beginning of all his great deeds; and
268c second, it is [taught at a stage when the teachings] for the sake of those of inferior capabilities have not yet been taught. Therefore the [teachings of] the *Avataṃsaka Sūtra* are analogous to milk. Next, without moving from his place of enlightenment he magically went to the Deer Park and preached the sermon on the Four Noble Truths as arising and perishing. This is analogous to cream emerging from milk. Next, he expounded the teachings of the

Vaipulya texts, the "Great Collection of Sutras," the *Vimalakīrti-nirdeśa Sūtra,* the *Viśeṣacinta-brahmaparipṛcchā Sūtra* and so forth, which praise the perfect and criticize the one-sided, extol the Mahāyāna and impugn the Hīnayāna. This is analogous to curds emerging from cream. Next he preached all of the *Prajñā-pāramitā Sūtras*, in which the explanation is left to Śāriputra, as the rich man passes on the household treasures to his son, and distinctions as to superior and inferior are integrated. This is analogous to butter emerging from curds. Next, the first four flavors are exposed as belonging ultimately to the Buddha-vehicle. This is analogous to ghee emerging from butter.

Q: The [teachings of] the *Avataṃsaka Sūtra* are the direct teaching of the Mahāyāna. Why are they analogous to milk?

A: This does not refer to it being light or heavy [in profundity], but merely means that it comes first. Therefore it corresponds to the first flavor.

Q: The *Mahāparinirvāṇa Sūtra* says that "the *Mahāparinirvāṇa Sūtra* emerges from the *Prajñā-pāramitā Sūtras*." Why does it not mention the *Lotus Sutra?* Why is the *Lotus Sutra* analogous to ghee?

A: The *Mahāparinirvāṇa Sūtra* is called "ghee," and the *Lotus Sutra* is called "a meal fit for the great King."

Q: Although you quote the phrase "a meal fit for the great King," this is evidence for the meaning but not the text.

A: The *Saddharmapuṇḍarīka-sūtra Upadeśa* says [in reference to the *Lotus Sutra*], "Of these Five Flavors, ghee is supreme." Therefore we know that the two Sutras are both analogous to ghee. Also, the Buddha Dīpa [Moon and Sun Glow] expounded the *Lotus Sutra* and then proclaimed that at midnight he would enter Nirvāṇa. In the same way this Buddha [Śākyamuni] also first expounded the *Avataṃsaka Sūtra* and later expounded the *Lotus Sutra.* When the Buddha was Kāśyapa he also did the same thing; in all cases he did not explain the *Mahāparinirvāṇa Sūtra.* In all these cases the *Lotus Sutra* is the last teaching and the last flavor. Now the Buddha utilizes the *Lotus Sutra* as ghee in order to bring to maturity those who are ready. He then [in the *Mahāparinirvāṇa Sūtra*] leads the remaining [sentient beings] to maturity through repeating [teachings concerning] *prajñā*-wisdom and leads those [of the fourth *Prajñā-pāramitā* period] to enter Nirvāṇa. Thus the *Mahāparinirvāṇa Sūtra* is used as the last teaching and last flavor. Also, the *Mahāparinirvāṇa Sūtra* says, "By receiving an assurance of Buddhahood in the *Lotus Sutra,* one perceives one's potential for enlightenment, attains the great fruit [of Buddhahood], and undertakes no more action, as when the autumn harvest is done and placed in winter storage."

Q: Are there any distinctions to be made between the Five Flavors and the Five Time Periods?

A: The Five Flavors are identical to the Five Time Periods. There is only the distinction of Dharma and analogy.

Q: Are the Five Time Periods clarified in the *Lotus Sutra?*

A: In the chapter on "Belief and Understanding" in the *Lotus Sutra* it says, "Accordingly he dispatched an attendant to follow quickly . . . but the poor son was terrified and fell to the earth." This refers to the first time period. It also says, "He secretly dispatched two men" who brought the son back through expedient means. This refers to the second time period. It also says, "At the end of this time there was mutual trust and he came and went without difficulty, though he still lived in the same place." This refers to the third time period. It also says, "The father knew that he would die before long. . . ." This refers to the fourth time period. It also says, "When facing his last moments, he ordered his son [to come, and the father revealed their true relationship]." This refers to the fifth period.

269a *Q:* The teachings of the Buddha's life include all of the Four Teachings. Why are the Five Flavors also established?

A: The Four Teachings are given in reference to the depth or shallowness of capabilities, and the Five Flavors clarify the order of the teaching. The purpose of interpreting all meaning and truth with the Four Teachings and the Five Flavors is to manifest the *Lotus Sutra* as the climax of the Buddha's life teachings.

Chapter III

The Meaning of the One Vehicle

All Buddhas appear in the world for one great purpose. Though distinctions are made as to the three vehicles, ultimately [they all] rely on One Vehicle. Therefore Śākyamuni descended to this world to be born in a royal palace, left home, and attained the Path according to his capability. He preached many different sermons; some were at first direct and later gradual, some were at first gradual and later direct, but all were taught as inducements to the *Lotus Sutra.* This is the meaning of the Sutra where it says, "The teachings of expedient means are exposed [like the opening of a gate] and the aspects of true reality revealed." There are four sections for interpreting this meaning. The first is the Explanation of Terms; the second is the Interpretation of the Essence; the third is Quotations from Scripture [i.e., Scriptural Support]; and the fourth is the Interpretation.

A. Explanation of Terms

Question: What is the meaning of the term "One Vehicle"?

Answer: "One" means non-dual and "vehicle" refers to a means of transportation.

Q: What are the meanings of "non-dual" and "a means of transportation"?

A: It is called "non-dual" because there are not two or three vehicles, and because it [the One Vehicle] transcends the relativity of two or three [vehicles]. It is called "a means of transportation" because practitioners ride on it to attain omniscience.

B. Interpretation of the Essence

Q: What is the essence of the One Vehicle?

A: There are two: the common essence and the distinctive essence.

Q: What are the meanings of "common essence" and "distinctive essence"?

A: The common essence is the true aspect of reality. The distinctive essences are the four categories of oneness.

Q: The common essence is understood, but what is meant by "the four categories of oneness" of the distinctive essences?

A: Oneness of reality, oneness of teaching, oneness of practice, and oneness of persons.

Q: What is the meaning of "the oneness of reality," and so forth?

A: Exposing the reality of the three vehicles as manifested in the reality of the One Vehicle is called "the oneness of reality." Exposing the teaching of the three vehicles as manifested in the teaching of the One Vehicle is called "the oneness of teaching." The practice of the three vehicles is brought in harmony with the practice of the One Vehicle; this is called "the oneness of practice." The people in the three vehicles are brought in harmony with those in the One Vehicle; this is called "the oneness of persons."

Q: Why is it said that the reality of the three vehicles is brought into harmony with the reality of the One Vehicle, and so forth?

A: Because the three vehicles are not the fundamental intent of the Buddha. The One Vehicle is the fundamental import of the Buddha.

C. Scriptural Support

Q: The meaning of the One Vehicle is established on the basis of what Sutra passages?

A: The *Lotus Sutra* says, "All Buddhas, the World Honored Ones, appear in this world for one great deed as cause and condition."

269b *Q:* What is the meaning of "one great deed as cause and condition"?

A: "One" refers to the one true reality that there are not three, five, seven, or nine vehicles. Therefore it is "one." It is called "great" because its nature is vast and expansive. It is called "deed" because it is the activity of all Buddhas who appear in this world. It is called "cause" because sentient beings who have the capability thus approach the Buddha. It is called "condition" because the Buddha responds in accordance with their capabilities.

Q: Although you have quoted this text, the meaning is still not clear. Are there other passages?

A: There are truly many passages. The *Lotus Sutra* says, "The words of all Buddhas and Tathāgatas are not vain delusions. There is no other vehicle but the one Buddha-vehicle." It also says, "In the Buddha-lands in the ten directions there is only one Buddha-dharma, not two and not three." It also says, "The appearance of all Buddhas in this world is only one true deed." It also says, "All the World Honored Ones expound the Path of the One Vehicle." It also says, "The words of all the Buddhas are not different. There is only one and not two vehicles." It also says, "It is widely said to the great multitude that all Bodhisattvas and Śrāvaka disciples are taught and transformed only with the way of the One Vehicle."

Also, the chapter on "Expedient Means" [in the *Lotus Sutra*] contains sections on five kinds of Buddhas. The first section on "All Buddhas" says, "All Buddhas preach the Dharma in accordance with what is appropriate." This [illustrates that] the three tentative [teachings: Tripiṭaka, Shared, and Distinct] are the exposition of expedient means. The Sutra says, "This Dharma cannot be understood through conceptualization or discrimination." This [illustrates] the One True [Perfect Teaching], which manifests true reality. Next, the section on the Buddhas of the past says, "All Buddhas utilize innumerable and incalculable expedient means and various stories, parables, and words to expound all Dharmas

for the sake of all sentient beings." This clarifies the exposition of the tentative. The Sutra says, "These Dharmas are all those of the One Buddha-vehicle." This clarifies the manifestation of the real. Next, the section on future Buddhas says, "Śāriputra, all future Buddhas should, upon appearing in this world, utilize innumerable and incalculable expedient means and various stories, parables, and words to expound all Dharmas for the sake of all sentient beings." This clarifies the exposition of the tentative. The Sutra says, "All of these Dharmas correspond to the One Buddha-vehicle. Therefore all sentient beings hear the Dharma from the Buddha and everyone ultimately attains universal wisdom." This clarifies the manifestation of the real. Next, the section on present Buddhas says, "Śāriputra, at the present time, in the immeasurable hundred thousand million billion Buddha-lands in the ten directions, in the many places where all Buddhas, World Honored Ones, benefit and pacify sentient beings, all of these Buddhas also utilize innumerable and incalculable expedient means and various stories, parables, and words to expound all Dharmas for the sake of sentient beings." This clarifies the exposition of the tentative. The Sutra says, "All of these Dharmas correspond to the One Buddha-vehicle. Therefore all sentient beings hear the Dharma from the Buddha and everyone ultimately attains universal wisdom." This clarifies the manifestation of the real. Next, in the section on the Buddha Śākyamuni it says,
269c "Śāriputra, I also now do the same. Knowing that all sentient beings have various desires and profound attachments, I therefore utilize various stories, parables, words, and the power of expedient means in order to preach the Dharma, in accordance with their inherent natures." This clarifies the exposition of the tentative. The Sutra says, "Śāriputra, in this way all attain the One Buddha-vehicle and universal wisdom." This clarifies the manifestation of the real.

Q: You said previously that the One Buddha-vehicle consists of the four categories of oneness. Why do you now speak only of the One Vehicle and not illustrate the four categories of oneness?

A: The sections on the five kinds of Buddhas all include the four categories of oneness.

Q: Which passages do you mean?

A: The section on "All Buddhas" says, "The exposing, signifying, awakening, and entering of the Buddhas' knowledge and insight"; this refers to "the oneness of reality." "Only to teach and transform Bodhisattvas" refers to "the oneness of persons." "All of his actions are constantly for one purpose" refers to "the oneness of practice." "He preaches the Dharma for the sake of sentient beings utilizing only the One Buddha-vehicle" refers to "the oneness of teaching." The section on past Buddhas says, "These Dharmas are all those of the One Buddha-vehicle," referring to "the oneness of teaching." "To hear the Dharma from all Buddhas" refers to "the oneness of persons." In the phrase "Ultimately everyone attains universal wisdom," this wisdom consists of both the knower and the known. That which is known is the "one reality," and the knower refers to "the oneness of practice." The sections on future Buddhas, present Buddhas, and the Buddha Śākyamuni can be known in the same way.

D. Interpretation

Q: To which of the four categories of oneness does the phrase "exposing, signifying, awakening, and entering" correspond?

A: To the oneness of reality.

Q: How many types of interpretation does this include?

A: There are two types. First I shall quote the *Saddharmapuṇḍarīka-sūtra Upadeśa* and discuss three interpretive categories, and then I shall utilize four types of interpretation based on the commentary [the *Fa-hua wen-chü* by Chih-i].

Q: What are the passages quoted in the discussion of three interpretive categories?

A: The *Saddharmapuṇḍarīka-sūtra Upadeśa* says, "First is the meaning of supremacy. There is no other deed except [the attainment of] universal wisdom. As the [*Lotus*] *Sutra* says, the Buddha's knowledge and insight are revealed in order to lead sentient beings to attain purity; therefore he appears in the world. Second, the meaning of sameness is: Śrāvakas, Pratyekabuddhas, and Buddhas are equal with regard to the Dharma Body. It is as the [*Lotus*] *Sutra* says, that the Buddha appears in the world because he wishes to signify the Buddha's knowledge and insight to sentient beings. Third, the meaning of the unknown: those of the two vehicles do not know the ultimate, One Buddha-vehicle. Therefore it is as the [*Lotus*] *Sutra* says, that the Buddha appears in the world because he wishes to awaken sentient beings concerning the Buddha's knowledge and insight. Fourth, the Buddha manifests immeasurable deeds of wisdom for the sake of leading them to be enlightened concerning the stage of Non-retrogression. It is as the *Lotus Sutra* says, that the Buddha wishes to lead sentient beings to enter the Buddha's knowledge and insight." Since the second and third categories are discussed in detail in the *Saddharmapuṇḍarīka-sūtra Upadeśa,* I shall not discuss them at length.

Next, four interpretations based on the commentary.

Q: What are the four types of interpretations?

270a *A:* (1) Interpretation according to levels, (2) interpretation of the four kinds of wisdom, (3) interpretation of the Four Doctrines, and (4) interpretation of the four ways of contemplating the mind.

Q: What is the gist of the interpretation according to levels?

A: The four words "exposing, signifying, awakening, and entering" are compared with the forty levels of attainment; therefore it is said to be an interpretation according to levels.

Q: How do they compare?

A: "Exposing" corresponds to the Ten Abodes. "Signifying" corresponds to the Ten Levels of Practice. "Awakening" corresponds to the Ten Levels of Merit Transference. "Entering" corresponds to the Ten Stages.

Q: Why does the word "exposing" correspond to the Ten Abodes, and so forth to the word "entering" corresponding to the Ten Stages?

A: On the first level of the Ten Abodes one destroys the delusion of ignorance, exposes the potential for Buddhahood, and perceives the true aspects of reality. Therefore the word "exposing" corresponds to the Ten Abodes. Also, within the Ten Levels of Practice the obstacle of delusions is already removed so that all the merits of the Dharma realm are manifestly indicated and clear. Therefore "signifying" corresponds to the Ten Levels of Practice. Next, within the Ten Levels of Merit Transference, obstacles are removed, the essence of reality is manifest, and the practice of the Dharma realm is clear; therefore "awakening" corresponds to the Ten Levels of Merit Transference. Next, within the Ten Stages, phenomenal appearances and reality are [understood to be] integrated and one can freely enter the sea of universal wisdom. Therefore "entering" corresponds to the Ten Stages.

Q: If, as you have explained above, this should be understood as successive stages, what about the meaning of the Perfect Teaching?

A: The virtuous qualities that are to come are already [latently] present in the causal levels. The good roots of the past are also contained in the resultant stages. It is analogous to moonlight, which dispels darkness, waxing and waning while the moon itself does not change.

Second, the interpretation according to the Four Wisdoms.

Q: What are the Four Wisdoms?

A: (1) Wisdom of the Path, (2) various wisdoms of the Path, (3) wisdom concerning [the emptiness of] everything, and (4) universal wisdom.

Q: To which teaching do these Four Wisdoms correspond?

A: These are the Four Wisdoms of the Perfect Teaching.

Q: How do they correspond with regard to "exposing, signifying, awakening, and entering"?

A: They correspond in the same way as the next example. [First = exposing, second = signifying, third = awakening, and fourth = entering.]

Third, the interpretation according to the Four Doctrines.

Q: What are the Four Doctrines?

A: (1) The doctrine of existence, (2) the doctrine of emptiness, (3) the doctrine of both emptiness and existence, and (4) the doctrine of neither emptiness nor existence.

Q: To which of the Four Teachings do these Four Doctrines correspond?

A: These are the Four Doctrines of the Perfect Teaching.

Q: How do they correspond with regard to "exposing," and so forth?

A: They correspond in the same way as above.

Q: The doctrines for understanding [reality] are four. Is the reality that is understood also four?

A: Although there are four [doctrines] for understanding [reality], the [reality] that is understood is one. For example, there are many outer gates for [entering] the king's palace, but the inside is one [that is, all gates lead into one place].

Fourth, interpretation with regard to contemplating the mind.

Q: How do you make distinctions according to "exposing" and so forth with regard to contemplating the mind?

A: Contemplate the principle of the threefold truth and the nature of the mind. To contemplate this clearly and purely is called "exposing." Though it is difficult to conceptualize the nature of the mind, to merge [the thoughts of] emptiness, conventional exist-
270b ence, and the Middle calmly, just as they are, is called "signifying." For the thoughts of emptiness, conventional existence, and the Middle to be three yet one, one yet three, is called "awakening." The thoughts of emptiness, conventional existence, and the Middle are not emptiness, conventional existence, nor the Middle, yet they equally illuminate emptiness, conventional existence, and the Middle. This is called "entering."

Q: What is the origin of these four interpretations?

A: The perception of reality depends on the level of attainment. The level of attainment depends on wisdom. The arousing of wisdom depends on doctrine. The penetrating understanding of doctrine depends on contemplation. Due to the practice of contemplation one understands doctrine. Due to the understanding of doctrine one attains wisdom. Due to the attainment of wisdom one establishes a certain level of attainment. Due to establishing a level of attainment one can perceive reality. [One] reality is perceived, therefore it is called "the oneness of reality."

Q: Does each of the four terms "exposing, signifying, awakening, and entering" include all four types of interpretation, and are the four terms all related?

A: Each term has these four interpretations, and each of the four interpretations is related to these four terms.

Q: How are the four terms related to the four interpretations?

A: The interpretation of Four Wisdoms is related to "exposing." The interpretation of contemplating the mind is related to "signifying." The Four Doctrines are related to "awakening." The Four Levels are related to "entering."

Q: Is there scriptural evidence for these four types of interpretation?

A: The *Saddharmapuṇḍarīka-sūtra Upadeśa* says the interpretation of Four Levels is made in order to "illustrate the stage of Non-retrogression." The treatise says that the interpretation of the Four Wisdoms is made in order that "the Tathāgata may illumine the truth." The treatise says that the interpretation of contemplating the mind is made for the sake of "the meaning of sameness." The treatise says that the interpretation of the Four Doctrines is made because "they do not know the ultimate state."

Q: It is interpreted that there are exceedingly many explanations given for interpreting "exposing, signifying, awakening, and entering." Why do you reduce it to one explanation?

A: There are exceedingly many explanations because we have not yet examined the unique contribution of the *Lotus Sutra*. The *Lotus Sutra*'s unique contribution is the doctrine of the One Vehicle, which is difficult to conceptualize. It cannot be fathomed by ordinary people, although it is praised by noble men. Teachers and disciples should know it. Now, relying on the meaning and following the text I shall summarize it in ten pairs by discussing its different features. (1) The assurance of imminent Buddhahood is given to those of the two vehicles [in the third chapter of the *Lotus Sutra,* "Parables"], and the Tathāgata's original enlightenment from the distant past is exposed [in the sixteenth chapter of the *Lotus Sutra,* "The Life Span of the Tathāgata"]. (2) Rejoicing [over hearing a verse from the *Lotus Sutra*] and praising it until it is passed on to the fiftieth person, whose benefit upon hearing it is to reach the highest stage of [the Bodhisattva, wherein one will attain] Buddhahood after this one life [is explained in the eighteenth chapter of the *Lotus Sutra,* "The Merits of Appropriate Joy"]. (3) [In the twelfth chapter, "Devadatta"] Śākyamuni indicates that the activity of overcoming the five major sins was his original teacher, and Mañjuśrī converts the eight-year-old dragon girl. (4) [In the eighteenth chapter, "The Merits of Appropriate Joy"] everyone, upon hearing one verse [from the *Lotus Sutra*], is given the assurance of Buddhahood; the merit accumulated by preserving the name of the *Lotus Sutra* is immeasurable. (5) [In the twenty-third chapter, "The Former Affairs of the Bodhisattva Bhaiṣajyaguru" it is explained that] if one hears [the message of] the *Lotus Sutra* and keeps its teachings, one can put an end to rebirth as a woman; if one hears, reads, and chants the *Lotus Sutra,* one will neither grow old nor die. (6) [In the nineteenth chapter, "The Good Qualities of the Dharma Teacher," it is explained how] the five types of Dharma teachers manifest and attain the qualities [of the Buddha]; while undertaking the four practices of serenity one dreams of entering the stages of the Ten Abodes. (7) [In the twenty-sixth chapter, "*Dhāraṇī,*" it explains that] if a man torments or disturbs [a Dharma teacher], his head will split into seven parts. One who pays homage has more than

ten blessings. (8) One life of the Buddha is now past and cut off, but its teachings are praiseworthy; the ten parables [of the *Lotus Sutra*] are presented. (9) [In the fifteenth chapter, "Welling Up out of the Earth," innumerable witnesses for the Buddha] arise out of the ground, and Ajita [the future Buddha Maitreya] does not know even one of them; the Dragon King of the lotus flower in the east does not yet know the basis. (10) [As is explained in the seventh chapter, "The Parable of the Magic Castle,"] the traces of [the Buddha's] transformations appeared three thousand incalculable [aeons ago]; and [as is explained in the chapter, "The Life Span of the Tathāgata," Buddhahood was] originally fulfilled five hundred
270c incalculable [aeons ago]. The phenomena of the original basis and the transformational traces [of the Buddha] are mysterious. This is not explained in all of the [other] Sutras. Such passages are found only in this *Lotus Sutra.* This is indicated on the basis of what is appropriate [according to the capabilities of sentient beings]. If not unique, what is it? Also, the other interpretations are made in order to lead to and prepare for this explanation. There are thus many [interpretations of] the Buddha's knowledge and insight.

Q: As you say, the subtle Dharma [of the *Lotus Sutra*] should be expounded quickly by the Buddha. Why did he not expound it for more than thirty years after he attained Buddhahood?

A: Because people were not ready and the time was not right. In the thirty-odd years after his attainment of Buddhahood he made distinctions in the One Buddha-vehicle and expounded three.

Q: For what reason did he now expound the real truth for the first time?

A: Because people were ready and the time was right, he expounded only the unique, subtle, One Vehicle.

Q: Is the doctrine of the One Vehicle in this *Lotus Sutra* and the doctrine of the One Vehicle in the *Avataṃsaka Sūtra,* the *Śrīmālādevī Sūtra,* and so forth, the same or different?

A: The term is the same but the meaning is different.

Q: What do you mean [when you say] that the meaning is different?

A: The doctrine of the One Vehicle in the *Avataṃsaka Sūtra,* the *Śrīmālādevī Sūtra,* and so forth, contains expedient means; but the doctrine of the One Vehicle in the *Lotus Sutra* rejects all expedient means. Therefore one can perceive that the meaning is different.

Q: What is the meaning of "containing expedient means" and "rejecting expedient means"?

A: In one the three [vehicles] exist outside [the One Vehicle]; therefore it contains expedient means. In the other the three do not exist outside, therefore it is said to reject [expedient means].

Q: How many causes are utilized in interpreting the One Vehicle that rejects expedient means?

A: Based on the *Saddharmapuṇḍarīka-sūtra Upadeśa,* four causes are given in interpreting the One Vehicle.

Q: What are the four causes?

A: These are the "exposing, signifying, awakening, and entering" expounded above.

Q: Are these four causes the same as or different from the "ten causes" in the *Mahāyāna Saṃgraha?*

A: These are all the same.

Q: What do you mean by these being the same?

A: Both treatises are the same in leading those whose nature is that of the two vehicles to enter the One Vehicle.

Q: What do you mean [when you say] that they are the same in entering the One Vehicle?

A: The *Saddharmapuṇḍarīka-sūtra Upadeśa* says, "Those who are of a determined nature to be Śrāvakas have roots that are still immature, and therefore the Buddha does not give them assurance of Buddhahood." The *Mahāyāna Saṃgraha* says, "Because [the emptiness of] their Dharmas and their selflessness are equal, [the Buddha] secretly expounded the One Vehicle."

Q: The passage "still immature" and the words "secret intention" are certainly not similar. Why do you say that "they are the same in entering"?

A: It has already been said that their roots are still immature, but it should be known that [the roots] will certainly mature. Also, the intention of the *Mahāyāna Saṃgraha* is that the time for the fulfillment [of Buddhahood] has not arrived. The meaning of "assurance of Buddhahood" is to "prepare one for the gift [of eventual Buddhahood]"; therefore it is called a "secret intention." It does not mean that they will not [eventually] fulfill Buddhahood. This treatise also says, "Those of an already determined Śrāvaka nature can become Bodhisattvas through further training of their roots." Therefore it is clearly known that even those of a determined nature of the two vehicles can fulfill Buddhahood. All things with form and consciousness have the nature of awakening. Is there any man or woman who cannot fulfill Buddhahood? If one believes in the universal fulfillment of Buddhahood, he will be given the fruit of Vairocana [of ultimate enlightenment]. If one argues over the fulfillment or nonfulfillment of Buddhahood, one should fear the possibility of falling into the Avīci hell. The Perfect Teaching and the perfect exposition are gathered in this text [the
271a *Lotus Sutra*]. If one reads and chants it, one can attain the wisdom of the Buddha.

Chapter IV

The Meaning of the Ten Suchlikes

The Ten Suchlikes, which are like Indra's net, are integrated into the ten realms of existence yet are distinct. The threefold truth is like a crystal in which the three thousand realms are contained and colorfully reflected. This is the objective realm illumined by the Tathāgata's true wisdom, the ultimate goal of the jeweled vehicle in the *Lotus Sutra*. From the first aspiration to the stage just before Buddhahood it is necessary to rely on this [teaching of the *Lotus Sutra*] and not on any other way. This is the meaning of "arousing [an understanding of] subtle objective reality." There are three parts to interpreting this meaning.

A. Introduction

Question: What are the Ten Suchlikes?

Answer: The chapter "Expedient Means" in the *Lotus Sutra* lists "suchlike appearance, suchlike nature, suchlike essence, suchlike power, suchlike activity, suchlike causes, suchlike conditions, suchlike results, suchlike retribution, and suchlike beginning and end being ultimately the same."

B. Interpretation

Q: Why are these called "suchlike appearance" and so forth to "suchlike beginning and end being ultimately the same"?

A: There is a general interpretation of their common features and a detailed interpretation of their distinct features. The general interpretation is that "appearance" refers to distinctions that are made in perceiving outer forms; therefore it is called "appearance." "Nature" refers to that which is inside oneself and does not change; therefore it is called "nature." That which is the central quality [of something] is the "essence." "Power" is the ability to influence. "Activity" refers to the activity of construction. "Causes" refers to direct causes. "Conditions" refers to auxiliary causes. "Results" refers to direct results. "Retribution" refers to the indirect results of retribution. "Beginning" refers to the first suchlike of appearance, "end" refers to the last suchlike of retribution, and "ultimately the same" refers to their integration.

Q: Do these Ten Suchlikes have numerous meanings?
A: They have shared and distinct meanings.

Q: What are they?
A: The shared meaning is that they all exist in one thought; the distinct meaning is that they are divided according to material and mental categories.

Q: What thoughts are meant by saying that "they all exist in one thought"?
A: This refers to a single thought of an ordinary person.

Q: What about dividing them according to material and mental categories?
A: Appearance and retribution exist only in the material category. Nature, causes, and results exist only in the mental category. Essence, power, activity, and conditions span both the material and mental categories. "Beginning and end both the same" should be known in accordance with this.

Q: What is the essence of these Ten Suchlikes?
A: The causes and effects of the ten Dharma realms are its essence.

Q: What are the "ten Dharma realms"?
A: (1) The Dharma realm of hell, (2) that of beasts, (3) that of hungry spirits, (4) that of *asuras*, (5) that of human beings, (6) that

of gods, (7) that of Śrāvakas, (8) that of Pratyekabuddhas, (9) that of Bodhisattvas, and (10) the Dharma realm of the Buddha.

Q: Do these ten Dharma realms include the Ten Suchlikes?
A: Each and every realm contains the Ten Suchlikes.

Q: If so, how many are causes and how many are results?
271b *A:* The first seven are causes, the next two are results, and the last one is both cause and result.

Q: What is the meaning of the distinct interpretation?
A: This is a classification into four parts according to similar tendencies.

Q: What are the four categories?
A: (1) The four evil destinies, (2) human beings and gods, (3) the two vehicles, and (4) Bodhisattvas and Buddhas.

Q: What are the Ten Suchlikes for the category of the four evil destinies?
A: The interpretations are exceedingly vast and cannot be exhausted. Now I shall abbreviate the complex renditions and present a simple summary. The four evil destinies have as their appearance the manifestation of suffering. Their nature is to be destined to accumulate evil. Their essence is to have their minds and bodies pounded and broken. Their power is to climb on swords and enter cauldrons [of boiling metal in pursuit of their desires]. Their activity is to do the ten immoral deeds. Their causes are the arousing of evil and defiled karma. Their conditions are passion, attachment, and so forth. Their results are the fruits of evil habits. Their retribution is further rebirth in the three evil destinies. The beginning and end are the same in that they all consist of ignorance.

Q: How about the Ten Suchlikes of human beings and gods?
A: The appearance of human beings and gods is that of manifesting pleasure. Their nature is to be destined to accumulate goodness. Their essence is to rise above their bodies and minds. Their power is to experience pleasure. Their activity is to keep the

five precepts and do the ten good deeds. Their causes are the pure white karma [of good deeds]. Their conditions are good passions and attachments. Their results are the fruit of good habits. Their retribution is to be human beings or gods. They are the same in that the existence of the beginning through the end is merely that of having conventional names.

Q: How about the Ten Suchlikes of the two vehicles?

A: The Ten Suchlikes of these realms are explained with reference to true nondefilement. Their appearance manifests Nirvāṇa. Their nature is neither white nor black [good nor evil]. Their essence is the fivefold Dharma Body [endowed with the virtues of morality, concentration, wisdom, liberation, and the knowledge-insight of liberation]. Their power is the ability to move about in or transcend [this world]. Their activity is to strive diligently. Their causes are those of undefiled, correct wisdom. Their conditions are the practices that are conducive to the Path. Their results are the fourfold fruit [of stream-winner to Arhat]. Those of the two vehicles have no retribution.

Q: Why is the arousing of the truth considered the result, while there is no discussion of retribution?

A: A condition of nondefilement is aroused, and this direct cause is rewarded by the attainment of a similar result. The condition of nondefilement has destroyed [the causes for] further rebirth, and so further rebirth does not occur. Therefore it is said that there is no retribution.

Q: If so, how do you explain that the first three fruits [of stream-winner and so forth] do have retribution?

A: A residue of conceptual delusions still remains to be severed; delusions remain for seven lifetimes. Some have one more rebirth, others are born in the realm of form; this is not retribution from [the condition of] nondefilement.

Q: Do you say that there is no retribution from the perspective of the Mahāyāna or the Hīnayāna?

A: This is Hīnayāna.

Q: How about from the perspective of the Mahāyāna?

A: From the perspective of the Mahāyāna, this "[condition of] nondefilement" still contains defilements.

Q: Why do you say that there are still defilements?

A: Although it is said to be lacking in defilements from the perspective of the Hīnayāna, from the perspective of the Mahāyāna this nondefilement is a cause, and ignorance a condition, for rebirth in this world of inconceivable transformations. Therefore there are still retributions.

271c *Q:* How about the Ten Suchlikes of the realms of the Bodhisattva and the Buddha?

A: A detailed discussion would include the fact that there are three types of Bodhisattvas.

Q: What are the three types of Bodhisattvas?

A: First, the Bodhisattva of the Tripiṭaka Teaching; second, the Bodhisattva of the Shared Teaching; and third, the Bodhisattva of the Distinct Teaching.

Q: How about the Ten Suchlikes of the Bodhisattva of the Tripiṭaka Teaching?

A: The appearance, nature, essence, power, and so forth, of Bodhisattvas of the Tripiṭaka Teaching are discussed from the perspective of their virtuous qualities. Their appearance is that of the Six Perfections of phenomena. Their nature is the goodness of human beings and gods. Their essence is the thirty-two major marks. Their power is the four universal vows as arising and perishing. Their activity is the practice of the Six Perfections of phenomena. Their causes are good karma. Their conditions are passions. Their results are the complete severance [of mistaken views and attitudes through] the thirty-four mental states [of eight kinds of patience, eight wisdoms, nine stages of non-obstruction, and nine liberations]. The Buddha has no retribution, but the Bodhisattvas are endowed with all ten [suchlike characteristics, including retribution]. They have not yet severed fundamental passions, so they experience retribution in the triple world.

The appearance, nature, and so forth of the Bodhisattvas of the Shared Teaching are discussed from the perspective of their nondefilement. Their appearance is that of Nirvāṇa with and without remainder. Their nature is that of undefiled wisdom. Their essence is the superior body and mind of transformation. Their power is the nonarising four universal vows. Their activity is the nonarising Six Perfections. Their causes are the direct causes of nondefilement. Their condition is the auxiliary path of arising and perishing. Their results are to sever remaining [negative] habitual tendencies. Those below the sixth stage have remaining deluded attitudes, so they experience retribution. Those above the sixth stage have exhausted all deluded attitudes and experience no further rebirth. If they make a vow to be reborn in this world, this is not real karmic retribution.

The Ten Suchlikes of the Bodhisattva of the Distinct Teaching are discussed in terms of their cultivation of the Middle Path as a practice of progressive contemplation. They realize emptiness through conventional existence, as in the first two Teachings. If, through [the realization of] emptiness, they transcend conventional existence, their appearance is the Buddha-dharmas, which are as numerous as the sands of the Ganges River. Their nature is a determination to reenter the cyclic world of birth and death. Their essence is the mind and body of worldly transformations. Their power is the four immeasurable universal vows. Their activity is the immeasurable Six Perfections. Their causes are true undefiled wisdom. Their condition is the auxiliary contemplation of conventional existence. Their result is the fulfillment of the contemplation of conventional existence. Their retribution is [to be reborn in this world of] transformation. If they realize the Middle Path, their appearance is [the Buddha-nature as] conditional cause, their nature is [the Buddha-nature as] the complete cause, their essence is [the Buddha-nature as] the direct cause, their power is the spontaneous four universal vows, their activity is the spontaneous Six Perfections, their causes are the adornments of wisdom, their conditions are the adornments of virtuous qualities, their result is unsurpassed enlightenment, and their reward is great Nirvāṇa.

Q: The Ten Suchlikes of the three types of Bodhisattvas are as you say. How about the Ten Suchlikes of the Dharma realm of the Buddha?

A: Their appearance is [the Buddha-nature as] conditional cause, their nature is [the Buddha-nature as] the complete cause, their essence is [the Buddha-nature as] the direct cause, their power is the spontaneous four universal vows, their activity is the spontaneous Six Perfections, their causes are the adornments of wisdom, their conditions are the adornments of virtuous qualities, their result is clear unsurpassed enlightenment, which is a great awakening, and their reward is great, perfect Nirvāṇa. Here "beginning and end being ultimately the same" means that the threefold truth of appearance, nature, and so forth is not
272a different from the ultimate threefold truth. Therefore it is called "the same."

Q: What do you mean [when you say] that the threefold truth of appearance, nature, and so forth is not different from the ultimate threefold truth?

A: The suchness of sentient beings and the suchness of the Buddha are equal; therefore it is said that they are equal in being empty [of substantial Being]. Sentient beings and the Buddha are equal. The Buddha and sentient beings are equal. Therefore it is said that they are equal in having conventional existence. Ordinary people and the sage all [partake of] true reality. Therefore it is said that they are the same [in all partaking of the reality of] the Middle.

Q: What do you mean [when you say] that sentient beings and the Buddha are equal, and that the Buddha and sentient beings are equal?

A: The Buddha assures sentient beings that they will surely attain Buddhahood. This is the meaning of "sentient beings and the Buddha are equal." The Buddha expounds on his deeds in his former lives. This is the meaning of "the Buddha and sentient beings are equal."

Q: Do each and every one of these suchlikes include the threefold truth?

A: They do include the threefold truth.

Q: What do you mean by "include"?

A: The term "such" of all the Ten Suchlikes refers to the meaning of emptiness. The conventional constructions, which are all different, such as appearance, nature, and so forth, refer to the meaning of conventional existence. The term "like" of all the Ten Suchlikes refers to the meaning of the Middle.

Q: If the text is read on this basis, what does it mean?

A: There are three "turnings" [of the phrase]. The first is [to emphasize "suchness" or emptiness] by reading it as "the appearances are *such,* the nature is *such* . . . the retributions are *such.*" The second is [to emphasize the conventional aspects by] reading it as "the *appearances* are so-and-so, the *nature* is so-and-so . . . and the *retributions* are so-and-so." The third is [to emphasize the aspect of the Middle by] reading it as "*suchlike* are the appearances, *suchlike* is the nature . . . and *suchlike* are the retributions."

Q: Why is this threefold distinction made?

A: Such distinctions are made in order to facilitate understanding. If one understands and tries to verbalize this, it is expressed as "emptiness is identical to conventional existence and the Middle, conventional existence is identical to the Middle and emptiness, and the Middle is identical to emptiness and conventional existence."

Q: What is the meaning of "emptiness is identical to conventional existence and the Middle," and so forth?

A: If emptiness is clarified with reference to suchness, then the emptiness of one is the emptiness of all. If appearances [and so forth] are clarified with regard to suchness, then the conventional existence of one is the conventional existence of all. If the Middle is discussed in terms of "likeness," then the Middleness of one is the Middleness of all.

Q: Is this [threefold truth of] emptiness, conventional existence, and the Middle [of being simultaneously empty and conventionally existent] included in one thought, or included in [many] different thoughts?

A: It is included in one thought.

Q: What do you mean [when you say] that it is included in one thought?

A: One thought in the mind truly has no substantial mark. This is called emptiness. But there is no dharma that it does not encompass. This is called conventional existence. It is neither one nor differentiated. This is called the Middle. Therefore it is known that each and every [thought] is suchlike. All contain the threefold truth. Each aspect of the threefold truth is present in one thought.

Q: Does the mind of one thought merely contain the threefold truth and the ten suchnesses?

A: It also contains the trichiliocosm of one hundred realms and a thousand suchnesses.

Q: What is the trichiliocosm of one hundred realms and a thousand suchnesses?

A: One Dharma realm contains Ten Suchlikes, so the ten Dharma realms contain one hundred suchlikes. Also, each Dharma realm contains the other nine Dharma realms, so there are one hundred Dharma realms and one thousand suchlikes. Also, one Dharma realm contains three kinds of worlds, so the one hundred Dharma realms contain three thousand worlds, a trichiliocosm.

Q: Why do you establish a trichiliocosm of one hundred realms and a thousand suchnesses?

A: If we do not organize phenomena in terms of the one hundred realms, it would not be complete, the thousand suchnesses could not be verbalized, and causality would be excluded.
272b Without the trichiliocosm, the world and we who live in it would not be exhaustively [explained].

Q: Is this [doctrine of] the Ten Suchlikes [the direct teaching of] the Dharma [as it truly is], or is it just [a teaching by] analogy?

A: This is [a direct teaching of] the Dharma, not just an analogy.

Q: What if it were [taught] by analogy?

A: There is the text in the chapter of "Parables" in the *Lotus Sutra* concerning the Great White Bull Cart.

Q: What if [the Ten Suchlikes as] both [the direct teaching of] the Dharma and as analogy are harmonized?

A: That which is called "suchlike appearance" in the text, which is the direct teaching of the Dharma, is explained as "adorned with a multitude of jewels" in the analogy. The Dharma of "suchlike nature" is analogously explained as "there was a Great White Bull Cart." The Dharma of "suchlike essence" is analogously explained as "that cart was high and vast." The Dharma of "suchlike power" is analogously explained as "also, on its top are spread out parasols and canopies." The Dharma of "suchlike activity" is analogously explained as "swift as the wind." The Dharma of "suchlike causes" is analogously explained as "mounting the jeweled cart, they played in all four directions." The Dharma of "suchlike conditions" is analogously explained as "there are also many attendants serving and guarding it." The Dharma of "suchlike results" is analogously explained as "leading directly to the seat of enlightenment."

Q: What is utilized to harmonize the [direct] teaching of the Dharma and [the teaching] as an analogy with regard to these Ten Suchlikes?

A: The texts that explain the Dharma [directly] refer to the fruit of Buddhahood as the true aspect of reality. The analogous explanation refers to the "grandly adorned great cart" as that which leads directly to the seat of enlightenment. The section concerning past lives [the first half of the *Lotus Sutra*] teaches the ultimate fruit of Buddhahood as the exposition of the tentative and the manifestation of the real. The section on the original basis [of the Buddha] [the second half of the *Lotus Sutra* teaches] that the eternally enlightened Buddha corresponds to the subtle Dharma. How can it be referred to as merely a harmonization [of the direct teaching] of the Dharma and [teaching through] analogy? This meaning is common to all from the stories of past lives to [the explanation of original Buddhahood in] the last half of the *Lotus Sutra.*

C. Final Summation

Q: Who knows these Ten Suchlikes?

A: "Only a Buddha and a Buddha can exhaust their reality," but an ordinary man of the Perfect Teaching can attain a partial knowledge. This is the fundamental principle of the *Lotus Sutra,* the core of all teachings, the key to interpreting the meaning, the refuge of all sentient beings, the basis of the aspiration for enlightenment, the functional essence of conventional devices, the foundation of delusion and awakening, the reality basis for the resultant virtuous qualities [of Buddhahood], the ultimate purpose of the Buddha's life, and the consummation of the Five Periods.

Q: Why are these ten meanings clarified?

A: If these ten meanings are understood, this explains all the differences [in the Buddha's teachings] and, unexpectedly, there is no contradiction.

Q: Are these Ten Suchlikes the subject that illuminates or the object that is illuminated?

A: They are the subtle objective realm that is to be illuminated.

Q: How can we come to know them?

A: The *Lotus Sutra* first praises the wisdom through which there is illumination, that is, the two tentative and real wisdoms of all Buddhas. Next, the objective realm that is to be illuminated is clarified as the Ten Suchlikes.

Q: What does this text say?

A: In the chapter on "Expedient Means" it says, "The wisdom of all Buddhas is exceedingly profound and immeasurable. This
272c gate of wisdom is difficult to understand and difficult to enter" to

"Only a Buddha and a Buddha can exhaust their reality, that all dharmas have suchlike appearance" and so forth.

Q: Why do you establish such a troublesome scheme?

A: The [*Fa-hua*] *hsüan-i* and [*Mo-ho*] *chih-kuan* have this as their central theme, and the doctrines of this Tendai school are richly summarized therein.

Q: What is forfeited if one does not understand this topic?

A: If one is deluded concerning this meaning, one naturally misses the thrust of the course of all the teachings, and the streams that branch out from the single teaching [of the Buddha] dry up.

Q: Are the Ten Suchlikes merely Dharma teachings concerning causality, or do they also include other Dharma teachings?

A: Whether of cause or result, whether of the world or its inhabitants, all [teachings] are contained in these [Ten Suchlikes] and are beyond conceptual understanding. An expansion of this [teaching] fills the entire universe. If one does not know it, on what basis can one transcend [this triple world]?

Q: Why is this so?

A: The Ten Suchlikes are identical to "all dharmas." All dharmas are identical to the three virtuous qualities [of Buddhahood]. The three virtuous qualities are identical to reality. Reality is identical to a single mind. If this meaning is understood, the vast sermons during [the last] eight years [of Śākyamuni's life] do not go beyond one single thought. [The Bodhisattvas who welled up out of the earth, as explained in the fifteenth chapter of the *Lotus Sutra,* praised Śākyamuni] for fifty short aeons, but it seemed to pass in a moment. For example, the sermons of the Buddha in his one life [of eighty years] are innately present in the mind, and the activity of Buddhas in the ten directions [in saving sentient beings] is clearly observable. The basic nature of the universe can be easily perceived, and the expositions taught in accordance [with the capabilities of sentient beings] all point to the reality of the innate potential [for Buddhahood]. This is explained in detail in the commentary [the *Fa-hua hsüan-i*].

Chapter V

The Meaning of the Twelvefold Conditioned Co-arising

Reality is unchanging and inherently has no marks of coming or going. The nature of phenomena is to conform to habitual tendencies and function in the realm of distinctions. Therefore Twelvefold Conditioned Co-arising revolves and creates karma, and the causes and results of the three ways [of craving, karma, and suffering] alternate without rest. If one is deluded concerning this reality, this inflames the cycle of birth and death. If one understands this meaning, the bonds of suffering are severed forever. The essential techniques for transcending this [triple] world are in this chapter. Now I shall clarify the meaning briefly in four parts. First, listing of the terms; second, scriptural support; third, correct interpretations; and fourth, classification into crude and subtle.

A. List of Terms

Question: What are the individual terms for the links of Twelvefold Conditioned Co-arising?

Answer: (1) Ignorance, (2) volitional activity, (3) consciousness, (4) name and form, (5) the six senses, (6) contact, (7) experience, (8) passion, (9) attachment, (10) existence, (11) rebirth, and (12) decay and death.

Q: How many kinds of Twelvefold Conditioned Co-arising are there?

A: There are four kinds of Twelvefold Conditioned Co-arising.

Q: What are these four?

A: (1) Twelvefold Conditioned Co-arising conceptually understood as arising and perishing, (2) Twelvefold Conditioned Co-arising conceptually understood as neither arising nor perishing, (3) Twelvefold Conditioned Co-arising beyond conceptual understanding yet arising and perishing, and (4) Twelvefold Conditioned Co-arising as beyond conceptual understanding and neither arising nor perishing.

Q: Why do you discuss four interpretations of conditioned co-arising?

A: The two types of conditioned co-arising that are conceptu-
273a ally understood are discussed for the sake of those of clever and dull faculties within this triple world. The two types of conditioned co-arising that are beyond conceptual understanding are discussed for the sake of those of clever and dull faculties in the transworldly realm.

B. Scriptural Support

Q: Is there any textual evidence for these four interpretations of Conditioned Co-arising?

A: The *Saddharma-smṛtyupasthāna Sūtra* says that an artist paints all shapes by distributing the five colors. There are incalculable beautiful and ugly pictures. The basis for these images is discovered in the hand of the artist. The *Ying lo ching* says that ignorance is the condition for volitional activity. Thus the Twelvefold [Links of Conditioned Co-arising] arise, and so forth until rebirth, [which is] the condition for decay and death, and thus the Twelvefold [Links of Conditioned Co-arising] arise again. This is evidence for Twelvefold Conditioned Co-arising conceptually understood as arising and perishing. The *Suvarṇaprabhāsa Sūtra* says, "The essential mark of ignorance is that of fundamentally lacking self[-nature]; it has existence only as the confluence of deluded conceptualizations concerning that which conditionally co-arises. . . . Thus I explain it, and I call it ignorance. Volitional activity, consciousness, name and form, the six senses, contact, experience, passion, attachment, existence, rebirth, decay and death, deluded sorrows, multifarious suffering, and karmic deeds are beyond conceptual understanding. The cycle of birth and death is limitless; revolving transmigration never rests. Fundamentally there is no arising, nor is there any confluence of immoral thoughts or creation of mental activity." This is evidence for Twelvefold Conditioned Co-arising conceptually understood as neither arising nor perishing. The *Avataṃsaka Sūtra* says, "The mind, like a skillful painter, creates the various aggregates. In all the world there is nothing that does not follow the creations of the mind." The *Ratnagotravibhāga* says, "There are four obstacles for those who dwell in the undefiled realm: conditions, marks, rebirth, and destruction. 'Conditions' refers to fundamental ignorance, which becomes the condition for volitional activity. 'Marks' refers to the combination of ignorance and volitional activity, which causes further rebirth. 'Rebirth' refers to the combination of fundamental ignorance and undefiled deeds, which causes the rebirth of the three types of mind-born bodies. 'Destruction' refers to the three types of mind-born bodies as the conditions for birth and death, which is an inconceivable transformation." This is evidence for Twelvefold Conditioned Co-arising beyond conceptual understanding yet arising and perishing. The *Mahāparinirvāṇa Sūtra* says, "Twelvefold Conditioned Co-arising is called the Buddha-nature." This is evidence for Twelvefold Conditioned Co-arising as beyond conceptual understanding and neither arising nor perishing.

C. Correct Interpretation

Q: What is the meaning of the passage quoted from the *Saddharma-smṛtyupasthāna Sūtra* that speaks of "distributing the five colors"?

A: The combination of ignorance with the most evil activity arouses the conditioned co-arising of the hellish realm, like painting with the color black. The combination of ignorance with middling evil activity arouses the conditioned co-arising of the realm of

beasts, like painting with the color red. The combination of ignorance with lesser evil activity arouses the conditioned co-arising of the realm of hungry spirits, like painting with the color blue. The combination of ignorance with lesser good activity arouses the conditioned co-arising of the realm of the *asuras*, like painting with the color yellow. The combination of ignorance with middling good activities arouses the conditioned co-arising of the realm of human beings, like painting with the color white. The combination of ignorance with the best good activity arouses the conditioned co-arising of the realm of gods, like painting with the most superior
273b white color. The analogy of the five colors has this meaning. The arousing of these six destinies should be known as having these causes.

Q: This Twelvefold Conditioned Co-arising consists of how many causes and how many results?

A: There are two causes from the past, five results of the present, three causes from the present, and two results of the future.

Q: What are the two causes from the past and so forth?

A: The two causes from the past are (1) ignorance and (2) volitional activity. The five results of the present are (1) consciousness, (2) name and form, (3) the six senses, (4) contact, and (5) experience. The three causes from the present are (1) passion, (2) attachment, and (3) existence. The two results of the future are (1) rebirth and (2) decay and death.

Q: We have now heard the names of the causes and results in the past, present, and future. What is the meaning of "conditioned birth" and "conditioned arising"?

A: The distinctions in meaning are revealed through the tetralemma.

Q: What are they?

A: (1) Conditioned arising but not conditioned birth, (2) conditioned birth but not conditioned arising, (3) both conditioned arising and conditioned birth, and (4) neither conditioned arising nor conditioned birth.

Q: What does this mean?

A: "Conditioned arising but not conditioned birth" refers to the two results of the future. "Conditioned birth but not conditioned arising" refers to the two causes from the past and the final physical death of the present life of an Arhat. "Both conditioned arising and conditioned birth" refers to all past and present dharmas except for the final physical death of the Arhat in the past and present. "Neither conditioned arising nor conditioned birth" refers to all unconditioned dharmas.

Q: How about if you establish Twelvefold Conditioned Co-arising in terms of time?

A: Ignorance refers to all times of bondage in the past. Volitional activity refers to all times of volitional activity in the past. Consciousness refers to the time of the mind of continuity and its concomitants. Name and form refers to the time when, though one has already experienced birth, one is still not endowed with the four sense organs and the six senses. The six senses refer to the time when the four sense organs have arisen and the six senses are perfected. Contact refers to the time when one does not distinguish between pleasure and pain, and does not try to avoid injury when being thrown into the fire, drowning in water, or coming into contact with poison or dangerous blades. Experience refers to the time when one knows pain and is conscious of pleasure, and avoids danger and injury; though one has no sensual desires, nevertheless one is corrupted by things. Passion refers to the time when consciousness of the three kinds of experiences [pain, pleasure, and neither-pain-nor-pleasure] is complete and one embraces sensual desires. Attachment refers to the time when one covets objects and thus seeks them in all directions. Existence refers to the time when the physical, verbal, and mental aspects arise due to the seeking of objects. Rebirth refers to the time when the present consciousness arises in the future. Decay and death refer to when the present name and form, and so forth, arise in the future.

Q: How many stages are there to the level of name and form?

A: There are five stages. There is a change every seven days after being conceived in the womb. The first week is called *kalala.* The second week is called *arbudam.* The third week is called *peśī,* as in the short and small medicine pestle. The fourth week is called
273c *ghana,* as in a stone pocket warmer. The fifth week is called *praśākhā.* These five [stages in] the womb expand and [the child] is in the mother's womb for thirty-eight weeks. This is called the time of name and form.

Q: Let us set aside the discussion of Twelvefold Conditioned Co-arising conceptually understood as neither arising nor perishing, and as beyond conceptual understanding yet arising and perishing. Now you should explain Twelvefold Conditioned Co-arising as beyond conceptual understanding and neither arising nor perishing.

A: This [understanding of] conditioned co-arising is the manifestation of reality as identical with phenomenal appearance for the sake of those with clever faculties.

Q: What does this mean?

A: Twelvefold Conditioned Co-arising refers to phenomenal appearances. Awakening the threefold Buddha-nature refers to reality.

Q: In what way do you distinguish the threefold Buddha-nature?

A: Ignorance, passion, and attachment are the path of craving. These correspond to the "Buddha-nature as complete cause." Volitional activity and existence are the path of karma; these correspond to "Buddha-nature as conditional cause." Consciousness, name and form, the six senses, contact, experience, rebirth, and decay and death are the path of suffering; these correspond to "Buddha-nature as the direct cause."

Q: Why do you identify the threefold Buddha-nature with these three paths?

A: Because the path of craving is identical with enlightenment, the path of karma is identical with liberation, and the path of suffering is identical with the Dharma Body.

Q: Craving and enlightenment, and delusion and awakening, are distinct. Is it not careless [to emphasize] the relative aspect of their meaning?

A: A distinction is made between delusion and awakening with regard to conditions, but since they are [fundamentally] unchanging, the essence of the defiled and of the pure are one. Therefore it is said that craving and enlightenment, and the cycle of birth and death and Nirvāṇa, are identical.

Q: On what basis do you know that Twelvefold Conditioned Co-arising is identical with the threefold Buddha-nature?

A: The *Mahāparinirvāṇa Sūtra* says, "Twelvefold Conditioned Co-arising is called the Buddha-nature."

Q: Why do you go out of your way to clarify Twelvefold Conditioned Co-arising?

A: The *Pañcaviṃśati-sāhasrikā-prajñā-pāramitā Sūtra* says, "If one is able profoundly to contemplate Twelvefold Conditioned Co-arising, then one can immediately sit on the seat of enlightenment." The [*Mo-ho*] *chih-kuan* says, "If one contemplates Twelvefold Conditioned Co-arising, then one fully fathoms the principle of the Middle Way. This is the Buddha Vairocana of the Perfect Teaching sitting on the seat of enlightenment with emptiness as his seat."

Q: Is there any distinction between [the teachings of] the *Mahāparinirvāṇa Sūtra* and the *Pañcaviṃśati-sāhasrikā-prajñā-pāramitā Sūtra?*

A: The *Mahāparinirvāṇa Sūtra* clarifies the cause, and the *Pañcaviṃśati-sāhasrikā-prajñā-pāramitā Sūtra* and the [*Mo-ho*] *chih-kuan* the result. Thus should it be known.

D. Classification into Crude and Subtle

Q: Which of the [interpretations of] conditioned co-arising are crude and which subtle?

A: The first three are tentative and thus crude, and the last one is real and thus subtle.

Q: What if one interprets the Five Flavors with regard to this classification of crude and subtle?

A: The Milk Teaching includes two interpretations of conditioned co-arising, one crude and one subtle. The Cream Teaching is just one crude interpretation. The Curds Teaching includes three crude interpretations and one subtle interpretation. The Butter Teaching includes two crude interpretations and one subtle interpretation. The *Lotus* Ghee [Teaching] merely expounds one subtle interpretation. Thus I have given a summary of the main ideas. Details are in the original text [the *Fa-hua hsüan-i*].

Chapter VI

The Meaning of the Two Truths

274a The real and mundane [truths] are difficult to know clearly. The Great Awakened One during his [stage of] causal practice disputed [with Mañjuśrī] over [the Two Truths as] emptiness or existence, for it is easy to be confused. The Hīnayāna Arhats are still in the dark. Therefore during the Liang period (502–56) the interpretations of the *Ch'eng shih lun* were various, and during the Ch'en dynasty (557–89) there was no agreement about criticizing or supporting the *Mūlamadhyamakakārikā*. Blind men stroke an elephant [and each reaches different conclusions], and blind children doubt [the existence of] a crane. Then there appeared the masters of Nan-yo and T'ien-t'ai, sages who were together on [Vulture] Peak [and heard the preaching of the *Lotus Sutra* directly]. [Chih-i] brought forth the Perfect Teaching and taught skillfully without stagnation. Seven levels [of the Two Truths] were classified; these were incorporated into five levels. All the treatises from the West [India] were mastered, and none of the virtuous people in the east could match him. Now I shall clarify the Two Truths in four sections: [I shall] first briefly summarize its meaning; second, clarify the correct understanding of the Two Truths; third, classify them as crude and subtle; and fourth, expose the crude and manifest the subtle.

A. A Brief Summary of the Meaning of the Two Truths

The term "Two Truths" is mentioned in many Sutras, but its principle is difficult to understand. The world is in an uproar and has debated this issue for a long time. A Sutra [the *Miao-sheng-ting ching*] says, "In the past the Buddha and Mañjuśrī had a dispute over the Two Truths, and they both fell into hell. It was not until the time of the Buddha Kāśyapa that their doubts were resolved satisfactorily." If these two sages in their causal stages [previous to attaining Buddhahood] were unable to understand completely, how is it possible for people with strong emotional passions?

Question: Śākyamuni, when he met Kāśyapa, was a Bodhisattva with two rebirths left [before attaining Buddhahood]. Why is it that he first understood the Two Truths [at this stage]? He should not have previously retrogressed to an evil destiny.

Answer: The word "previous" is to be interpreted broadly. Why is it necessary to limit his first emergence from evil destinies to his life [as a Bodhisattva] with two rebirths left? Also, a Bodhisattva with two rebirths left is surely dwelling in the stage just before Buddhahood. There are many levels to this stage. The Distinct and Perfect [Teachings] do not have this doctrine. In the Shared Teaching one is already free from the evil destinies and will never relapse after the stage of [severing mistaken] views. [Therefore] this must refer to the Tripiṭaka Bodhisattva, who, when he has arrived at his life [as a Bodhisattva] with two rebirths left, has still not severed all delusions, and understands the Two Truths for the first time. Thus this meaning cannot be faulted. To have previously retrogressed to evil destinies can also be interpreted in this way.

Q: If the Tripiṭaka Bodhisattva does retrogress, but the Bodhisattvas of the other Three Teachings do not, then why does it say in the *Suvarṇaprabhāsa Sūtra* that those in the Ten Stages are afraid of tigers, wolves, and lions?

A: If one is killed by an evil friend, one can fall into hell. If one is killed by an evil elephant, one does not fall into hell. Thus for [a Bodhisattva of] the Perfect Teaching to have a physical body means that he can ascend or transcend the Ten Stages within this life. This means that though one has already destroyed all passions and has no karma for falling into hell, one still has a physical body that cannot avoid evil beasts. The physical body of Bodhisattvas of the other Teachings cannot ascend the Ten Stages within one life.

They merely perform practice and gain understanding, so they have passions and [can fall into hell if attacked by] tigers and wolves and so forth.

However, those who have attachments are various. Seng-min of the Chuang-yen temple says that the Two Truths are transcended in Buddhahood and is thus criticized by [Chih-tsang,] the master of the *Mūlamadhyamakakārikā*. What reality is illumined and what delusions destroyed by this Buddha-wisdom? The *Ch'eng shih lun* masters of the Liang period were attached to the worldly truth in different ways. The interpretations of the *Mūlamadhyamakakārikā* during the Ch'en period were various. Some criticized the interpretation of the Two Truths by the twenty-three
274b scholars in days of old and established their own interpretations of the Two Truths. The various interpretations new and old each quoted different scriptural proofs, and each held fast to only one text and did not believe the others. Now, I do not agree. The different explanations in the Sutras and treatises are all good tentative expedient means of the Tathāgata. His explanations are various and different because he knows their capacities and desires. Briefly there are three differences: that in accordance with the feelings [of the listener]; that in accordance with the feelings [of the listener] and the wisdom [of the Buddha]; and that in accordance with the wisdom [of the Buddha].

The exposition in accordance with the feelings of the listener refers to [the teaching of the Buddha that takes into account] the fact that the feelings and natures [of sentient beings] are not the same. Therefore the exposition is different in accordance with their feelings. As the *Mahāvibhāṣā-śāstra* says, there are immeasurable varieties of the supreme worldly Dharma. It is the same for the real ultimate [truth]. How much more so for the others! It is like the feelings of blind men when various analogies [such as a shell, rice, snow, or a crane] are given for [the color of] milk. The blind men hear different explanations [but cannot understand] and argue over [the meaning of] the color white. Is it not milk [and therefore white]? Of all the masters, none has penetrated this meaning and thus each is attached to one text. They promote their own opinions and argue, denying each other's opinions, believing one and not believing another. What vigorous bickering! They do not know which is correct. If they have scriptural evidence, these are all interpretations of the Two Truths in accordance with human feelings. Those who lack any scriptural evidence are all wrong.

Exposition in accordance with both the feelings [of the listener] and the wisdom [of the Buddha]. The Two Truths spoken in accordance with the feelings [of the listener] are all of the mundane [truth]. If one is awakened concerning the truth of reality, this should be called the real [truth]. The real [truth] is only one. The [*Mahāparinirvāṇa*] *Sūtra* says, "That which is perceived in the minds of worldly people is called the worldly truth. That which is perceived in the minds of transworldly people is called the truth of supreme meaning."

That in accordance with [the Buddha's] wisdom refers to the sage's awakening concerning reality. This is not merely a perception of the real but also a complete understanding of the mundane. Therefore the [*Viśeṣacinta-brahmaparipṛcchā*] Sutra says, "Ordinary people are active in the world but do not know the characteristics of the world. The Tathāgata is active in the world and understands clearly and completely the characteristics of the world."

If one understands these three meanings and refers to the Sutras and treatises, [one should realize that] although there are various explanations [concerning the Two Truths], each and every truth contains these three meanings.

B. The Correct Understanding of the Two Truths

Q: What are the names of the Two Truths?
A: First, the mundane truth; and second, the real truth.

Q: What is the meaning of the mundane and real truths?
A: If one discusses the meaning succinctly, [one can say] merely that the crux of the nature of reality is the real truth, and the

Twelvefold Conditioned Co-arising of ignorance is the mundane truth. If [the meaning is] discussed extensively, there are seven categories of the Two Truths. Each of these categories of Two Truths also has three categories, so all together there are twenty-one [interpretations of] the Two Truths. If one utilizes the first category of the Two Truths, one can destroy all mistaken sayings and exhaust all attachments, as the fire at the end of an era burns up [everything] and does not leave even a mustard seed behind. How much more so [are the effective results of] expanding on the later interpretations of the Two Truths, which go beyond the limits of language and are not within the capacity of human feelings to fathom!

Q: Why do you identify the nature of reality and ignorance with the real and mundane truths?

A: The single nature of reality is contrasted with ignorance. Ignorance is delusion, which is the beginning of the real [truth], before the aspiration [for enlightenment]. The real [truth] is not unrelated to the mundane [truth]; therefore it is called the mundane "truth." The nature of reality as a whole connotes ignorance. From beginningless time, when was it [the nature of reality] not real? Therefore it is called "the real truth."

274c *Q:* If so, do you mean to establish the Two Truths with regard to one Dharma? You should establish the Two Truths in terms of two Dharmas.

A: There are Two Truths with regard to only one Dharma. The mundane [truth] refers to the hundred realms and thousand suchnesses, and the real [truth] refers to their mutual integration in one thought.

Q: The meaning of the nature of reality and ignorance as one type of the Two Truths is sufficient; why do you establish seven categories of Two Truths?

A: People's minds are crude and shallow. They do not realize this profound subtlety. One must "blaze the trail" and point out its profundity.

Q: What are the seven categories?

A: (1) "Real existence" is the mundane, and "the extinction of this true existence" is the real. (2) "Illusory existence" is the mundane, and "identifying this illusory existence as empty" is the real. (3) "Illusory existence" is the mundane, and "identifying illusory existence as both empty and non-empty" is the real. (4) "Illusory existence" is the mundane, and "the identity of illusory existence with emptiness and non-emptiness, so that all dharmas are included in emptiness and non-emptiness" is the real. (5) "Illusory existence and the identity of illusory existence with emptiness" is all called the mundane, and "neither existence nor emptiness" is the real. (6) "Illusory existence and the identity of illusory existence with emptiness" is all called the mundane, and "neither existence nor emptiness, so that all dharmas are included in 'neither existence nor emptiness'" is the real. (7) "Illusory existence and the identity of illusory existence with emptiness" is the mundane, and that "reality includes existence, includes emptiness, and includes neither existence nor emptiness" is the real.

Q: How many different names do these seven categories of the Two Truths have?

A: Briefly, they have three kinds of dissimilarity.

Q: What are these passages?

A: In the [*Fa-hua*] *hsüan-i* the terms are listed as above. The [*Fa-hua hsüan-i*] *shih ch'ien* [of Chan-jan] says, "In the *Mahāparinirvāṇa Sūtra* it says, 'The five aggregates converge and these are given names; this is called the worldly truth. The aggregates are understood as having no [substantial] aggregate or name. There is no second [aggregate] apart from the aggregates. This is called the truth of supreme meaning.' The commentary [on the *Mahāparinirvāṇa Sūtra* by Kuan-ting] says, 'These are the Two Truths of names and no names.' The Sutra says, 'For the existence of dharmas, names, and reality to have existence is the truth of supreme meaning. For the existences of dharmas and names not to have real existence is called the worldly truth.' The commentary says, 'These are the Two Truths of reality and non-reality.' The

Sutra says, 'It is like [the fact that] the self, people, sentient beings, life spans, knowledge and insight, and so forth are made up of aggregates, realms, sense organs, and their objects, and thus are like the hair of a tortoise or the horns of a rabbit. This is called the worldly truth. [The Four Noble Truths of] suffering, the causes of suffering, the extinction of suffering, and the Path, are the real truth.' The commentary says, 'These are the Two Truths of being: definite and indefinite.' The Sutra says, 'There are five types of worldly dharmas: the realm of names, the realm of words, the realm of bonds, the realm of dharmas, and the realm of attachment. This is called the worldly truth. (The text of the Sutra gives details.) The mind that does not have warped views concerning these five dharmas is called the truth of supreme meaning.' The commentary says, 'These are the Two Truths of the Dharma and non-Dharma.' The Sutra says, 'The destruction that is death by burning is called the worldly truth. That which is not death by burning is called the truth of supreme meaning.' The commentary says, 'These are the Two Truths of burning and not burning.' The
275a Sutra says, 'The existence of eight kinds of suffering is called the worldly truth. The non-existence of eight kinds of suffering is called the truth of supreme meaning.' The commentary says, 'These are the Two Truths of suffering and non-suffering.' The Sutra says, 'It is like one man being called many names, but he is born from his parents. This is called the worldly truth. For things to arise from the confluence of Twelvefold Conditioned Co-arising is called the truth of supreme meaning.' The commentary says, 'The Two Truths of confluence.'"

Q: Why are there seven categories of the Two Truths?

A: The Buddha obliquely exposed seven layers with regard to seven capabilities.

Q: What are these seven layers?

A: The [*Fa-hua*] *hsüan*[*-i*] *shih ch'ien* says, "(1) Tripiṭaka, (2) Shared, (3) Shared advancing to Distinct, (4) Shared advancing to Perfect, (5) Distinct, (6) Distinct advancing to Perfect, and (7) Perfect."

Q: These have already been explained as the Four Teachings. Why are they now formed into seven [categories]?

A: In order to expand the Buddha's original intention and fulfill the potential of sentient beings based on past deeds.

Q: What are the meanings of the "Shared advancing to Distinct," "Shared advancing to Perfect," and "Distinct advancing to Perfect"?

A: If one perfects an insight into reality from within concentration, one advances from the reality of this realm of the [triple] world to that of the transworldly reality.

Q: Why is this so?

A: Both the Tripiṭaka Teaching and the Shared Teaching clarify the reality of this realm of the [triple] world, and both the Distinct Teaching and the Perfect Teaching clarify the transworldly reality. Both the Shared Teaching and the Distinct Teaching overlap both realities; therefore only "advancing from the Shared to the Distinct" is clarified.

Q: According to this meaning, there is only one "advancement." Why does the [*Fa-hua*] *hsüan-i* establish three "advancements"?

A: The first six kinds of Two Truths are methods of teaching. [The teachings] previous to the *Lotus Sutra* do not go beyond the level of those with tentative capabilities. Therefore there are the two meanings of [those in] the Shared and Distinct advancing to the Perfect.

Q: Why is there no advancement out of the Tripiṭaka Teaching?

A: The Tripiṭaka Teaching deals only with the realm of the [triple] world which is non-integrated. Hīnayanists gain their enlightenment; therefore advancement [to higher levels] is not discussed. The remaining six are Mahāyāna. If one wishes to advance, one can escape [from the lower stage to the higher]. Therefore it is called "advancement."

Q: If there is no advancement [for those of the Tripiṭaka Teaching], do they have no encounter [with the final revelation of the ultimate truth in the *Lotus Sutra*]?

A: The meaning of advancement is different from the meaning of "encountering." Thus at the time before encounter [with the message of the *Lotus Sutra*], there is no discussion of advancement [to the Distinct or Perfect Teachings].

Q: The last five categories of the seven categories of the Two Truths include the threefold [truth]. Why are they called "Two Truths"?

A: Though the meaning includes the threefold [truth], it is still encompassed within the Two Truths.

Q: What does it mean for the meaning to "include the threefold [truth]"?

A: Illusory existence is the mundane [truth]; emptiness is the real [truth]; and innate emptiness is the Middle.

Q: In which truth are the Middle and emptiness included?

A: If they are included in the mundane truth, this is like the Distinct Teaching, which is called "the Two Truths of the true included in the mundane." If they are included in the real truth, it is like the Distinct and Perfect Teachings, which "enter" the Shared and are called "the Two Truths of the Middle included in the real." The Perfect Teaching is called "the real and mundane [truths] that are beyond conceptual understanding." If one rigorously realizes the intent [of this doctrine], one will not overlook any details in the names and interpretation of the meaning.

275b *Q:* What is the meaning of the Two Truths of real existence in the Tripiṭaka Teaching?

A: That the aggregates, senses, sense organs, and their objects and so forth are all real dharmas. The multifarious and infinite phenomena produced by these real dharmas are called the mundane truth. The extinction of this mundane reality and attaining an encounter with the real is called the real truth.

Q: What is signified by "multifarious and infinite phenomena"?

A: This refers to the marks of the world and its inhabitants.

Q: What are the texts that are evidence for this interpretation of the Two Truths?

A: The *Pañcaviṃśati-sāhasrikā-prajñā-pāramitā Sūtra* says, "Emptiness is visible form and visible form is emptiness."

Q: What is the meaning of this Sutra text?

A: It is through the extinction of the mundane that one says that visible form is empty. Since visible form is not really extinguished, emptiness is visible form.

Q: If so, why does it say in the [*Fa-hua hsüan-i shih*] *ch'ien* that "[for this interpretation of the Two Truths,] visible form has real existence and is said to be 'unextinguishable'. Though it cannot be extinguished, it is said that 'visible form is empty' because of its transiency."

A: The mundane is merely visible form. It is said that "emptiness is visible form" because of the analysis of the extinction of visible form [as lacking in substantial Being]. The meaning of saying "though it cannot be extinguished . . . because of its transiency" is as follows: it is said that "visible form is emptiness" because, even though it is said to be transient, visible form is not extinguishable.

Q: Does this [interpretation of] the Two Truths include the three meanings of "[teaching] according to feelings, according to feelings and wisdom, and according to wisdom"?

A: These are included. The other Two Truths are like this.

Q: What is the meaning of "[teaching] according to feelings and wisdom," and so forth?

A: "According to feelings" refers to giving various explanations of the teachings [according to the capacity of the listener]. "According to wisdom" refers to explaining reality as it corresponds to people. "According to feelings and wisdom" refers to the two meanings as relative. All should be taught and determined [in this way] so that there is no confusion.

Q: What is the meaning of the Two Truths of "illusory existence and the illusions as empty"?

A: "Illusory existence" refers to the mundane [truth]. Illusory existence cannot be realized [since it is empty and lacks substantial Being]; therefore this is the real [truth].

Q: Does this [interpretation of] the Two Truths have the same meaning as the previous one?

A: It is in opposition to the previous one. The reason is that [for the first interpretation,] when there is real existence, there is no real [truth], and when existence is extinguished there is no mundane [truth]. Thus the meaning of the Two Truths [as one integrated reality] is not established. The Two Truths of illusory existence and the illusions as empty are mutually identical.

Q: How do you know that the Two Truths are mutually identical?

A: The *Pañcaviṃśati-sāhasrikā-prajñā-pāramitā Sūtra* says, "Visible form is identical to emptiness, and emptiness is identical to visible form." Thus the meaning of the Two Truths as the mutual identity of emptiness and visible form is established.

Q: What is the meaning of the Two Truths of illusory existence as both empty and not empty?

A: The mundane [truth] is not different from the previous [interpretation]. There are three types of the real [truth] which are not the same. The one type of mundane [truth] goes with the three types of the real [truth] and thus there are three types of Two Truths.

Q: What are their characteristics?

A: The *Pañcaviṃśati-sāhasrikā-prajñā-pāramitā Sūtra* explains "neither with outflows [of passion] nor without outflows." A person [of the Shared Teaching], though he may be without outflows and thus not mundane, is not completely lacking in outflows for he has a remainder of attachments. This is one of the categories of the Two Truths. Next, a person [of the Distinct Teaching] who hears "neither outflows nor no outflows" denies both extremes and distinctly manifests the reality of the Middle [which is the simultaneous denial of both extremes]. This reality of the Middle is the real [truth]. This is one of the categories of the Two Truths. Next, there

is the person [of the Perfect Teaching] who hears "neither outflows
275c nor no outflows" and thereupon knows that both negations correctly manifest the Middle Path, and that the activity of the Middle Path, reality itself, is great and vast, so that all reality is "neither with outflows nor without outflows." This is one of the categories of the Two Truths.

Q: Why do people hear the same thing yet understand differently and accept varying interpretations?

A: "Both outflows and no outflows" is basically a Shared doctrine. Both are negated in order to fulfill their karma from the past. "Both emptiness and non-emptiness" is basically a Distinct doctrine. "Reality [all dharmas] as it is" is basically a Perfect doctrine. Thus there are three kinds of people who accept differing interpretations of this one Dharma [of the real truth].

Q: Why do these three kinds of people accept differing interpretations?

A: What they hear is not the same, because of their [varying] capabilities and aspirations.

Q: Why are there varieties of [this interpretation of] the Two Truths?

A: Since the faculties of the Bodhisattvas of the Shared Teaching are sharp or dull, their arousal of understanding is not the same.

Q: What do you mean [by saying] that they are not the same in sharpness or dullness?

A: The dull ones are the same as those of the two vehicles; they approach [the message of] the *Lotus Sutra* and encounter [the possibility of] advancement. The clever ones have already adhered to the Middle Path, so though they contemplate the mundane truth of illusory existence in the same way, they are each different in their grasp of the real [truth]. Therefore those of Distinct and Perfect capabilities arouse and fulfill three distinct [possibilities], in contrast to the dull who remain [attached to a one-sided view of] emptiness.

Q: What is the meaning of the three distinct [possibilities]?

A: Wisdom that one-sidedly realizes the real [truth] fulfills the Two Truths of the Shared [Teaching]. Wisdom that realizes the real [truth] as non-emptiness fulfills the Two Truths of the Shared advancing to the Distinct [Teaching]. Wisdom that realizes the real [truth] as the non-emptiness of all reality fulfills the Two Truths of the Shared advancing to the Perfect [Teaching].

Q: If the realization of wisdom by these three kinds of people is not the same, is their understanding of the mundane also different?

A: The understanding of the mundane [truth] by the three kinds of people is not the same. If a one-sided view of the real is established, then there is also an understanding of mundane [reality] as illusory. If the real as non-emptiness is established, then the mundane is understood as the Buddha-dharmas that are as numerous as the sands of the Ganges. If the real [truth] as the true aspects of reality is realized, then there is also an understanding of the mundane [truth] as transworldly and beyond conceptual understanding.

Q: Is there evidence for these three who enter wisdom differently?

A: The *Pañcaviṃśati-sāhasrikā-prajñā-pāramitā Sūtra* says, "There are Bodhisattvas who from their first aspiration for enlightenment are in conformance with the wisdom [that understands the emptiness] of all things. There are Bodhisattvas who, from their first aspiration for enlightenment, enjoy supranormal powers and purify a Buddha-land. There are Bodhisattvas who, from their first aspiration for enlightenment, immediately sit on the seat of enlightenment like a Buddha."

Q: What is the meaning of the Two Truths of the Distinct Teaching?

A: Illusory existence and non-existence are the mundane [truth], and neither existence nor non-existence is the real [truth].

Q: Why are existence and non-existence the mundane [truth], and neither existence nor non-existence the real [truth]?

A: The duality of existence and non-existence is the mundane [truth]. The Middle Path of the non-duality of neither existence nor non-existence is the real [truth].

Q: Why is this interpretation of the Two Truths called that of the Distinct Teaching?

A: Those of the two vehicles hear of this [interpretation of] the real and mundane, but none of them can understand it, and they are as deaf and dumb. Therefore it is identified with the Distinct Teaching.

Q: Is there evidence for [this interpretation of] the Two Truths?

276a *A:* The *Mahāparinirvāṇa Sūtra* says, "Maitreya and I both discussed the worldly truth, and when the five hundred Śrāvakas heard it they said that we expounded on the real truth . . . What can be said of the transworldly truth of supreme meaning?"

Q: What is the meaning of the Two Truths of the Distinct advancing to the Perfect?

A: The mundane is the same as in the Distinct Teaching, but the real truth is different.

Q: How is the real truth different?

A: Those of the Distinct Teaching say that only non-emptiness is reality. If one wishes to manifest this reality, it is necessary to utilize the expedient means of conscious practices. Therefore it is said that all reality is not empty. Those of the Perfect Teaching hear of reality as not empty and thereupon completely know all Buddha-dharmas without exception. Therefore it is said that all dharmas are not empty.

Q: What is the meaning of the Two Truths of the Perfect Teaching?

A: For all dharmas to be the Middle is the real [truth]; the hundred realms and thousand suchnesses, and the fundamental emptiness of the thousand suchnesses, is the mundane [truth]. These are the Two Truths that are beyond conceptual understanding.

Q: Why are these Two Truths called the Two Truths that are beyond conceptual understanding?

A: The real is identical to the mundane, and the mundane is identical to the real, like the Maṇi jewel.

Q: Why are the Two Truths of the Perfect Teaching compared to the Maṇi jewel?

A: The real truth is analogous to the jewel itself, and the mundane truth is analogous to its function. The function is identical to the jewel, and the jewel is identical to its function. It is non-dual yet two; so is the distinction of real and mundane.

Q: The [idea of] mutual identity in this Teaching overlaps with the Shared Teaching. Is there any difference?

A: That [Shared Teaching] refers to mutual identity within this worldly realm. This [Perfect Teaching] refers to mutual identity in the transworldly realm.

Q: In what sense are they mutually identical?

A: "Identity" in this [Perfect] Teaching is the graded threefold truth of the Distinct Teaching as mutually identical. When the graded [threefold truth] becomes [mutually] identical, then [the meaning of] identity in this [Perfect] Teaching is fulfilled. Therefore it is known that the Two Truths, from those of the Distinct Teaching to those of the Shared and Tripiṭaka Teaching, are fundamentally subtle and [mutually] identical, and it is human feelings [and capacities] that are different.

Q: What is wrong with the threefold truth of the Distinct Teaching that is not yet mutually identical?

A: It is the same as an inferior [interpretation of] emptiness.

[*Q:* . . .] and how about "in accordance with feelings and wisdom," and so forth?

A: The *Lotus Sutra* says, "The Buddha, in various and sundry conditions, utilizes analogies to expound [the Dharma] skillfully. His mind is peaceful like the sea. I hear it and the chains of doubt are severed."

Q: What is the meaning of this passage?

A: "Various and sundry conditions" refers to [teaching] "according to feelings." Thus it refers to pre-*Lotus Sutra* teachings. The "peaceful mind" and "severance of doubts" refer to the teachings within the *Lotus Sutra.* Thus it refers to [teaching] "according to wisdom." If [teaching according to] feelings and wisdom are in contrast [to each other], this is the third teaching.

Q: The real and mundane [truths] as in contrast to each other should refer to the mundane [truth of] existence and the real [truth of] non-existence in the Tripiṭaka Teaching, or to the "illusory existence and the emptiness of the illusions" in the Shared Teaching. Why are the real and mundane [truths] still not the same upon advancing to the Distinct Teaching?

A: This can be put into a tetralemma. (1) The mundane [truth] is differentiated and the real [truth] is one. (2) The real [truth] is differentiated and the mundane [truth] is one. (3) The real and mundane [truths] are differentiated and in contrast. (4) The real and mundane [truths] are one yet in contrast.

276b *Q:* How does this tetralemma correspond to the seven categories of the Two Truths?

A: In the Tripiṭaka and Shared Teachings, the real [truth] is one but the mundane [truth] is differentiated. For the two people [Śrāvakas and Pratyekabuddhas] who enter the Shared Teaching, the real [truth] is differentiated and the mundane [truth] is one. In the Distinct Teaching, the real and mundane [truths] are all differentiated and in contrast. For those who advance from the Distinct to the Perfect Teaching, the mundane [truth] is one but the real [truth] is differentiated. In the Perfect Teaching the real and mundane [truths] are not differentiated yet in contrast.

Q: The [*Fa-hua*] *hsüan-i* classifies the first two Teachings as both belonging to "[teaching] according to feeling." The [*Mo-ho*] *chih-kuan,* in classifying the three conventionalities, says that only the Tripiṭaka corresponds to "[teaching] according to feeling" and that the rest are "[teaching] in accordance with reality."

These are the teachings of one man but the two meanings are in disagreement.

A: There are three distinctions here. First, the [*Mo-ho*] *chih-kuan* refers to the relativity of the Hīnayāna. Therefore the Tripiṭaka Teaching alone is said to correspond to "[teaching] according to feelings." The [*Fa-hua*] *hsüan-i* refers to the relativity of the two realities of the tentative and the real. Therefore the first two [Tripiṭaka and Shared Teachings] are both said to correspond to "[teaching] according to feeling." Second, the [*Mo-ho*] *chih-kuan* is concerned throughout with discussing contemplative practice, therefore it criticizes [only] the Tripiṭaka as "[teaching] according to feelings." The [*Fa-hua*] *hsüan-i* profoundly discusses the intentions of the *Lotus Sutra.* It is necessary that only the Middle Path be "in accordance with reality." Third, the [*Mo-ho*] *chih-kuan* clarifies the three conventionalities. The three conventionalities are the mundane [truth]. The two mundane [truths] in the Tripiṭaka and Shared Teachings are different in being identical and non-identical. Therefore the [*Mo-ho*] *chih-kuan* classifies them as different with regard to phenomenal appearance and reality. The [*Fa-hua*] *hsüan-i* classifies the Two Truths. In both [the Tripiṭaka and Shared Teachings] the Two Truths are tentative and have not encountered the reality of the Middle. [Therefore] both correspond to "[teaching] according to feelings."

C. Classification into Crude and Subtle

Q: Of these seven levels of the Two Truths, which are crude and which subtle?

A: The Two Truths of real existence is an incomplete doctrine. It lures those of dull faculties to dispose of the dung of frivolous arguments. The meaning of the Two Truths is not fulfilled, so this doctrine is crude. The Two Truths as illusory is a complete doctrine; it is a teaching for those of sharp faculties. All three people [Śrāvakas, Pratyekabuddhas, and Bodhisattvas] realize the true aspects of reality. Compared to the previous one, this is subtle. In the same way, it is crude compared to the later ones in that it perceives only emptiness. Those who advance from the Shared to the Distinct [Teaching] are able to perceive non-emptiness; this is subtle. Since it is not integrated with regard to reality, it is crude. The advancement from the Shared to the Perfect [Teaching] is subtle. It is not different from the later ones in subtlety, but it is crude in including the expedients of the Shared Teaching. The Two Truths of the Distinct Teaching do not include the expedients of the Shared Teaching; in this sense it is subtle. In the sense that its teaching is not integrated in discussing reality, it is crude. The advancement from Distinct to Perfect is integrated with regard to reality; thus it is subtle. It is crude in that it includes the expedients of the Distinct Teaching. Only the Perfect Two Truths is the correct, direct, supreme Path; therefore it is subtle, and so forth.

Q: How about comparing the seven levels of Two Truths with the teaching of the Five Flavors?

A: The Milk Teaching includes three kinds of Two Truths: the Distinct, the Perfect, and advancing from the Distinct to the Perfect. It is two parts crude and one part subtle. The Cream Teaching is only the Two Truths of real existence, so it is merely crude. The Curds Teaching includes the seven levels of the Two Truths, six crude and one subtle. The Butter Teaching includes six levels, five crude and one subtle. The *Lotus Sutra* only has the one Perfect Two Truths, and not the six expedient ones. It is only subtle and not
276c crude. The reason why it is called subtle is to be found here. This is a relative classification into crude and subtle.

D. Exposing the Crude and Revealing the Subtle

Q: The Tathāgatas of the past, present, and future basically appear in the world in order to lead sentient beings to be exposed to the Buddha's knowledge and insight. Why do you explain all these various and different interpretations of the Two Truths, some simple and some complicated, and some beyond conceptual understanding?

A: These are inducements to [the message of] the *Lotus Sutra.* The Tathāgata is eternally quiescent yet his transformations permeate the universe. Truly he does not discriminate, first deliberately planning and later taking action to save [sentient beings]. With his innate powers of compassionate goodness he [spontaneously] guides sentient beings to attain enlightenment.

Q: Someone has said that from the sermons in the Deer Park, all [sermons taught by the Buddha Śākyamuni] are inducements to [the message of] the *Lotus Sutra.* How about this interpretation?

A: This interpretation is not acceptable. [The period of the Buddha's sermons from] the sermon on the seat of enlightenment [the *Avataṃsaka Sūtra*] is also a limited period for inducements to [the message of] the *Lotus Sutra.* Alas, in this way these inducements [the message of the *Lotus Sutra* performed in the forty-five-year preaching career of Śākyamuni] are of a limited period. The inducements to the *Lotus Sutra* have been performed, all for the sake of sentient beings, from the time of Mahābhijñājñānābhibhū until now. Even these are of a limited period. Expedient means [leading to] the *Lotus Sutra* have been performed, all for the sake of sentient beings, from the time of the original attainment of Buddhahood. Even these are of a limited period. Expedient means [leading to] the *Lotus Sutra* have been performed, all for the sake of sentient beings, from the time [the Buddha] originally practiced the Bodhisattva Path. The *Lotus Sutra* says, "I originally made a vow that I would universally lead all sentient beings to attain this same Path." Thus should it be known. How can it be said that the inducements are performed only in the present [life of the Buddha as Śākyamuni]?

Q: Those originally transformed have already realized the truth and come to an end. Why do you discuss the tentative transformations [of the Buddha] as eternal?

A: [The idea that] "those originally transformed have already realized the truth and come to an end" is in itself one extreme. Those who have not yet realized [Buddhahood] are, like the above expedient means, without end. Therefore know that the real teachings of the *Lotus Sutra* embrace all the Sutras. It is the original intention [of the Buddha] in appearing in the world, the true significance of all the teachings. People do not perceive this reality, but only the phenomenal appearances of conditioned co-arising. If they do not cease being haughty, their tongues will rot in their mouths. If they realize this essence they will profoundly perceive [the meaning of] the seven and twenty-one categories [of the Two Truths]. There are immeasurable doctrines [of the Buddha] with vast and far-reaching meaning. Further, they are mutually interrelated, from the shallow to the profound, some apparent and some hidden. The horizontal [identities] are all included and the vertical [grades of teachings and practice] are culminated. All is consummated in [the message of] the *Lotus Sutra*.

Part Two

THE PRACTICE OF CONTEMPLATION

Chapter I

The Meaning of the Four Samādhis

The four types of regulating and rectifying bring about the illumination of perfect quiescence in one life. The five categories of preparatory practices train one's uncontrolled physical, verbal, and mental actions. Though one experiences craving, one nevertheless can gain enlightenment concerning *bodhi*-wisdom. By contemplating [the cycle of] birth and death one is awakened to Nirvāṇa. One crosses over this realm of delusion on the raft of practice, and thus completes this doctrine. Where else can one seek the torch of wisdom [that illumines] this dark room? A detailed interpretation of the meaning of this [practice] requires establishing three sections. The first is the introduction, the second is scriptural support, and the third is interpreting its fulfillment.

277a

A. Introduction

Question: How many parts are there in this section?

Answer: There are two parts. The first lists the names, and the second interprets the names.

1. List of Names

Q: What is the list of names?

A: (1) The Constantly Sitting Samādhi; (2) the Constantly Walking Samādhi; (3) the Half-walking and Half-sitting Samādhi; and (4) the Neither-walking-nor-sitting Samādhi.

2. Interpretation of the Names

Q: What is the interpretation of the names?

A: "Samādhi" refers to regulating, rectifying, and concentrating.

Q: What is regulated to justify calling it "regulating and rectifying"?

A: Physical, verbal, and mental [activity] are regulated and rectified.

Q: How do you know that "samādhi" means regulating and rectifying?

A: The *Ta chih tu lun* says, "A good mind dwells in one place without moving. This is called samādhi."

Q: What is the meaning of this treatise passage?

A: "One place" refers to the Dharma realm. In [the state of] cessation and contemplation one can concentrate without wavering. With these four practices as conditions, one contemplates the mind, and with these conditions one regulates and rectifies [physical, verbal, and mental activity]. Therefore it is called "samādhi."

Q: From what languages are the terms "samādhi" and "regulating and rectifying"?

A: "Samādhi" is Sanskrit and "regulating and rectifying" is Chinese.

Q: "Regulating and rectifying" is the same [in all Buddhist practice]. Why is it called "Constantly Sitting," and so forth?

A: Regulating and rectifying is common [to all Buddhist contemplation]; "Constantly Sitting" is a distinctive type [of contemplation].

B. Scriptural Support

Q: On what Sutra is the Constantly Sitting Samādhi based?

A: It is based on the two *Prajñā-pāramitā Sūtra*s, the *Ārya-saptaśatikā-nāma-prajñā-pāramitā Sūtra* [Sutra Explained by

Mañjuśrī], and the *Wen-shu-shi-li wen ching* [Questions by Mañjuśrī]; and it is called "the Single Practice Samādhi."

Q: [In these Sutras the practice] is only called "Single Practice" and is not called "Constantly Sitting." Why then are these quoted as evidence for this practice?

A: "Single Practice" refers to its doctrinal content and "Constantly Sitting" refers to the physical regulations.

Q: Why is this [practice] called the "Single Practice" in these Sutras?

A: One singly contemplates the Dharma realm. Therefore it is also called "the Lotus Samādhi."

C. Interpretation of Its Fulfillment

1. The Constantly Sitting Samādhi

Q: How many parts are there to cultivating this samādhi?

A: There are two parts. First, clarifying the method, and second, clarifying the encouragement of its cultivation.

Q: What is the method [of cultivating this practice]?

A: (1) Physically one does what one should, and does not do what one should not. (2) Verbally one speaks or maintains silence [at the appropriate times]. (3) Mentally one maintains a state of cessation and contemplation.

Q: What is the meaning of physically doing what one should and not doing what one should not?

A: It means to maintain physically a posture of constantly sitting and to avoid walking, standing, or lying down.

Q: Should this samādhi be cultivated in a place with other people, or should one cultivate it alone?

A: It can be done in a place with other people, but it is better to do it alone.

Q: If done with other people, with whom should it be done? How is it to be done alone?

A: "A place with other people" refers to the people in the Meditation Hall, and not to the crowd in a noisy marketplace. To cultivate alone means to stay in a single quiet room, or in a lonely spot in the woods.

Q: What seat should one sit in?

A: One should stay on a single coarse chair, with no other seats by one's side.

Q: For how long a period [should this continue]?

A: Ninety days is one period.

277b *Q:* Why is one period determined as ninety days?

A: Because cultivating the way for one summer is the teaching of a thousand sages.

Q: Are there any breaks in practice during this period?

A: The time must be continuous, without even the slightest interruption, except for walking meditation, meals, and so forth.

Q: What is the meaning of "verbally speaking or maintaining silence"?

A: If one's practice is progressing normally, one should maintain silence. One speaks to remove obstacles.

Q: What is meant by "removing obstacles"?

A: Internal and external obstacles collect in a mind of correct thoughts. Then one should chant the name of a single Buddha, be repentant, and perform confession.

Q: Why should this be done?

A: A person who pulls a heavy load with his own power does not advance, but if he temporarily enlists some nearby aid, it can be lifted easily. The practitioner is the same. If his mind is weak and he is not able to eliminate obstacles, he should chant the Buddha's name and request protection, or the evil conditions will not be overcome.

Q: If so, then one should chant the Buddha's name and recite Sutras and spells. Why do you say that reciting Sutras and spells is noisy [and interferes with] quiet?

A: Where did I say that? I meant that reciting Sutras and spells is noisier than maintaining silence. How much more so the conversations of the secular world!

Q: Is this [maintenance of silence] limited to the "Constantly Sitting Samādhi"?

A: The avoidance of recitation is limited to this [samādhi]. The avoidance of speech is common to all four.

Q: The beginner in contemplation does not have a complete [understanding of] doctrine. How can he maintain and achieve these Four Samādhis?

A: He should approach someone who understands *prajñā*-wisdom and cultivate and study according to his instructions. Then he can enter the Single Practice Samādhi and/or [the samādhi in which one concentrates on] following one's own thoughts [as they arise in the mind].

Q: Of the three [physical, verbal, and mental] activities, which activity is the key to entering samādhi?

A: Physical and verbal [activities] are auxiliary to mental [activities] in perfecting the capacity to approach the Buddha.

Q: If this is so, then why do the [*Fa-hua*] *hsüan*[-*i*] and [*Fa-hua*] *wen*[-*chü*] discuss the meaning of the capacity of the mind?

A: That is not the same meaning of "mind" as here.

Q: Third, what is the meaning of "a mind of cessation and contemplation"?

A: Sit upright with correct thoughts and dispel all evil fancies. Identify the objects of cognition with the Dharma realm and integrate your thoughts with the Dharma realm.

Q: What is the meaning of "identifying the objects of cognition" and "integrating one's thoughts"?

A: "Identifying the objects of cognition" refers to cessation, and "integrating one's thoughts" refers to contemplation.

Q: "Identifying the objects of cognition" and "integrating one's thoughts" thus refer to cessation and contemplation. What is meant by the Dharma realm?

A: "Cessation and contemplation" refers to the action of contemplation; the Dharma realm is the object of contemplation. Whether identifying or thinking, it is none other than the Dharma realm. Whether through cessation or contemplation, quiescent illumination is simultaneous.

Next is the clarification of the "Exhortation to Practice."

Q: What is the "Exhortation to Practice"?

A: One praises the virtuous qualities [gained from cultivating this practice] to encourage the practitioner.

Q: What are these virtuous qualities?

A: The reality of the Dharma realm is the true Dharma of the Buddha.

Q: This is cultivated by whom?

A: The practitioners of the perfect and immediate [teachings] hear this and are not surprised. They realize this Dharma and so they dwell in the stage of Non-retrogression.

[*Q:* Why are they not surprised?

A: Because they follow the Dharma that they heard from Mañjuśrī.] (This section is found in another text. Cf. T. No. 2366, p. 277, footnote 11.)

Q: There are many methods of practice. Why do you recommend this one?

A: The Single Practice Samādhi includes all methods. If one
277c diligently practices it without indolence, then any and all can perceive the Buddha. Therefore it is said that the monks and nuns who heard this Dharma and were not surprised thereupon followed the Buddha and abandoned lay life. Laymen and laywomen

who heard this Dharma and believed represent [those who] truly take refuge [in the Buddha].

Q: Are there texts supporting these words of praise?

A: These texts are taken from the *Ārya-saptaśatikā-nāma-prajñā-pāramitā Sūtra* and the *Wen-shu-shi-li wen ching.* The regulations for the practice of the Four Samādhis are each distinctive, but all take the Dharma realm as their object of rest. Details are contained in the *Chih-kuan ju-hsing* [*ch'uan hung chüeh*] and so forth.

2. The Constantly Walking Samādhi

Second, the "Constantly Walking Samādhi " is distinctive in its method of practice [i.e., one walks while chanting the name of Amida] but the same in length [ninety days]. The original text [the *Mo-ho chih-kuan*] expands on this in detail, so I shall not outline it here.

3. The Half-sitting and Half-walking Samādhi

Third, there is a distinct one-volume manual concerning the "Half-sitting and Half-walking Samādhi." It was written by Chih-i himself and is well known in the world. I shall not repeat it here.

4. The Neither-walking-nor-sitting Samādhi

Fourth, there are three parts to the section on the "Neither-walking-nor-sitting Samādhi:" (1) interpreting the name, (2) scriptural support, and (3) correct interpretation.

a) Interpretation of the Name

Q: Why is it called "Neither-walking-nor-sitting"?

A: The above [samādhis] exclusively utilize walking and sitting. This [samādhi] is different from the above. In order to complete the tetralemma it is called "Neither-walking-nor-sitting." Actually it includes walking, sitting, and all other modes of activity.

b) Scriptural Support

Q: What textual support is there for this samādhi?

A: The *Pañcaviṃśati-sāhasrikā-prajñā-pāramitā Sūtra* calls it the "samādhi of the awakened mind"; one is perfectly conscious and fully aware of all the tendencies of one's mind. The great master of Nan-yüeh called it "following one's own thoughts." When a thought arises, one cultivates samādhi. Therefore, though three names are established, this is actually only one method.

c) Correct Interpretation

Q: How many methods of practice are there for this samādhi?

A: There are four: first, with reference to all the Sutras; second, with reference to all good things; third, with reference to all evil things; and fourth, with reference to all neutral things. The methods of practice found in all the Sutras but not included in the first three [samādhis] are contained in [the fourth samādhi of] following one's own thoughts.

Q: What is the meaning of the first—that with reference to all the Sutras?

A: The features of this practice are discussed mostly with reference to the *Ch'ing kuan-yin ching* [Sutra on Petitioning Avalokiteśvara].

Q: What are its features?

A: At a quiet location adorn a place of meditation with banners, parasols, incense, and lamps. Petition images of Amitābha and the two Bodhisattvas Avalokiteśvara and Mahāsthāmaprāpta, which are placed on the western side. Provide toothpicks and clean water. If beneficial, smear the body with ashes on the left and right, bathe, be purified, put on a new robe, and begin practice on a ceremonial day. One should properly face in a westerly direction, throw one's five-limbed body to the ground, pay homage to the Three Treasures [the Buddha, Dharma, and Sangha], the seven Buddhas, Śākya-
278a muni, Amitābha, the three *dhāraṇīs*, the two Bodhisattvas, and the noble assembly. After paying homage, kneel, burn incense, and scatter flowers. Concentrate your mind with utmost sincerity in

the usual manner. When the offering is finished, sit erect with a proper mind-set and assume the lotus position. Fix your thoughts and count your breaths, one thought for ten breaths. After completing ten thoughts, rise and burn incense. For the sake of sentient beings petition the above Three Treasures three times. After this petition, chant the names of the Three Treasures thrice, then chant [the name of] Avalokiteśvara. Put together the ten fingers and palms of the hands and recite the four-line verses. When this is finished, also chant the Three Sectioned Spells, either once or seven times, depending on the time of night. After chanting, repent and make confession, remembering your own shortcomings. Make these public and be cleansed, and then pay homage to the above objects of petitions. Then one person [should] climb to a high place to recite or chant this Sutra text. The others should listen attentively. In the morning and early evening this method should be followed. At other times the regular practices are followed.

Q: Second, what is "the consideration of all good things"?

A: This is divided into two parts. First is the discrimination of the four phases of a thought, and next is the consideration of all good things.

Q: What are, first, "the four phases of a thought"?

A: The mind and consciousness have no form and cannot be seen, but four features can be discriminated: previous to the thought, imminent thought, the thought proper, and the completed thought. "Previous to the thought" refers to the mind before [a thought] arises. "Imminent thought" refers to the mind in which [a thought is] just about to arise. "The thought proper" refers to the dwelling [of a thought] due to contact with an object. "The completed thought" refers to the end of [mental] contact with an object. If one is able completely to understand these four [phases], then one can understand their marks as integrated and their marklessness.

Q: [In the phase] previous to thought, [the thought] has not yet arisen, and in [the phase of] thought completed, [the thought has] already ended. These are integrated and non-dual. If non-dual, they are without marks. How can they be contemplated?

A: Although [the thought] has not yet arisen [in the phase of] "previous to thought," it is not ultimately nothingness. It is like a person who has not yet performed an action but later performs this action. One cannot say that there is no person just because he has not yet performed a certain action. If one determines that there is no person, then who later performs the action? Since there is a person who has not yet performed the action, an action can then be performed. The mind is also like this. Because there is [a phase] "previous to thought," the imminent thought can come to pass. If there were no phase previous to thought, how could one attain an imminent thought? For this reason, although the phase previous to thought does not exist [in itself], neither can it be said that ultimately this phase of thought is nothingness. As for [the phase of] thought completed, although [the thought] is extinguished it can be contemplated. Similarly, a person who has finished an action cannot be said to be nothingness. If one determines that that person does not exist, then who has performed the previous action? The phase of thought completed, the extinguishing of the mind, is also like this. One cannot say that it is an eternal extinguishing. If it means an eternal extinguishing, this is the heresy of annihilationism, a denial of cause and effect. Therefore, though [the thought] is already extinguished in the phase of thought completed, it can be contemplated.

Q: Next, what does it mean to consider good things?

A: Good things are many, but here they can be abbreviated as the Six Perfections. If one has possession of all the sense objects, he should be even-minded in [his perception of them through] the six senses. If one has no material possessions [to practice the Perfection of giving], he should perform the six actions. Even-
278b mindedness [concerning six objects] and performance [of six actions] together make twelve subjects.

Q: What is meant by the six senses and the six actions?

A: [The perceptions of] color, sound, odor, taste, touch, and dharmas are called the six senses. The performances of the activities of walking, standing, sitting, lying down, speaking, [and silence, eating, or general movement] are the six actions. This should be known with reference to the above, and I shall not go into detail.

Q: Third, what is the meaning of considering all evil things by following one's own thoughts?

A: The following clarifies the contemplation of evil. Although one first contemplates the good, its obstructions never cease. We drown in our cravings and there is no time when they do not arise. If we contemplate others, evil is again immeasurable. At times there is much greed, at other times there is much breaking of the precepts, or much anger, or much sloth, or much imbibing of wine. It is easy to lose one's zeal; there will certainly be failures. Who is there who has never made a mistake? Those who have left lay life and practice apart from the secular world, yet are incomplete [in their practice] and desire to accept the white robe, are not [true] practitioners of the Path. These should cultivate the wisdom of contemplation in the midst of evil, as in the time of the Buddha, when lay people [who] had wives and children, and government officials and those with secular duties, were all able to attain the Path. In the case of Aṅgulimāla, the more he murdered, the more he had compassion. Jeta and Mālikā drank wine but kept [the other] precepts. Vasumitrā indulged in sex yet remained pure. Devadatta's heretical views were [ultimately] correct. If it had been impossible to cultivate the Path in the midst of all that evil, then all of these people would have remained ordinary ignorant people forever. Since the Path exists in the midst of evil, though there are many obstructions to practice one can attain sagehood. Therefore know that evil does not hinder the Path. Also, the Path does not hinder evil. The stream-winner's carnal desires grew even greater; Pilinda was still arrogant; Śāriputra became angry. Yet what loss or gain was there in their state of nondefilement?

Q: Some people abound in covetous desires, seething with defiled craving. Even if they attempt to overcome and suppress [these cravings], they progressively increase. How can they be overcome?

A: Simply allow one's thoughts to go where they will. How can one know this? If the obstructions [to attaining virtue] do not arise, one would have no opportunity to cultivate contemplation. It is analogous to a situation in which the fishing line is weak and the baited fish strong so that it cannot be forcibly hauled in. In this case one simply directs the baited hook to enter the fish's mouth and then allows the fish to dive or surface freely according to its proximity. It can be gathered in before long. Cultivating contemplation with regard to the obstacles [to virtue] is the same. The obstacles are like the evil fish, and contemplation is like the baited hook. If there is no fish, the baited hook is of no use. If the fish are numerous and large, so much the better. All will follow after the baited hook and not reject it. The obstructions will give in before long to the attempt to bring them under control.

Q: Do not these obstructions and the nature of reality mutually hinder each other?

A: If the obstructions [really] hindered the nature of reality, then the nature of reality would be destroyed. If the nature of reality [really] hindered the obstructions, then the obstructions could not arise. One should know that the obstructions and the nature of reality are indivisible. The arising of the obstructions is indivisible from the arising of the nature of reality. The ceasing of the obstructions is indivisible from the ceasing of the nature of reality.

278c *Q:* Is there scriptural support for this position?

A: The *Wu-hsing ching* says, "Covetous desire is indivisible from the Path. It is the same for anger and ignorance. In this way all of the Buddha-dharma is contained within these three passions. If a person seeks enlightenment apart from covetous desires, [he is as far from the Buddha's teaching] as heaven from the earth. Covetous desire is indivisible from enlightenment." The

Vimalakīrtinirdeśa Sūtra says, "By practicing the non-Way [that which is not the Path], one achieves the Buddha's Path." "All sentient beings are indivisible from the mark of enlightenment, so they cannot attain it again. They are indivisible from the mark of Nirvāṇa, so they cannot gain further extinction." "Liberation is defined, for those who are haughty, as detachment from lust, anger, and ignorance. For those who are not haughty it is explained that lust, anger, and ignorance are indivisible from liberation." "All the defilements are the seeds of the Tathāgata." There is no duality or distinction in the color of the mountains or the flavor of the sea. Therefore contemplate all evil as [integrated with] incomprehensible reality.

Q: Fourth, what is the meaning of contemplating neither good nor evil?

A: This refers to dharmas that are neutral and indeterminate. Details are in the [*Mo-ho*] *chih-kuan*.

Q: Why did you avoid [discussing] the two middle samādhis yet clarify this samādhi?

A: The other two samādhis are either limited or require complete cultivation. Only the samādhi of following one's own thoughts can be contemplated constantly by both monks and lay persons. Even though one is burdened with the duties of a royal court, one should not avoid [this practice].

Thus I have abbreviated the general meaning [from the *Mo-ho chih-kuan*].

Chapter II

The Meaning of the Three Categories of Delusions

The conscious mind is dark and depressed; it has wandered from the right path and does not improve. The nature of the mind is to be noisy and cluttered, and it rejects the jeweled vehicle instead of accepting it. This is due to the dominance of cravings, which obstruct the sun of wisdom like a dark cloud, and the prevalence of the cycle of birth and death, which causes the boat of contemplation to sink in the sea of suffering. Thus the three wisdoms are hidden of themselves, and the three virtuous qualities are not manifest because of this. Therefore practice is required. Now in order to clarify this meaning I shall divide it into three parts: first, the introduction; second, scriptural support; and third, the interpretation.

A. Introduction

Question: What are the names of the Three Categories of Delusions?

Answer: (1) Deluded views and attitudes, (2) minute delusions, and (3) the delusion of ignorance.

B. Scriptural Support

Q: Treatises such as the *Daśabhūmika-sūtra Śāstra* all refer to the obstacle of cravings and the wisdom obstacle. Why do you now propose Three Categories of Delusions?

A: This [Tendai] school exposes Three Categories of Delusions based on the *Pañcaviṃśati-sāhasrikā-prajñā-pāramitā Sūtra* and the *Ta chih tu lun.*

Q: Of the two obstacles, which is expanded to make three categories?

A: The wisdom obstacle includes both phenomenal appearances and reality; therefore it is the one which is expanded.

Q: Of the minute and ignorance [categories of delusion], which refers to phenomenal appearances and which to reality?

A: The obstacle to wisdom concerning phenomenal appear-
279a ances corresponds to the minute delusions, and the obstacle to wisdom concerning reality corresponds to the delusion of ignorance.

C. Interpretation

The interpretation consists of four parts. First is the explanation of the Three Categories of Delusions; next is the interpretation concerning severing the delusions; the third concerns the Three Categories of Delusions and the manifestation of the subtle Dharma; and the fourth concerns the severance of delusions and the fulfillment of Buddhahood.

1. The Three Categories of Delusions

The explanation of the Three Categories of Delusions consists of three parts: first, clarification of deluded views and attitudes; next, clarification of the minute delusions; and last, interpretation of the delusion of ignorance.

a) Clarification of Deluded Views and Attitudes

First, the clarification of deluded views and attitudes.

Q: Does this refer to deluded views *and* attitudes, or to deluded views-attitudes?

A: It means deluded views *and* attitudes.

Q: What is the meaning of "deluded views"?

A: "Views" refers to views concerning reality. The views themselves are not identical to delusion. When the views are [in accordance with] reality, then delusions are severed. "Deluded views" are so named in accordance with understanding [or lack of it]. However, they are so named not simply in accordance with understanding. They are also so called on the basis of their essence. This means that they are called "views" when they are not in accordance with reality, are definitely mistaken discriminations, and are clearly one-sided views. These are what are named "[deluded] views."

Q: How many kinds of these deluded views are there?

A: In general there are four: (1) four single views, (2) four plural views, (3) four inclusive views, and (4) four nonverbal views.

Q: What is the meaning of the four single views?

A: Attachment to [substantial] Being, attachment to nothingness, attachment to both Being and nothingness, and attachment to neither Being nor nothingness.

Q: Through what ways do these attachments arise?

A: There are many ways for attachments to arise, but they can be explained with reference to [a mistaken belief in a substantial] self.

Q: How many types of cravings are included in the first [deluded] view of Being?

A: There are eighty-eight afflictions and cravings.

Q: What are these eighty-eight [afflictions and] cravings?

A: There are thirty-two afflictions of the realm of desire, twenty-eight of the realm of form, and the same [twenty-eight] for the formless realm.

Q: What are the distinct names for the thirty-two afflictions of the realm of desire, and so forth?

A: As for the realm of desire, there are ten [afflictions] that correspond to the truth of suffering: (1) the affliction of covetous desires, (2) the affliction of hatred, (3) the affliction of stupidity, (4) the affliction of arrogance, (5) the affliction of doubt, (6) the affliction of the mistaken view of a Self, (7) the affliction of extreme views, (8) the affliction of heretical views, (9) the affliction of attachment to these views, and (10) the affliction of attachment to precepts. There are seven that correspond to the truth of the causes of suffering: [the above ten] except for the mistaken view of a Self, extreme views, and [deluded] views [stemming] from attachment to precepts. There are also seven that correspond to the truth of extinction: the same as those for the truth of the causes of suffering. There are eight that correspond to the truth of the Path: [the above ten] except for the mistaken view of a Self and extreme views. Therefore there are thirty-two.

For the realm of form there are twenty-eight [afflictions]. There are nine afflictions that correspond to the truth of suffering: [the above ten] except for hatred. There are six afflictions that correspond to the truth of the causes of suffering: [the above ten] except for hatred, mistaken view of a Self, extreme views, and [deluded] views [stemming] from attachment to precepts. There are six afflictions that correspond to the truth of extinction: again the same as the truth of the causes of suffering. There are seven afflictions that correspond to the truth of the Path: [the above ten] except for hatred, the mistaken view of a Self, and extreme views. Therefore there are twenty-eight afflictions for the realm of form.

The formless realm is the same [as the realm of form].

279b *Q:* What are those [afflictions] from that named "the affliction of covetous desires" to that called "views [stemming] from attachment to precepts"?

A: To be attracted and attached to something without becoming weary is named "having covetous desires." An angry and spiteful mind is named "hatred." To be deluded and imperfect is named "the affliction of stupidity." To be confident in oneself and take others lightly is named "the affliction of arrogance." To be skeptical and uncertain is named "the affliction of doubt." To discriminate falsely a [substantial] Self in the midst of the senses, their organs, and objects, and act according to this false discrimination, is named "the view of a Self." A mind that is attached to extremes is named "extreme views." To accept heretical thought as true is named "heretical views." To view as true that which is false is named "attachment to views." To accept as precepts those things that are not real precepts is called "the view of attachment to precepts."

Q: Why are they all called "cravings," or "tormenting scourges"?

A: They are "tormenting" because they are vociferous torments, and they are scourges because they are oppressive troubles.

Q: Why are they called "afflictions"?

A: They are called "afflictions" due to their domineering oppressiveness. These cravings ["tormenting scourges"] constantly oppress the mind and spirit of the practitioner who is swirling through [the cyclic existence of] this triple world.

Q: Are all of these eighty-eight afflictions "sharp afflictions," or are they all "dull afflictions"?

A: Fifty-two of the afflictions are dull and thirty-six are sharp.

Q: All of the deluded views should be sharp afflictions. Why do they include some dull afflictions?

A: The delusions of dull afflictions contain both "illusion concerning reality" and "illusion concerning phenomenal appearances." Here only the extreme of "illusion concerning reality" is included.

Q: When are [deluded] views and attitudes severed?

A: One severs the delusion of illusion concerning reality at the time of recognizing the validity of the Four [Noble] Truths, and one severs the delusion of illusion concerning phenomenal appearances at the time of cultivating the Path. Insight and cultivation are not the same, and reality and phenomenal appearances are also different.

Q: Are these eighty-eight afflictions and the sixty-two [mistaken] views the same or different?

A: One incorporates each of the eighty-eight afflictions by considering the sixty-two mistaken views. It is also said that "the sixty-two mistaken views are the same as including all extreme views."

Q: What are the distinctive names of the sixty-two mistaken views?

A: There are various interpretations of this. To give one meaning, there are sixty-two mistaken views in considering the triple world and five aggregates.

Q: How many attachments are there?

A: With reference to the five aggregates of the past there are the four possibilities of the tetralemma. With reference to the present and future, there are the four possibilities of the tetralemma for each.

Q: What are the four possibilities of the tetralemma for the past and the four possibilities of the tetralemma for the present and future?

A: The four possibilities of the tetralemma for the past are (1) thus-gone, (2) not thus-gone, (3) both thus-gone and not thus-gone, and (4) neither thus-gone nor not thus-gone. With reference to the five aggregates, there are twenty-five aggregates.

The four possibilities of the tetralemma for the present are (1) eternal, (2) transient, (3) both eternal and transient, and (4) neither eternal nor transient. These also have twenty-five aggregates.

The four possibilities of the tetralemma for the future are (1) the extreme of Being, (2) the extreme of nothingness, (3) both
279c the extreme of Being and the extreme of nothingness, and (4) neither the extreme of Being nor the extreme of nothingness. These also have twenty-five aggregates.

The three times [past, present, and future] combined together make sixty [mistaken views]. There are sixty-two by adding the two [mistaken views of] annihilationism and eternalism.

Also, there are [the sixty-two mistaken views categorized in the *Fan wang ching* as] the past [eighteen] mistaken views and the future [forty-four] mistaken views. The singular view of Being is abbreviated in this way. The view of nothingness, both Being and nothingness, and neither Being nor nothingness are each likewise.

There are also the four plural views, the four inclusive views, and the four nonverbal views. These are explained in the commentary [the *Mo-ho chih-kuan*], so I shall not give a protracted explanation here.

Next is the clarification of deluded attitudes. First I shall clarify the meaning of "attitude" and later interpret how it fosters [delusions].

Q: Why are they called "deluded attitudes"?

A: They are called deluded attitudes because these delusions are severed through [the severance of] conceptual attitudes and considered rationalization.

Q: Which delusions are signified by the term "conceptual attitudes"?

A: The afflictions of covetousness, hatred, stupidity, and arrogance. These four afflictions are called "conceptual attitudes."

Q: How many kinds of these cravings are there?

A: In short there are ten. Broadly speaking, there are eighty-one degrees.

Q: What are their names?

A: The ten are as follows: Four [covetousness, hatred, stupidity, and arrogance] correspond to the realm of desire. Three, [the above four] minus hatred, correspond to the realm of form. The same [three] correspond to the formless realm.

The eighty-one degrees are as follows. The three realms consist of nine stages. Each of the nine stages has nine degrees, so together there are eighty-one degrees.

Q: What are the nine stages of the three realms?

A: The realm of desire consists of one stage, the realm of form consists of four stages, and the formless realm consists of four stages. Together they make nine stages.

Q: What are the nine degrees of each stage of these nine stages?

A: In each and every stage there are three degrees: intense, moderate, and mild. Each of these three degrees also has three degrees. Thus each stage consists of [the degrees of] extremely intense, moderately intense, mildly intense, intensely moderate, moderately moderate, mildly moderate, intensely mild, moderately mild, and mildly mild. Thus there are nine times nine degrees of the nine stages for a total of eighty-one degrees. This is a list of their names. Further interpretation is in the commentary [the *Mo-ho chih-kuan*].

Next, the interpretation of how it fosters delusion.

Q: How many delusions are fostered by the nine degrees [of cravings] in the realm of desire?

A: They foster seven.

Q: Why do the delusions that do the fostering number nine degrees, while the delusions that are fostered number only seven?

A: The one extremely intense degree fosters two [delusions]; the three degrees of moderately intense, mildly intense, and intensely moderate each foster one, the moderately moderate and mildly moderate together foster one, the three mild degrees together foster one. The content of the two higher realms is explained in detail in the commentary [the *Mo-ho chih-kuan*].

b) Clarification of the Minute Delusions

Q: What is the meaning of "minute [delusions]"?

A: The prevalence of ignorance is very great; therefore they are called "minute."

Q: How does one interpret this minuteness?

280a *A:* There are many methods of clarifying this issue. One method is to classify it into five parts: (1) the disease of deluded views and attitudes, (2) the basis of deluded views and attitudes, (3) the causes and conditions for the arising of deluded views and attitudes, (4) the time for the arising of deluded views and attitudes, and (5) many-layered deluded views and attitudes.

Q: Laying aside for now the first four, what is the meaning of "many-layered deluded views and attitudes"?

A: The three conventionalities emerge [in response to] the first mistaken view of Being. The four possibilities of the tetralemma, and practices for oneself and for saving others, emerge [in response to] the three conventionalities. Thus their number is immeasurable. The mistaken view of Being is like this. How much more so the mistaken views of nothingness, both Being and nothingness, and neither Being nor nothingness. They are incalculable, so they are called "minute." Further clarification can be found in the commentary [the *Mo-ho chih-kuan*], so I shall refrain from explaining it exhaustively.

c) Clarification of the Delusion of Ignorance

Q: What is properly signified as "ignorance"?

A: The wisdom obstacle is properly signified as ignorance.

Q: What does this mean?

A: The two wisdoms [attained from contemplating emptiness and conventional existence] that seek the wisdom of the Middle should be called the wisdom obstacle.

Q: Why is that called the "wisdom obstacle"?

A: There are three interpretations in understanding this "wisdom obstacle." (1) It is called wisdom obstacle because wisdom acts as an obstacle. (2) It is an obstacle because wisdom is being obstructed. (3) It is called "wisdom obstacle" because it refers to both the obstacle and [that which is] obstructed.

Q: What wisdom is acting as an obstacle?

A: The wisdoms attained from contemplating emptiness and conventional existence both destroy delusions; therefore they are called "wisdom." However, now the Middle Path is sought, and these wisdoms in turn produce delusion. These obstruct the attainment of the wisdom of the Middle; therefore they are called wisdom obstacles. They receive their name from the fact that they act as obstacles. Also, since these wisdoms obstruct the wisdom of the Middle, they are obstacles to wisdom. Since this [wisdom of the

Middle] is being obstructed, they are called [wisdom obstacles]. Also, the delusions are an obstacle, and that which is being obstructed is the wisdom of the Middle; therefore it is called the "wisdom obstacle." [The wisdom obstacle] refers to both the obstacle and that which is obstructed.

At the first level of interpretation, both parts of the term "wisdom obstacle" correspond to an active obstacle. At the second level of interpretation, both parts of the term "wisdom obstacle" correspond to the object of obstruction. At the third level of interpretation, the term "wisdom" corresponds to the object [of obstruction], and the term "obstacle" to the act [of obstruction].

Q: Cravings refer to the mind of delusion. Only they should be called obstacles. Wisdom refers to the Dharma of clear understanding. How can there be wisdom that is an obstacle?

A: There are two kinds of wisdom: the wisdom of enlightenment and wisdom based on consciousness. The wisdom based on consciousness discriminates, penetrates to the essence [of reality], and is in conformity with certain marks [of reality]. It is called wisdom because it is in conformity with certain marks. It is called wisdom because it penetrates to the essence and is in conformity with certain marks. However, if one penetrates to the essence by discriminating, this wisdom based on consciousness becomes an obstacle [to more profound insight]; therefore it is explained as an obstacle.

Q: Although I have now heard this explanation, it is not yet clear. What is the gist?

A: The wisdom of enlightenment is the wisdom of the Buddha and the Bodhisattvas. Wisdom based on [discriminative] consciousness is the wisdom of those of the two vehicles. The wisdom of those of the two vehicles, though it can be called wisdom, is not yet in full accordance with true reality, so its meaning is closer
280b to that of [discriminative] consciousness. It is able to destroy cravings, so in that sense it should be called wisdom. In being different from the essence [of reality] and so forth, it is interpreted [merely] as the wisdom based on [discriminative] consciousness.

This wisdom is different from the essence of reality; therefore it is called "different in essence." This wisdom is in conformity with the marks [of the two vehicles]; therefore it is called "in conformity with certain marks [of reality]." It is in conformity with the wisdom of the two vehicles, but it is different from the wisdom of the Buddha. Since it obstructs the wisdom of the Buddha, it is called a wisdom obstacle.

Q: Concerning the delusion of ignorance, there are two different varieties: that of the worldly and that of the transworldly. Which ignorance are you refering to in speaking of a wisdom obstacle?

A: The *Ju ta-ch'eng lun* [Introduction to the Mahāyāna] says, "Transworldly ignorance is the wisdom obstacle. The wise sages are already detached from worldly ignorance." Details concerning ignorance as the two varieties of (a) illusion concerning phenomenal appearances and (b) illusion concerning reality, and the delusions that arise alongside of or independent of cravings, at the time of sowing or at the time of fruition—these are all discussed in the text [the *Mo-ho chih-kuan*], so I shall not go into details here.

2. The Severance of Delusions

Second, the clarification of severing delusions is divided into four sections: the delusions severed in the Four Teachings.

a) The Tripiṭaka Teaching

Q: Which of these Three Categories of Delusions are severed in the Hīnayāna Tripiṭaka Teaching?

A: The Tripiṭaka Teaching utilizes the wisdom of analyzing dharmas and merely severs [the first category of deluded] views and attitudes. The delusions of the other two categories are not severed.

Q: What is meant by severing deluded views and attitudes?

A: Those at the lower and the higher levels of ordinary people both overcome [deluded] views and attitudes. Those at the level of the four causal and resultant stages of sagehood have severed these delusions.

Q: What does it mean to "sever delusions"?

A: At the causal and resultant stages of the stream-winner, eighty-eight deluded views and attitudes are severed. At the causal and resultant stages of the once-returner, the first six of the nine degrees [of delusions] in the realm of desire are severed. At the causal and resultant stages of the non-returner, the last three degrees [of the nine degrees of delusions in the realm of desire] are severed. At the causal and resultant stages of the Arhat, the seventy-two classes of deluded attitudes in the two superior realms [of form and the formless] are severed. Pratyekabuddhas exhaustively sever the deluded views and attitudes of the three realms and overcome all their habitual propensities. The Bodhisattva practices the Six Perfections for three incalculable aeons, sows the seeds for the thirty-two marks of a Buddha for one hundred aeons, and then, under the Bodhi tree, severs the [active] afflictions themselves and their habitual propensities.

Q: Concerning the nine degrees of delusions in the realm of desire, how many degrees are severed in order to lose what rebirths?

A: The *Abhidharmakośabhāṣya* says, "One becomes a wandering sage with two or three [remaining] rebirths upon severing the third and fourth degrees in the realm of desire. One enters the causal stage of the once-returner upon severing the fifth degree. One attains the resultant stage of the once-returner upon severing the sixth [degree]."

Q: What is the meaning of this text?

A: The interpretation is as follows: to sever the first three degrees means to lose four rebirths. Three rebirths remain, which are fostered by the [remaining] six degrees [of delusions]; one [in this state] is called a "wandering sage with three [remaining] rebirths." If one advances and severs the [delusions of] intensely moderate degree, another rebirth is lost. Together with the previous ones this means the loss of five rebirths. Two rebirths

remain; one [in this state] is called a "wandering sage with two rebirths." If one further severs the [delusions of] moderately moderate degree, one rebirth is not yet lost and one is called a potential "once-returner." If one further severs the [delusions of] mildly moderate degree, one has in general lost six rebirths, along with the previous [severance of the delusions of] moderately moderate [degree]. The remaining three [delusions of] mild degree
280c foster one rebirth, so such a person is called a "once-returner."

Q: Why is one who has severed the first and fifth degrees not called a "wandering sage"?

A: There is never anyone who severs the second but not the third [degree of delusions] before ending his life, and there is never one who severs the fifth but not the sixth [degree of delusions] before ending his life.

Q: Why is this so?

A: When the sage initiates his great practice, it is certain that he will not fail to sever exhaustively the great degrees of delusions before his life is over. Also, there is not one degree that is able to obstruct this result. Therefore one who has severed the fifth will certainly attain [severance of] the sixth. The severance of delusions and cultivation of enlightenment is explained in detail in the commentary [the *Mo-ho chih-kuan*], so I shall abbreviate and not expand on it here. It is not that it is not explained.

b) The Shared Teaching

Q: Which delusions in the three categories are severed by the Mahāyāna Shared Teaching?

A: The wisdom belonging to practitioners of this Teaching, [which comes] from contemplating the essence of dharmas [as empty of substantial Being], severs deluded views and attitudes and also a small part of the minute [delusions], but it does not yet sever [the delusion of] ignorance.

Q: What does it mean to sever deluded views and attitudes and minute [delusions]?

A: These are severed stage by stage in the Ten Stages.

Q: What are these Ten Stages?

A: (1) The stage of parched wisdom, (2) the stage of potential, (3) the stage of eight endurances, (4) the stage of insight, (5) the stage of thinner [delusions], (6) the stage of freedom from desires, (7) the stage of completion, (8) the stage of Pratyekabuddhahood, (9) the stage of Bodhisattvahood, and (10) the stage of Buddhahood.

Q: What delusions are severed on these Ten Stages?

A: The deluded views are overcome in the first stage of parched wisdom. This corresponds to the lower level of ordinary people. The deluded views are also overcome in the stage of potential. This corresponds to the higher level of ordinary people. The eighty-eight afflictions are severed in the two stages of eight personalities and insight. The six classes of deluded attitudes in the realm of desire are severed in the stage of thinner [delusions]. The nine classes of deluded attitudes in the realm of desire are severed in the stage of freedom from desires. The seventy-two classes of deluded attitudes in the realm of form and formlessness are severed in the stage of conclusion. The active afflictions of the triple realm are severed and their habitual propensities removed in the stage of the Pratyekabuddha. Both active afflictions and their habitual propensities, and also ignorance concerning the mental and physical realms, are severed in the stage of the Bodhisattva. Unlike those of the two vehicles, [Bodhisattvas] arouse compassion and vow to benefit sentient beings. In the stage of the Buddha one completely exhausts all active delusions and their habitual propensities and, passing through the eight features [of a Buddha's life], attains Buddhahood under a Bodhi tree.

c) The Distinct Teaching

Q: Which of the delusions in the three categories are severed in the Mahāyāna Distinct Teaching?

A: Those of this Teaching utilize a gradual contemplation to overcome and sever the delusions in the three categories.

Q: In what stage are the delusions in the three categories overcome, and in what stage are they severed?

A: The [deluded] views and attitudes of the triple realm are overcome on the level of the Ten Levels of Faith. The [deluded] views are severed on the level of the first Abode. Deluded attitudes are severed and extinguished from the second to the seventh Abode. The habitual propensities are severed from the eighth to the tenth Abode. The minute delusions of the transworldly realm are removed on the next Levels of Practice. The delusions of ignorance are overcome by cultivating the contemplation of the Middle through advancing to the Ten Levels of Merit Transference. One is first enlightened concerning the Middle Path in the next Ten Stages. The methods of attaining Buddhahood in the one hundred realms are in these stages. Next, on the Level of Preliminary Awakening one further severs and removes one degree of
281a ignorance, and the Middle Path is partially enlightened. Finally, upon advancing to the Level of Subtle Awakening one severs and removes one [final] degree of ignorance. This should be called ultimate Subtle Awakening.

d) The Perfect Teaching

Q: Which delusions in the three categories are severed and removed in the One-Vehicle Perfect Teaching?

A: Those of this teaching sever delusions with wisdom from a non-gradual contemplation. This consists of five degrees and fifty-two levels. The five degrees refer to the ordinary person at a lower level; therefore severance of delusions is not discussed. [Deluded] views are severed at the first of the Ten Levels of Faith. Deluded attitudes are severed from the second to the seventh Levels of Faith. The minute delusions of this realm [i.e., the triple world] and the transworldly realm are severed from the eighth to the tenth Levels of Faith. Next, ten degrees of ignorance are severed on the levels of the Ten Abodes. In addition, the Middle Path is completely illumined, and the eight features of the life of attaining Buddhahood begin at these levels. Next, ten degrees of ignorance are severed and removed, and enlightenment concerning the complete Middle Path is attained on the Ten Levels of Practice. Next, the exhaustive extinguishing of ten degrees of ignorance and attainment of the complete Middle Path is approached on the Ten Levels of Merit Transference. Next, ten degrees of ignorance are destroyed and extinguished, and the complete Middle Path is mastered on the levels of the Ten Stages. One enters the Level of Preliminary Awakening upon further extinguishing one degree of ignorance. One climbs to the fruition of Subtle Awakening with the severance of one final degree of ignorance.

3. Manifestation of the Subtle Dharma by Means of the Three Categories of Delusions

Q: What is meant by manifesting subtle [reality] without destroying the deluded nature?

A: The essence of the three kinds of delusions is indivisible from the nature of reality. The three kinds of delusions are transformed and produced due to stupidity and illusion. The basis of the four virtuous qualities is also ignorance, because the four virtuous qualities are made manifest through awakening enlightenment. It is analogous to when cold comes and solidifies water into ice, or heat comes and melts the ice and transforms it into water. There is no contaminated water detached from pure water, and one dips for water after breaking the hard ice on top. It is analogous to when one falls asleep and one's mind is transformed and has various dreams. Phenomenal appearances in the world are like this. The dharmas of mental dreams are also like this. Therefore one seeks enlightenment in the passionate mind. One gains Nirvāṇa within the visible form of the cycle of birth and death. Therefore the *Chu-fa wu-hsing ching* says, "Carnal desires are indivisible from the Path. Hatred and stupidity are also likewise." The *Vimalakīrtinirdeśa Sūtra* says, "Cravings are indivisible from enlightenment. The cycle of birth and death is indivisible from Nirvāṇa." The *Mahāparinirvāṇa Sūtra* says, "Ignorance is converted and changed into enlightenment." The Buddha explains true enlightenment in this way frequently. Are these not texts that manifest subtle [reality] with regard to delusions?

Q: What is the meaning of "the nature of reality"?

A: This refers to the mind, which is pure by nature. We abandon our raft at the quay of yonder shore; verbal discussion is not necessary in the garden of awakened enlightenment. Thus I have given the general meaning; how can any questions be added?

4. The Severance of Delusions and the Fulfillment of Buddhahood

Q: What does it mean for the practitioners of the Four Teachings to sever delusions and [attain] the fruit of enlightenment?

A: Those of the two vehicles, of the Tripiṭaka Teaching, are basically involved in their own salvation and do not seek the
281b fruit of Buddhahood. After a conversion of their mind they can attain mastery. Bodhisattvas, however, after three hundred incalculable aeons, fulfill the Buddhahood of the inferior vehicle by severing their bonds in a single moment through the thirty-four [correct] states of mind at the preparatory level. The lad of the Himalayas offered soft grass, and the Tathāgata accepted it and attained perfect awakening. Thus one [person] fulfilled the Buddha Path on a seat of grass under a tree. This is an inferior Buddha of transformation.

Next, those of the two vehicles in the Shared Teaching are the same as the Tripiṭaka Teaching. However, Bodhisattvas attain the enlightenment of Buddhahood sitting on an angel's robe beneath a seven-jeweled tree by severing deluded views and attitudes and minute delusions and their habitual propensities, with the wisdom that comes when one's final single thought corresponds [to reality as emptiness]. This is a superior Buddha of transformation.

Next, the practitioners of the Distinct Teaching cultivate practices over a period of time to attain the wisdom [gained] from gradual contemplation, and they fulfill the Buddhahood of Subtle Awakening under a seven-jeweled tree. This is a Buddha with a body accepted for the sake of saving others.

Next, the methods of the practitioners of the Perfect Teaching are different from [those of] the previous three. The reason is that with the threefold contemplation in a single thought [realizing that reality simultaneously has the threefold aspects of emptiness, conventional existence, and the Middle], one [realizes that] all is integrated and that there is not one color nor scent that is not the Buddha-nature. Without traversing the three aeons one immediately completes the practice of a [Bodhi]sattva, and without transcending one thought, one directly approaches the fruit of [the ultimate Buddha Mahā]vairocana. One fulfills perfect awakening on a seat of space. The triple body [of the Buddha] is perfectly complete, and there is no one [who is] superior. This result is truly the goal of this [Tendai] school.

In praise it is said:

After Kuśinagara [where the Buddha entered final
Nirvāṇa],
In the midst of the era of the semblance Dharma,
The two sages of Mt. Nan-yo and Mt. T'ien-t'ai
And the two leaders Chan-jan and Saichō
Firmly established the Path for the myriad years,
And its doctrine crowned all schools.

In the Tenchō period (824–834)
Buddhism again flourished.
The Emperor mercifully requested
A presentation of the admirable [doctrines].
Therefore, of the luxuriant meanings
I have outlined just a few.

End of *The Collected Teachings of the Tendai Lotus School,* in one fascicle.

Colophon

The *Collected Teachings* is a composition by Master [Gi]shin of Mt. Hiei. Whether on teachings or on the practice of contemplation, it is an outline of the 80,000 doctrines in the twelvefold scripture, a summary of the essentials concerning all the subjects of this [Tendai] school, rolled up in many pages. It should be recognized as a substantial vessel of scholarship. It is also a book that has reached the attention of the Emperor. It has already been officially presented to the court. How can it not be transmitted? In the past it was popular, but it became old with the years. Since there are not a few errata [in the text], I am now correcting and editing it, adding punctuation, having catalpa wood plates carved, and bringing it to print. It is hoped that this work by such a virtuous elder will not disappear for a thousand years.

On a propitious day in the middle of the winter of 1649.
Inscribed by an anonymous private monk.

Glossary

Note: The terms in this glossary have been chosen and defined according to their usage in *The Collected Teachings of the Tendai Lotus School*. The definitions do not necessarily reflect the meanings of the terms in other contexts. This glossary is not intended as a comprehensive collection of T'ien-t'ai/Tendai terms.

Abhidharma ("incomparable Dharma"): a body of treatises that analyze the Buddha's teachings. One of the "three stores" (q.v.) of the Buddha's teachings.

Ajita: a name for Maitreya (q.v.). Used by Śākyamuni in the fifteenth chapter of the *Lotus Sutra*.

Amitābha (Jp. Amida): the Buddha of infinite life and infinite light. The object of contemplation in the Constantly Walking Samādhi (q.v.).

anāgāmin ("non-returner"): one who will never again return to or be reborn in this world of desires.

Aṅgulimāla: the name of a bandit who set out to kill a thousand people. The Buddha was to be his one thousandth victim, but instead Aṅgulimāla became the Buddha's disciple. He serves as an example of swift rather than gradual attainment.

Arhat: one who has attained ultimate sagehood. One who has killed the traitor of passions, who will have no more rebirths, and who is worthy of homage.

aspiration, first (*bodhicitta*): the initial volition, intent, or hope to attain enlightenment.

Avalokiteśvara: a Bodhisattva of compassion. One of the attendants of Amitābha (q.v.).

Avīci hell: the lowest and most painful of the various levels of hells. The eighth of the eight hot hells.

Bhaiṣajyaguru: a Bodhisattva who is the central figure in the twenty-third chapter of the *Lotus Sutra*. A Bodhisattva of healing.

Bodhisattva ("enlightened being"): one who aspires for Buddhahood and takes the four great [Bodhisattva] vows (q.v.). A follower of the Mahāyāna. One who works for the enlightenment of others and not just himself.

Bodhi tree: the tree under which the Buddha attained enlightenment in meditation.

Buddha-land: a world or realm in which a particular Buddha dwells.

Buddha-nature: the potential in all beings to attain Buddhahood. The capacity for enlightenment, given the right conditions. The ultimate nature of reality. Synonymous with other terms that attempt to describe the indescribable, such as "suchness," the true features (of reality), and the Dharma realm (q.v.).

cessation (*śamatha*): concentration and stillness of the mind. Putting an end to delusions and mental afflictions. Both the action of stilling the mind and the quiescence attained thereby. Usually paired with contemplation (q.v.).

cessation and contemplation (*śamatha-vipaśyanā*): in Tendai, a broad term that includes all Buddhist practices and methods used to attain the goal of Buddhahood. The attainment of cessation and contemplation is like being able to see to the bottom of a pond when the water is still and clear of obstructions.

Chan-jan: the sixth T'ien-t'ai patriarch. The authoritative commentator on Chih-i's (q.v.) major works.

Chih-i: the founder of the T'ien-t'ai (Jp. Tendai) Buddhist tradition of thought and practice.

Constantly Sitting Samādhi: one of the Four Samādhis (q.v.). A method of Buddhist practice whereby one sits in meditation for a period of ninety days. Also referred to as the Single Practice Samādhi.

Constantly Walking Samādhi: one of the Four Samādhis (q.v.). A method of Buddhist practice whereby one concentrates on and chants the name of Amitābha (Jp. Amida) (q.v.) while walking for a period of ninety days.

contemplation (*vipaśyanā*): the practice of meditation to attain wisdom. Both the practice of meditation and the insight gained thereby. Usually paired with cessation (q.v.).

contemplation of evil: to contemplate evil thoughts and desires as they arise in the mind. The type of contemplation recommended for the Neither-walking-nor-sitting Samādhi (q.v.).

conventional existence. *See* threefold truth.

dāna-pāramitā: the perfection of charity. *See also* Six Perfections.

Deer Park: the location of the Buddha's first sermon after his enlightenment under the Bodhi tree (q.v.), where he gave the sermon on the Four Noble Truths (q.v.).

deluded views and attitudes: all of the explicit mistaken views and attitudes that afflict human beings, outlined in detail in *The Collected Teachings of the Tendai Lotus School.* The first of the Three Categories of Delusions (q.v.).

delusion of [fundamental] ignorance: the fundamental tendency toward ignorance that remains even after one has severed all of the explicit and subtle delusions. The third of the Three Categories of Delusions (q.v.).

Devadatta: a cousin of Śākyamuni, who promoted heretical views, caused a schism in the Sangha, and even tried to kill Śākyamuni. The subject of the twelfth chapter of the *Lotus Sutra.*

dhāraṇī incantation: the idealization of a Buddhist principle in a verse or phrase that contains spiritual power.

Dharma Body: one of the triple body [of the Buddha] (q.v.). The essence of reality; the fundamental beginningless and endless truth.

Dharma realm: the sphere of ultimate reality. *See also* Ten [Dharma] realms.

Dharma supreme in the world, the level of: one of the sub-levels of attainment in the Tripiṭaka Teaching (q.v.). The highest level of the stages of attainment reached by ordinary people.

dhyāna-pāramitā: the perfection of meditation. *See also* Six Perfections.

Dīpa (Full name Candrasūryapradīpa ["Moon and Sun Glow"]): the Buddha who appears in the *Lotus Sutra* as the name of numerous previous incarnations of the Buddha.

Dīpaṃkara: according to the *Lotus Sutra,* a Buddha who appeared in the past and prophesied the appearance of Śākyamuni.

Distinct advancing to Perfect: to make a spiritual quantum leap from the level of the Distinct Teaching (q.v.) to that of the Perfect Teaching (q.v.).

Distinct Teaching: one of the Four Teachings (q.v.). The teachings of the Buddha taught apart from the Tripiṭaka and Shared Teachings (q.v.), only for Bodhisattvas and not for the other two of the three vehicles (q.v.).

dragon girl: the eight-year-old daughter of the Dragon King Sāgara who, in the chapter on Devadatta (q.v.) in the *Lotus Sutra,* is said to have attained enlightenment.

eighty-eight afflictions: part of the obstacle of delusions (q.v.). The thirty-two afflictions of the realm of desire, the twenty-eight of the realm of form, and the twenty-eight of the formless realm. *See also* three realms.

emptiness. *See* threefold truth.

entering conventional existence from emptiness: to reaffirm conventional reality after or on the basis of a realization of emptiness. Cf. threefold truth.

expedient means (*upāya*): the skillful ways, methods, or teachings that are used to guide people to enlightenment. An indirect or incomplete method of leading people, in contrast to a direct and full use of the real truth (q.v.).

exposing, signifying, awakening, and entering: a phrase from the *Lotus Sutra* connoting that the one great purpose of the Buddha in appearing in this world is to expose and signify the Buddha-dharma, thus helping sentient beings to become awakened to and enter or realize the Buddha-dharma.

fifty-two [Bodhisattva] levels: the Ten Levels of Faith (q.v.), Ten Abodes (q.v.), Ten Levels of Practice (q.v.), Ten Levels of Merit Transference (q.v.), Ten Stages (q.v.), the Level of Preliminary Awakening, and the Level of [Supreme] Subtle Awakening (q.v.).

five aggregates: the five aspects of which a human being consists—form, sensation, conception, volition, and consciousness.

Five Flavors: an analogy that compares the various teachings of the Buddha to stages in the refinement of milk, based on an analogy in the *Mahāparinirvāṇa Sūtra.* The Five Flavors are milk (*Avataṃsaka Sūtra*), cream (*Āgama Sūtras*), curds (*Vaipulya Sūtras*), butter (*Prajñāpāramitā Sūtras*), and ghee (*Mahāparinirvāṇa Sūtra* and *Lotus Sutra*).

fivefold Dharma Body: the five virtues of the Dharma Body (q.v.)—morality, concentration, wisdom, liberation, and the knowledge-insight of liberation.

five meditations for putting the mind at rest: (1) to put the mind at rest by means of compassion, (2) counting one's breaths, (3) meditating on conditioned co-arising, (4) meditating on impurities, and (5) being mindful of the Buddha.

five preliminary grades: the five preliminary levels of practice and attainment for a disciple of the Buddha—(1) joy, (2) reading and chanting the Sutras, (3) preaching the Dharma, (4) preliminary practice of the Six Perfections (q.v.) along with contemplation (q.v.), and (5) proper keeping of the Six Perfections.

Five [Time] Periods: the Tendai classification of the historical teachings of Śākyamuni. The periods of (1) the *Avataṃsaka Sūtra,* (2) the Deer Park, (3) the *Vaipulya Sūtras*, (4) the *Prajñāpāramitā Sūtras*, and (5) the *Lotus Sutra* and *Mahāparinirvāṇa Sūtra.*

formless realm. *See* three realms.

four categories of oneness: (1) the oneness of reality (q.v.), (2) the oneness of teaching (q.v.), (3) the oneness of practice (q.v.), and (4) the oneness of persons (q.v.).

Four Doctrines: (1) the doctrine of existence, (2) the doctrine of emptiness, (3) the doctrine of both emptiness and existence, and (4) the doctrine of neither emptiness nor existence. *See also* threefold truth.

four great [Bodhisattva] vows: "Though there are unlimited sentient beings, I vow to save them; though there are unlimited passions, I vow to sever them; though there are inexhaustible doctrines, I vow to know them; though the Buddhist Path is supreme, I vow to fulfill it."

four interpretations of Twelvefold Conditioned Co-arising: four levels of understanding of Twelvefold Conditioned Co-arising (q.v.)—(1) as arising and perishing, (2) as neither arising nor perishing, (3) as immeasurable, or as beyond conceptual understanding, yet arising and perishing, and (4) as spontaneous, or as beyond conceptual understanding and neither arising nor perishing. These four interpretations correspond respectively to the four categories of the Four Teachings (q.v.).

four methods of instruction: four methods the Buddha uses to present the Dharma to his audience, called *siddhanta:* (1) the worldly, (2) the individual, (3) the therapeutic, and (4) the supreme.

Four Noble Truths: one of the basic teachings of the Buddha—(1) that all is suffering, (2) that the causes of suffering are our passionate attachments, (3) that these passionate attachments can be extinguished, and (4) that there is a way to realize this goal.

four phases of a thought: the four phases that a thought passes through—(1) previous to the thought, (2) imminent thought, (3) the thought proper, and (4) the completed thought.

Four Samādhis: the fourfold Tendai system for cultivating concentrated contemplation—(1) the Constantly Sitting Samādhi (q.v.), (2) the Constantly Walking Samādhi (q.v.), (3) the Half-walking and Half-sitting Samādhi (q.v.), and (4) the Neither-walking-nor-sitting Samādhi (q.v.).

four single views: part of the obstacle of delusions (q.v.). (1) Attachment to substantial Being, (2) attachment to nothingness, (3) attachment to both Being and nothingness, and (4) attachment to neither Being nor nothingness.

four supranormal concentrative states: the four *dhyānas*. Four levels of concentration, each with a number of different grades.

Four Teachings: the Tendai doctrinal classification system of all the Buddha's teachings into four categories—(1) the Tripiṭaka Teaching (q.v.), (2) the Shared Teaching (q.v.), (3) the Distinct Teaching (q.v.), and (4) the Perfect Teaching (q.v.).

four unexplainables: the teaching, based on a discussion in the *Mahāparinirvāṇa Sūtra,* that the arising of dharmas, their non-arising, both, and neither are all unexplainable and beyond conceptual understanding.

four warped views: that the world is (1) permanent, (2) full of pleasure, (3) possessed of selfhood, and (4) pure, as opposed to transient, full of pain, lacking selfhood, and impure.

Four Wisdoms: the wisdom of the Path; various wisdoms of the Path; omniscience, or wisdom concerning the emptiness of everything; and universal wisdom.

Govinda: a wise prime minister who divided the world into seven equal parts to satisfy seven kings who were fighting each other.

habitual propensities: the fundamental tendencies toward delusion and passionate attachment that remain even after one has removed or conquered the explicit passions.

hair of a tortoise: an analogy for something that does not really exist or for emptiness. *See also* horns of a rabbit; threefold truth.

Half-walking and Half-sitting Samādhi: one of the Four Samādhis (q.v.). Includes methods of cultivating contemplation that involve various activities, such as the *Vaipulya* repentance practice of ritual purity, and the Lotus Samādhi (q.v.), which focuses on practices based on the *Lotus Sutra.*

Hīnayāna: smaller or inferior vehicle, in contrast to the Mahāyāna (q.v.), the larger or greater vehicle. A derogatory term for the inferior teachings prior to the Mahāyāna. The Tripiṭaka Teaching (q.v.) that posits the three vehicles, or ways, of the Śrāvaka (q.v.), Pratyekabuddha (q.v.), and Bodhisattva, in contrast to the One Vehicle (q.v.) of the Mahāyāna.

horns of a rabbit: an analogy for something that does not really exist or for emptiness. The rabbit may appear to have horns but actually does not, so the "horns of a rabbit" are empty. *See also* hair of a tortoise; threefold truth.

Hui-ssu. *See* Nan-yo.

Identity in Contemplative Practice: the third level of the Six Identities (q.v.). The realization of identity attained through practice of the Buddha-dharma.

Identity in Outer Appearance: the fourth level of the Six Identities (q.v.). The level of realization when one begins to "resemble" the Buddha.

Identity in Partial Realization of the Truth: the fifth level of the Six Identities (q.v.). The level of realization on which the three virtuous qualities (q.v.) are partially manifested.

Identity in Reality: the first level of the Six Identities (q.v.). The basic state of sentient beings, in which they are inherently endowed with the three virtuous qualities (q.v.) of the Dharma Body (q.v.), *prajñā*-wisdom, and liberation.

Indra: the creator-god of Indian mythology.

Indra's net: an analogy in the *Avataṃsaka Sutra* that illustrates the interpenetration of all reality; a net that extends throughout the universe with perfect crystal balls in each mesh that reflect all the other crystal balls.

Jambudvīpa: "roseapple continent," which, in Indian Buddhist cosmology, refers to this world.

Jeta: a son of King Prasenajit who, along with his mother Mālikā (q.v.), drank alcoholic beverages but kept the other precepts and was praised by the Buddha for doing so.

Kali: a king who, out of jealousy, cut off the hands, feet, ears, and nose of Kṣānti the hermit (q.v.).

Kāśyapa (or Kassapa): the sixth of the seven Buddhas (q.v.).

Kātyāyanīputra: the author of a number of important *Abhidharma* (q.v.) texts.

Khāṇuśikhin: the second of the seven Buddhas (q.v.).

kṣānti-pāramitā: the perfection of patience. *See also* Six Perfections.

Kṣānti the hermit (Kṣāntivādi-ṛṣi): a model of patience and forbearance, who endured his suffering when King Kali (q.v.), out of jealousy, cut off his hands, feet, ears, and nose.

Kuśinagara: the site of Śākyamuni's death and final Nirvāṇa.

Level of Subtle Awakening: the supreme and final of the fifty-two [Bodhisattva] levels (q.v.) of attainment leading to Buddhahood.

Lotus Samādhi: a method of contemplation based on the *Lotus Sutra* in which one single-mindedly contemplates the Dharma realm (q.v.).

Mahābhijñājñānābhibhū ("Victorious through Great Penetrating Knowledge"): the Buddha who is the central figure in the seventh chapter of the *Lotus Sutra*.

Mahāsthāmaprāpta ("Gainer of Great Strength"): a Bodhisattva, one of the attendants of Amitābha (q.v.).

Mahātyāgavat, Prince: a model for the virtue of diligence. When the prince lost his Maṇi jewel (q.v.) in the sea, he diligently tried to recover it by scooping the water out of the sea.

Mahāyāna: the great vehicle. The supreme teaching of the Buddha. The idea that all beings are destined for Buddhahood.

Maitreya: the future Buddha, currently still a Bodhisattva.

Mālikā: the wife of King Prasenajit who, along with Jeta (q.v.), drank alcoholic beverages but kept the other precepts and was praised by the Buddha for doing so.

Maṇi jewel: a wish-fulfilling jewel.

Mañjuśrī: a Bodhisattva of wisdom.

Māra: the evil one. The tempter. The personification of evil desires and passions and of the temptations of this world.

Middle Path. *See* threefold truth.

milk, analogy of the color of: an analogy in the *Mahāparinirvāṇa Sūtra* that illustrates the inability of non-Buddhists to understand the Dharma, just as a blind person cannot truly know the color of milk even if it is compared to that of a shell, rice, snow, or a white crane.

minute delusions: the more subtle delusions, or tendencies, that remain even after one has severed all of the explicit delusions. The second of the Three Categories of Delusions (q.v.).

mundane truth (*saṃvṛti-satya*): the way the world is viewed by those without a complete understanding of the truth. The conventional, provisional reality of this world. Also called the worldly truth, in contrast to the real truth (q.v.).

Nan-yo, Master of: Hui-ssu (515–77), Chih-i's (q.v.) master and second patriarch of the T'ien-t'ai lineage.

Neither-walking-nor-sitting Samādhi: one of the Four Samādhis (q.v.). The cultivation of contemplation in any and all aspects of life by contemplating each thought as it arises in the mind. Also called the samādhi of the awakened mind (q.v.) and the samādhi of following one's own thoughts (q.v.).

nine liberations: nine of the thirty-four enlightened mental states (q.v.) that sever obstacles to true knowledge.

nine non-obstructions: nine of the thirty-four enlightened mental states (q.v.) that sever obstacles to true knowledge.

Non-retrogression: a high stage of attainment from which one will no longer retrogress to a lower stage.

obstacle of delusions (*kleśāvaraṇa*): the body of delusions that obstruct the attainment of enlightenment. *See also* wisdom obstacle.

one great deed: the teaching of the *Lotus Sutra* that the Buddha appears in this world for one great purpose—to reveal the way to Buddhahood.

oneness of persons: that those of the three vehicles (q.v.) ultimately all belong to the One Vehicle (q.v.), and that all are destined for Buddhahood.

oneness of practice: that ultimately the practices of the three vehicles (q.v.) are included in that of the One Vehicle (q.v.).

oneness of reality: the ultimate teaching that reality is integrated and one.

oneness of teaching: that the final teaching of the Buddha is the One Vehicle (q.v.) and not the three vehicles (q.v.), and that ultimately the teachings of the Buddha are one and noncontradictory.

One Vehicle (*ekayāna*): the teaching of the *Lotus Sutra* that all beings are destined for the single goal of Buddhahood, and that there is only one vehicle, not three vehicles (q.v.), on which to attain enlightenment.

pāramitā. *See* Six Perfections.

parched wisdom, stage of: the first of the Ten Stages (q.v.) in the Shared Teaching (q.v.).

patience, the level of: one of the sub-levels of attainment in the Tripiṭaka Teaching (q.v.). The level of longing for patience through contemplation of the Four Noble Truths (q.v.).

perfectly integrated threefold truth: the realization of the Middle Path as the simultaneous affirmation of and correct insight into both emptiness and conventional existence. *See also* threefold truth.

Perfect Teaching: one of the Four Teachings (q.v.). The direct and complete teaching of the Buddha-dharma.

Pilinda: a disciple of the Buddha who did not show "proper" respect to the god of the Ganges River.

prajñā-pāramitā: the perfection of wisdom. *See also* Six Perfections.

Pratyekabuddha ("solitary buddha"): one who attains enlightenment without the benefit of hearing the Buddha's teachings and thus has middling wisdom and insight. Also, "one who is awakened concerning conditions" based on insight into conditioned co-arising. Cf. three vehicles.

Preliminary Awakening, Level of: the fifty-first of the fifty-two levels of attainment leading to Buddhahood.

Puśya: a Buddha before whom a previous incarnation of Śākyamuni chanted verses for seven days with such great concentration that he forgot to put one of his feet on the ground.

realm of desire. *See* three realms.

realm of form. *See* three realms.

real truth (*paramārtha-satyā*): the ultimate truth, the way things truly are, in contrast to the mundane truth (q.v.). Also called the truth of supreme meaning.

reward body of enjoyment: the body of the Buddha that is his reward or recompense for attaining enlightenment. One aspect of the triple body [of the Buddha] (q.v.).

Saichō: the transmitter of T'ien-t'ai Buddhism and founder of the Tendai school in Japan.

sakṛdāgāmin ("once-returner"): one who, after finishing this life, will be reborn in this world only one more time before attaining enlightenment.

Śākyamuni: the sage of the Śākya clan. Gautama, the historical Buddha.

samādhi: the Buddhist practice of regulating, rectifying, and concentrating the mind, and the state attained thereby.

samādhi of following one's own thoughts: another name for the Neither-walking-nor-sitting Samādhi (q.v.). The practice of concentrating on each thought as it arises in the mind.

samādhi of the awakened mind: another name for the Neither-walking-nor-sitting Samādhi (q.v.). A state of concentration wherein one is perfectly conscious and fully aware of all the tendencies of one's mind.

Śaṅkhācārya the hermit: a model for the virtue of meditation. When a bird built a nest in his hair while he was meditating, he did not move until the eggs hatched and the birds flew away.

Śāriputra: one of the original disciples of the Buddha, "the foremost of the wise."

seven Buddhas: a line of seven Buddhas that culminates in the appearance of Śākyamuni, preceded by Vipassin (or Vipaśyin), Khāṇuśikhin, Vessabhū, Koṇḍañña, Konāgamana, and Kassapa (or Kāśyapa).

Shared advancing to Distinct: to make a spiritual quantum leap from the level of the Shared Teaching (q.v.) to that of the Distinct Teaching (q.v.).

Shared advancing to Perfect: to make a spiritual quantum leap from the level of the Shared Teaching (q.v.) to that of the Perfect Teaching (q.v.).

Shared Teaching: the second of the Four Teachings (q.v.). The teaching that is shared by all of the three vehicles (q.v.), and that is common to both the Hīnayāna (q.v.) and the Mahāyāna (q.v.).

śīla-pāramitā: the perfection of keeping the precepts. *See also* Six Perfections.

Single Practice Samādhi: another name for the Constantly Sitting Samādhi (q.v.).

Sivi (or Śivi), King: a previous incarnation of Śākyamuni, during which he sacrificed his own body to an eagle to save the life of a dove.

six actions: the activities of walking, standing, sitting, lying down, speaking (and silence), and general movement.

six destinies: the first six of the ten [Dharma] realms (q.v.), from hell to that of the gods. The "evil" realms.

Six Identities: the six levels of understanding the integrated nature of all reality: Identity in Reality (q.v.), Verbal Identity (q.v.), Identity in Contemplative Practice (q.v.), Identity in Outer Appearance (q.v.), Identity in Partial Realization of the Truth (q.v.), and Ultimate Identity (q.v.).

Six Perfections: the six virtues (*pāramitās*) that allow one to reach the other shore of enlightenment: charity (*dāna*), keeping the precepts (*śīla*), patience (*kṣānti*), diligence (*vīrya*), meditation (*dhyāna*), and wisdom (*prajñā*).

six senses: sight, hearing, smell, taste, touch, and consciousness. The perception of color, sound, odor, taste, touch, and mental phenomena.

sixteen truths: sixteen aspects of the Four Noble Truths (q.v.): the four aspects of suffering, namely transiency, suffering, emptiness, and selflessness; the four causes of suffering, namely the direct causes, assembled causes, birth, and conditions; the four aspects of extinction, namely extinction, quiescence, wonderfulness, and separation; and the four aspects of the way, namely the Path, Thusness, practice, and liberation.

Śrāvaka ("voice hearer" or "one who hears" the teachings of the Buddha): a disciple of the Buddha. In Tendai, the disciple of the Buddha who follows the Tripiṭaka Teaching (q.v.) of the *Āgama* Sutras and thus has wisdom and insight inferior to the Mahāyāna Bodhisattva's. Cf. three vehicles.

srotāpanna ("stream-winner"): a beginner on the Buddhist Path; one who has just "entered the stream."

summit of concentration: one of the sub-levels of attainment in the Tripiṭaka Teaching (q.v.), consisting of attainment of the four supranormal concentrative states (q.v.) and further clarification of the sixteen truths (q.v.).

supranormal powers: the six supranormal powers of a sage—(1) the divine eye, (2) the divine ear, (3) knowing other people's minds, (4) knowing one's past lives, (5) exhausting all passions, and (6) supranormal physical feats such as flying through the air.

Sutasoma (or Śrutasoma), King: a model of the virtue of keeping the precepts, especially the one against lying.

Sutra: text that contains the words of the Buddha. The "Dharma source"—the source of verbal teachings concerning the Dharma. One of the "three stores" (q.v.) of the Buddha's teachings.

Ten Abodes: the second ten of the fifty-two [Bodhisattva] levels (q.v.) leading to Buddhahood—(1) aspiration, (2) maintenance, (3) cultivation, (4) noble rebirth, (5) completion of expedients, (6) rectification of the mind, (7) non-retrogression, (8) childlike goodness, (9) Dharma-prince, and (10) anointment.

ten [Dharma] realms: the ten destinies or realms of rebirth—the realms of (1) hell-dwellers, (2) beasts, (3) hungry spirits, (4) *asuras*, (5) human beings, (6) gods, (7) Śrāvakas (q.v.), (8) Pratyekabuddhas (q.v.), (9) Bodhisattvas, and (10) Buddhas.

Ten Levels of Faith: the first ten of the fifty-two [Bodhisattva] levels (q.v.) leading to Buddhahood: (1) faith, (2) mindfulness, (3) diligence, (4) wisdom, (5) concentration, (6) non-retrogression, (7) merit transference, (8) preservation of the Dharma, (9) discipline, and (10) (fulfillment of) vows.

Ten Levels of Merit Transference: the fourth ten of the fifty-two [Bodhisattva] levels (q.v.) leading to Buddhahood: (1) salvation of sentient beings, (2) indestructibility, (3) equality with all the Buddhas, (4) pervading the universe, (5) inexhaustible virtue, (6) correspondence with all solid good roots of non-differentiation, (7) awakening of equality with all sentient beings, (8) the manifestation of Suchness, (9) unrestrained and unattached liberation, and (10) the immeasurable Dharma realm (q.v.).

Ten Levels of Practice: the third ten of the fifty-two [Bodhisattva] levels (q.v.) leading to Buddhahood, characterized as (1) joyful, (2) beneficial, (3) lacking in hate, (4) unexhausted, (5) unconfused, (6) attractive, (7) unattached, (8) honored, (9) exemplary, and (10) true.

Ten Stages: the ten Bodhisattva stages (*bhūmis*) of attainment in the Shared Teaching (q.v.)—the stages of (1) parched wisdom (q.v.), (2) potential, (3) eight endurances, (4) insight, (5) lesser delusions, (6) freedom from desires, (7) completion, (8) Pratyekabuddhahood, (9) Bodhisattvahood, and (10) Buddhahood. Or, the fifth ten of the fifty-two [Bodhisattva] levels (q.v.) leading to Buddhahood in the Distinct Teaching (q.v.), characterized as (1) joyful, (2) undefiled, (3) clear, (4) radiant wisdom, (5) difficult to conquer, (6) face to face with reality, (7) far-reaching, (8) immovable, (9) good, and (10) Dharma-cloud.

Ten Suchlikes: the ten features of reality, a Tendai classification based on a passage in the chapter "Expedient Means" in the *Lotus Sutra*. The ten "suchlike" features are (1) appearance, (2) nature, (3) essence, (4) power, (5) activity, (6) causes, (7) conditions, (8) results, (9) retribution, and (10) beginning and end being ultimately the same.

tentative and real: the Tendai teaching that there are tentative and real aspects of the Buddha's teachings, Buddhist practices, the capacities of sentient beings, and reality itself.

tetralemma: four possible options. Classically stated: (1) A, (2) not A, (3) both, or (4) neither. An alternate form is (1) A, (2) B, (3) both A and B, and (4) neither A nor B.

thirty-four enlightened mental states: the sixteen mental states (i.e., eight of patience and eight of wisdom) that sever mistaken views, plus the eighteen attitudes (i.e., nine of non-obstruction and nine of liberation) that sever obstacles to true knowledge.

thirty-two major marks: the major physical features possessed by a Buddha, such as images of wheels on the soles of his feet and a natural topknot of flesh on his forehead.

Three Categories of Delusions: all of the delusions that afflict human beings—(1) explicit deluded views and attitudes (q.v.), (2) minute delusions (q.v.), and (3) the delusion of [fundamental] ignorance (q.v.).

threefold Buddha-nature: the three causes of attaining Buddhahood. The potential to attain Buddhahood, analyzed as having three aspects: (1) the "direct cause," that all beings are endowed with the nature of Buddhahood by participating in reality; (2) the "complete cause," the wisdom that illumines this nature; and (3) the "conditional causes," the practices or conditions that bring about wisdom.

threefold truth: (1) emptiness—the true nature of things, which is empty of independent self-existence, (2) conventional existence—the truth that all things, though empty, have a conventional or provisional reality, and (3) the Middle Path—the simultaneous, balanced, and complete realization of both emptiness and conventional existence. *See also* perfectly integrated threefold truth.

three realms: (1) realm of desire—this world of desires, (2) realm of form—the realm experienced by one in this world who has severed all desires but still experiences the world as form, and (3) formless realm—the realm that has no form but consists of only the other four of the five aggregates (q.v.); the realm of experience of one who has severed all desires and attachment to form but has still not experienced enlightenment.

three stores: Sutras (q.v.), *Vinaya* (q.v.), and *Abhidharma* (q.v.).

three thousand realms: a Tendai term for the entire universe. The ten (Dharma) realms (q.v.) from hell to Buddhahood interpenetrate each other to produce one hundred realms. Each of these realms has the features of the Ten Suchlikes (q.v.), producing a thousand realms. Each of these is characterized by three "spheres"—(1) the aggregates, (2) the realm of sentient beings, and (3) the lands they occupy—producing three thousand realms.

Three Treasures: the Buddha, the Dharma, and the Sangha. The three sources of refuge for a Buddhist. Also known as the "three jewels."

three vehicles: the ways of the Śrāvaka (q.v.), Pratyekabuddha (q.v.), and Bodhisattva, in contrast to the One Vehicle (q.v.) of the Mahāyāna.

three virtuous qualities: the three ideals of the Dharma Body (q.v.), *prajñā*-wisdom, and liberation.

T'ien-t'ai, Mount: the site of the temple(s) that served as headquarters for Chih-i (q.v.).

transcendent realm: the realm of experience dwelt in by those who have transcended the delusions and passions of the worldly realm (q.v.).

Tripiṭaka Teaching: the first of the Four Teachings (q.v.). The teachings of the Buddha found in the "three stores (Tripiṭaka)" (q.v.) of the *Āgama* Sutras, the *Vinaya* (q.v.), and the *Abhidharma* (q.v.).

triple body [of the Buddha]: the Dharma Body (q.v.), the reward body (q.v.), and the transformation body (i.e., the historical Buddha).

truth of supreme meaning. *See* real truth.

Tuṣita Heaven: one of the heavens of Indian Buddhist cosmology. The heaven where Śākyamuni resided before being born in this world, and where Maitreya (q.v.), the future Buddha, currently resides.

Twelvefold Conditioned Co-arising: the twelvefold cycle of causes and conditions that make up the human condition: (1) ignorance, (2) volitional activity, (3) consciousness, (4) name and form, (5) the six senses (q.v.), (6) contact, (7) experience, (8) passion, (9) attachment, (10) existence, (11) rebirth, and (12) decay and death.

twenty-three scholars [of the Liang]: a group, presided over by Prince Chao-ming of the Liang dynasty, that carried on a famous debate (around A.D. 520 or 521) on the meaning of the Two Truths (q.v.).

two methods of contemplating emptiness: (1) to realize emptiness by analyzing dharmas (i.e., the method of the Tripiṭaka Teaching [q.v.]) and (2) to realize emptiness by direct insight into their essential nature. Cf. threefold truth.

two obstacles: the two types of obstacles to the attainment of perfect enlightenment—(1) the obstacle of delusions (q.v.) and (2) the wisdom obstacle (q.v.).

Two Truths: the real truth (q.v.) and the mundane truth (q.v.).

Ultimate Identity: the sixth level of the Six Identities (q.v.). The level of realization on which both wisdom and the severance of passions are perfected and the three virtuous qualities (q.v.) are completely manifested.

Vasumitrā: in the *Avataṃsaka Sūtra,* the twenty-fifth of the fifty-three "good friends" that Sudhana visited on his journey to enlightenment. Vasumitrā engaged in sexual intercourse ("embraces and kisses") to create opportunities to share the Dharma with her companions.

Verbal Identity: the second level of the Six Identities (q.v.). The level of realization attained by hearing the verbal teaching of the Buddhadharma.

Vinaya: the body of precepts that define the activity and lifestyle one must maintain in order to realize the extinction of passions and ignorance. The code for Buddhist monks and nuns. One of the "three stores" (q.v.) of the Buddha's teachings.

Vipaśyin: the first of the seven Buddhas (q.v.).

Vīrya-pāramitā: the perfection of diligence. *See also* Six Perfections.

warming up: one of the sub-levels of attainment in the Tripiṭaka Teaching (q.v.). Arousing approximate understanding through mindfulness and attaining insight into the sixteen aspects of the Four Noble Truths (q.v.). *See also* sixteen truths.

White Bull Cart, Great: the single, great vehicle (instead of three inferior vehicles) that the wise father gave to his children in the parable of the burning house in the *Lotus Sutra*.

wisdom obstacle (*jñeyāvaraṇa*): both the more subtle obstacles to wisdom (beyond the obstacle of delusions) and (in Tendai) the middling "wisdom" that itself obstructs the attainment of a higher wisdom. *See also* obstacle of delusions.

worldly realm: the everyday realm of passions and delusions. *See also* transcendent realm.

Selected Bibliography

Chappell, David, ed. *T'ien-t'ai Buddhism: An Outline of the Fourfold Teachings*. Tokyo: Daiichi Shobō, 1983.

Donner, Neal. "Chih-i's Meditation on Evil." In *Buddhist and Taoist Practice in Medieval Chinese Society,* edited by David W. Chappell, 49–64. Honolulu: University of Hawaii Press, 1987.

———. "Sudden and Gradual Intimately Conjoined: Chih-i's T'ien-t'ai View." In *Sudden and Gradual Approaches to Enlightenment in Chinese Thought,* edited by Peter N. Gregory. Honolulu: University of Hawaii Press, 1987.

Donner, Neal, and Daniel B. Stevenson. *The Great Calming and Contemplation: A Study and Annotated Translation of the First Chapter of Chih-i's* Mo-ho chih-kuan. Honolulu: University of Hawaii Press, 1993.

Groner, Paul. *Saichō: The Establishment of the Japanese Tendai School.* Berkeley Buddhist Studies Series 7. Seoul: Po Chin Chai, 1984.

Hurvitz, Leon. *Chih-i (538–597): An Introduction to the Life and Ideas of a Chinese Buddhist Monk.* Mélanges chinois et bouddhiques, 12 (1960–62). Brussels: Institut belge des hautes études chinoises, 1962.

Lu K'uan-yü. "Śamatha-vipaśyanā for Beginners" (*T'ien-t'ai hsiao chih kuan*). In *The Secrets of Chinese Meditation.* New York: Samuel Weiser, 1964.

Magnin, Paul. *La vie et l'oeuvre de Huisi (515–577)* (*Les origines de la secte bouddhique chinoise du Tiantai*). Paris: École Française d'Extrême-Orient, 1979.

McMullin, Neil. "The Sanmon-Jimon Schism in the Tendai School of Buddhism: A Preliminary Analysis." *Journal of the International Association of Buddhist Studies* 7 (1984): 83–105.

Mimaki, Katsumi, and Jacques May. "Chūdō." In *Hōbōgirin: Dictionnaire Encyclopédique du Bouddhisme d'après les Sources Chinoises et Japonaises,* fascicle 5 (1979): 456–470. Tokyo: Maison franco-japonaise.

Ng Yu-Kwan. *T'ien-t'ai Buddhism and Early Mādhyamika.* Honolulu: University of Hawaii Press, 1993.

Petzold, Bruno. *Die Quintessenz der T'ien-t'ai-(Tendai-)Lehre.* Wiesbaden: Otto Harrassowitz, 1982.

Rhodes, Robert F. "Saichō's *Mappō Tōmyōki: The Candle of the Latter Dharma.*" *Eastern Buddhist* 13 (1980): 79–103.

———. "The Four Extensive Vows and Four Noble Truths in T'ien-t'ai Buddhism." *Annual Memoirs of the Otani University Shin Buddhist Comprehensive Research Institute* 2 (1984): 53–91.

———. "Annotated Translation of the *Ssu-chiao-i* (On the Four Teachings)." *Annual Memoirs of the Otani University Shin Buddhist Comprehensive Research Institute* 3, 4 (1985, 1986): 27–101, 93–141.

Robert, Jean-Noël. *Les Doctrines de l'École Japonaise Tendaï au début du IXe Siècle: Gishin et le Hokke-shû gi shû.* Paris: Maisonneuve & Larose, 1990.

Stevenson, Daniel B. "The Four Kinds of Samādhi in Early T'ien-t'ai Buddhism." In *Traditions of Meditation in Chinese Buddhism,* edited by Peter N. Gregory, 45–97. Honolulu: University of Hawaii Press, 1986.

Swanson, Paul L. "Chih-i's Interpretation of *Jñeyāvaraṇa:* An Application of the Threefold Truth Concept." *Annual Memoirs of the Otani University Shin Buddhist Comprehensive Research Institute* 1 (1983): 51–72.

———. *Foundations of T'ien-t'ai Philosophy: The Flowering of the Two Truths Theory in Chinese Buddhism.* Berkeley: Asian Humanities Press, 1989.

———. "T'ien-t'ai Chih-i's Concept of Threefold Buddha Nature—A Synergy of Reality, Wisdom, and Practice." In *Buddha Nature: A Festschrift in Honor of Minoru Kiyota.* Reno: Buddhist Books International, 1990.

Weinstein, Stanley. "The Beginnings of Esoteric Buddhism in Japan: The Neglected Tendai Tradition." *Journal of Asian Studies* 34 (1974): 177–191.

Index

A List of the Volumes of the BDK English Tripiṭaka (First Series)

Abbreviations

Ch.: Chinese
Skt.: Sanskrit
Jp.: Japanese
T.: Taishō Tripiṭaka

Vol. No.		Title	*T.* No.
1, 2	*Ch.*	Ch'ang-a-han-ching (長阿含經)	1
	Skt.	Dīrghāgama	
3–8	*Ch.*	Chung-a-han-ching (中阿含經)	26
	Skt.	Madhyamāgama	
9-I	*Ch.*	Ta-ch'eng-pên-shêng-hsin-ti-kuan-ching (大乘本生心地觀經)	159
9-II	*Ch.*	Fo-so-hsing-tsan (佛所行讃)	192
	Skt.	Buddhacarita	
10-I	*Ch.*	Tsa-pao-ts'ang-ching (雜寶藏經)	203
10-II	*Ch.*	Fa-chü-p'i-yü-ching (法句譬喩經)	211
11-I	*Ch.*	Hsiao-p'in-pan-jo-po-lo-mi-ching (小品般若波羅蜜經)	227
	Skt.	Aṣṭasāhasrikā-prajñāpāramitā-sūtra	
11-II	*Ch.*	Chin-kang-pan-jo-po-lo-mi-ching (金剛般若波羅蜜經)	235
	Skt.	Vajracchedikā-prajñāpāramitā-sūtra	

Vol. No.		Title	T. No.
20-I	*Ch.*	Shêng-man-shih-tzŭ-hou-i-ch'eng-ta-fang-pien-fang-kuang-ching (勝鬘師子吼一乘大方便方廣經)	353
	Skt.	Śrīmālādevīsiṃhanāda-sūtra	
20-II	*Ch.*	Chin-kuang-ming-tsui-shêng-wang-ching (金光明最勝王經)	665
	Skt.	Suvarṇaprabhāsa-sūtra	
21–24	*Ch.*	Ta-pan-nieh-p'an-ching (大般涅槃經)	374
	Skt.	Mahāparinirvāṇa-sūtra	
25-I	*Ch.*	Fo-ch'ui-pan-nieh-p'an-liao-shuo-chiao-chieh-ching (佛垂般涅槃略說教誡經)	389
25-II	*Ch.*	Pan-chou-san-mei-ching (般舟三昧經)	418
	Skt.	Pratyutpannabuddhasammukhāvasthitasamādhi-sūtra	
25-III	*Ch.*	Shou-lêng-yen-san-mei-ching (首楞嚴三昧經)	642
	Skt.	Śūraṅgamasamādhi-sūtra	
25-IV	*Ch.*	Chieh-shên-mi-ching (解深密經)	676
	Skt.	Saṃdhinirmocana-sūtra	
25-V	*Ch.*	Yü-lan-p'ên-ching (盂蘭盆經)	685
	Skt.	Ullambana-sūtra (?)	
25-VI	*Ch.*	Ssŭ-shih-êrh-chang-ching (四十二章經)	784
26-I	*Ch.*	Wei-mo-chieh-so-shuo-ching (維摩詰所說經)	475
	Skt.	Vimalakīrtinirdeśa-sūtra	
26-II	*Ch.*	Yüeh-shang-nü-ching (月上女經)	480
	Skt.	Candrottarādārikāparipṛcchā	
26-III	*Ch.*	Tso-ch'an-san-mei-ching (坐禪三昧經)	614
26-IV	*Ch.*	Ta-mo-to-lo-ch'an-ching (達摩多羅禪經)	618
	Skt.	Yogācārabhūmi-sūtra (?)	
27	*Ch.*	Yüeh-têng-san-mei-ching (月燈三昧經)	639
	Skt.	Samādhirājacandrapradīpa-sūtra	
28	*Ch.*	Ju-lêng-ch'ieh-ching (入楞伽經)	671
	Skt.	Laṅkāvatāra-sūtra	

Vol. No.		Title	*T.* No.
29-I	*Ch.*	Ta-fang-kuang-yüan-chio-hsiu-to-lo-liao-i-ching (大方廣圓覺修多羅了義經)	842
29-II	*Ch.*	Su-hsi-ti-chieh-lo-ching (蘇悉地羯羅經)	893
	Skt.	Susiddhikaramahātantrasādhanopāyika-paṭala	
29-III	*Ch.*	Mo-têng-ch'ieh-ching (摩登伽經)	1300
	Skt.	Mātaṅgī-sūtra (?)	
30-I	*Ch.*	Ta-p'i-lu-chê-na-ch'êng-fo-shên-pien-chia-ch'ih-ching (大毘盧遮那成佛神變加持經)	848
	Skt.	Mahāvairocanābhisambodhivikurvitādhiṣṭhāna-vaipulyasūtrendrarāja-nāma-dharmaparyāya	
30-II	*Ch.*	Chin-kang-ting-i-ch'ieh-ju-lai-chên-shih-shê-ta-ch'eng-hsien-chêng-ta-chiao-wang-ching (金剛頂一切如來眞實攝大乘現證大教王經)	865
	Skt.	Sarvatathāgatatattvasaṃgrahamahāyānābhi-samayamahākalparāja	
31–35	*Ch.*	Mo-ho-sêng-ch'i-lü (摩訶僧祇律)	1425
	Skt.	Mahāsāṃghika-vinaya (?)	
36–42	*Ch.*	Ssŭ-fên-lü (四分律)	1428
	Skt.	Dharmaguptaka-vinaya (?)	
43, 44	*Ch.*	Shan-chien-lü-p'i-p'o-sha (善見律毘婆沙)	1462
	Pāli	Samantapāsādikā	
45-I	*Ch.*	Fan-wang-ching (梵網經)	1484
	Skt.	Brahmajāla-sūtra (?)	
45-II	*Ch.*	Yu-p'o-sai-chieh-ching (優婆塞戒經)	1488
	Skt.	Upāsakaśīla-sūtra (?)	
46-I	*Ch.*	Miao-fa-lien-hua-ching-yu-po-t'i-shê (妙法蓮華經憂波提舍)	1519
	Skt.	Saddharmapuṇḍarīkopadeśa	
46-II	*Ch.*	Fo-ti-ching-lun (佛地經論)	1530
	Skt.	Buddhabhūmisūtra-śāstra (?)	
46-III	*Ch.*	Shê-ta-ch'eng-lun (攝大乘論)	1593
	Skt.	Mahāyānasaṃgraha	
47	*Ch.*	Shih-chu-p'i-p'o-sha-lun (十住毘婆沙論)	1521
	Skt.	Daśabhūmika-vibhāṣā (?)	

Vol. No.		Title	*T.* No.
48, 49	*Ch.*	A-p'i-ta-mo-chü-shê-lun (阿毘達磨俱舍論)	1558
	Skt.	Abhidharmakośa-bhāṣya	
50–59	*Ch.*	Yü-ch'ieh-shih-ti-lun (瑜伽師地論)	1579
	Skt.	Yogācārabhūmi	
60-I	*Ch.*	Ch'êng-wei-shih-lun (成唯識論)	1585
	Skt.	Vijñaptimātratāsiddhi-śāstra (?)	
60-II	*Ch.*	Wei-shih-san-shih-lun-sung (唯識三十論頌)	1586
	Skt.	Triṃśikā	
60-III	*Ch.*	Wei-shih-êrh-shih-lun (唯識二十論)	1590
	Skt.	Viṃśatikā	
61-I	*Ch.*	Chung-lun (中論)	1564
	Skt.	Madhyamaka-śāstra	
61-II	*Ch.*	Pien-chung-pien-lun (辯中邊論)	1600
	Skt.	Madhyāntavibhāga	
61-III	*Ch.*	Ta-ch'eng-ch'êng-yeh-lun (大乘成業論)	1609
	Skt.	Karmasiddhiprakaraṇa	
61-IV	*Ch.*	Yin-ming-ju-chêng-li-lun (因明入正理論)	1630
	Skt.	Nyāyapraveśa	
61-V	*Ch.*	Chin-kang-chên-lun (金剛針論)	1642
	Skt.	Vajrasūcī	
61-VI	*Ch.*	Chang-so-chih-lun (彰所知論)	1645
62	*Ch.*	Ta-ch'eng-chuang-yen-ching-lun (大乘莊嚴經論)	1604
	Skt.	Mahāyānasūtrālaṃkāra	
63-I	*Ch.*	Chiu-ching-i-ch'eng-pao-hsing-lun (究竟一乘寶性論)	1611
	Skt.	Ratnagotravibhāgamahāyānottaratantra-śāstra	
63-II	*Ch.*	P'u-t'i-hsing-ching (菩提行經)	1662
	Skt.	Bodhicaryāvatāra	
63-III	*Ch.*	Chin-kang-ting-yü-ch'ieh-chung-fa-a-nou-to-lo-san-miao-san-p'u-t'i-hsin-lun (金剛頂瑜伽中發阿耨多羅三藐三菩提心論)	1665
63-IV	*Ch.*	Ta-ch'eng-ch'i-hsin-lun (大乘起信論)	1666
	Skt.	Mahāyānaśraddhotpāda-śāstra (?)	

Vol. No.		Title	T. No.
63-V	*Ch.* *Pāli*	Na-hsien-pi-ch'iu-ching (那先比丘經) Milindapañhā	1670
64	*Ch.* *Skt.*	Ta-ch'eng-chi-p'u-sa-hsüeh-lun (大乘集菩薩學論) Śikṣāsamuccaya	1636
65	*Ch.*	Shih-mo-ho-yen-lun (釋摩訶衍論)	1668
66-I	*Ch.*	Pan-jo-po-lo-mi-to-hsin-ching-yu-tsan (般若波羅蜜多心經幽賛)	1710
66-II	*Ch.*	Kuan-wu-liang-shou-fo-ching-shu (觀無量壽佛經疏)	1753
66-III	*Ch.*	San-lun-hsüan-i (三論玄義)	1852
66-IV	*Ch.*	Chao-lun (肇論)	1858
67, 68	*Ch.*	Miao-fa-lien-hua-ching-hsüan-i (妙法蓮華經玄義)	1716
69	*Ch.*	Ta-ch'eng-hsüan-lun (大乘玄論)	1853
70-I	*Ch.*	Hua-yen-i-ch'eng-chiao-i-fên-ch'i-chang (華嚴一乘教義分齊章)	1866
70-II	*Ch.*	Yüan-jên-lun (原人論)	1886
70-III	*Ch.*	Hsiu-hsi-chih-kuan-tso-ch'an-fa-yao (修習止觀坐禪法要)	1915
70-IV	*Ch.*	T'ien-t'ai-ssŭ-chiao-i (天台四教儀)	1931
71, 72	*Ch.*	Mo-ho-chih-kuan (摩訶止觀)	1911
73-I	*Ch.*	Kuo-ch'ing-pai-lu (國清百録)	1934
73-II	*Ch.*	Liu-tsu-ta-shih-fa-pao-t'an-ching (六祖大師法寶壇經)	2008
73-III	*Ch.*	Huang-po-shan-tuan-chi-ch'an-shih-ch'uan-hsin-fa-yao (黄檗山斷際禪師傳心法要)	2012 A
73-IV	*Ch.*	Yung-chia-chêng-tao-ko (永嘉證道歌)	2014
74-I	*Ch.*	Chên-chou-lin-chi-hui-chao-ch'an-shih-wu-lu (鎭州臨濟慧照禪師語録)	1985
74-II	*Ch.*	Wu-mên-kuan (無門關)	2005

Vol. No.		Title	T. No.
74-III	*Ch.*	Hsin-hsin-ming (信心銘)	2010
74-IV	*Ch.*	Ch'ih-hsiu-pai-chang-ch'ing-kuei (勅修百丈清規)	2025
75	*Ch.*	Fo-kuo-yüan-wu-ch'an-shih-pi-yen-lu (佛果圜悟禪師碧巖録)	2003
76-I	*Ch.* *Skt.*	I-pu-tsung-lun-lun (異部宗輪論) Samayabhedoparacanacakra	2031
76-II	*Ch.* *Skt.*	A-yü-wang-ching (阿育王經) Aśokarāja-sūtra (?)	2043
76-III	*Ch.*	Ma-ming-p'u-sa-ch'uan (馬鳴菩薩傳)	2046
76-IV	*Ch.*	Lung-shu-p'u-sa-ch'uan (龍樹菩薩傳)	2047
76-V	*Ch.*	P'o-sou-p'an-tou-fa-shih-ch'uan (婆藪槃豆法師傳)	2049
76-VI	*Ch.*	Pi-ch'iu-ni-ch'uan (比丘尼傳)	2063
76-VII	*Ch.*	Kao-sêng-fa-hsien-ch'uan (高僧法顯傳)	2085
76-VIII	*Ch.*	T'ang-ta-ho-shang-tung-chêng-ch'uan (遊方記抄:唐大和上東征傳)	2089-(7)
77	*Ch.*	Ta-t'ang-ta-tz'ŭ-ên-ssŭ-san-ts'ang-fa-shih-ch'uan (大唐大慈恩寺三藏法師傳)	2053
78	*Ch.*	Kao-sêng-ch'uan (高僧傳)	2059
79	*Ch.*	Ta-t'ang-hsi-yü-chi (大唐西域記)	2087
80	*Ch.*	Hung-ming-chi (弘明集)	2102
81–92	*Ch.*	Fa-yüan-chu-lin (法苑珠林)	2122
93-I	*Ch.*	Nan-hai-chi-kuei-nei-fa-ch'uan (南海寄歸内法傳)	2125
93-II	*Ch.*	Fan-yü-tsa-ming (梵語雜名)	2135
94-I	*Jp.*	Shō-man-gyō-gi-sho (勝鬘經義疏)	2185
94-II	*Jp.*	Yui-ma-kyō-gi-sho (維摩經義疏)	2186
95	*Jp.*	Hok-ke-gi-sho (法華義疏)	2187

Vol. No.		Title	*T.* No.
96-I	*Jp.*	Han-nya-shin-gyō-hi-ken (般若心經秘鍵)	2203
96-II	*Jp.*	Dai-jō-hos-sō-ken-jin-shō (大乘法相研神章)	2309
96-III	*Jp.*	Kan-jin-kaku-mu-shō (觀心覺夢鈔)	2312
97-I	*Jp.*	Ris-shū-kō-yō (律宗綱要)	2348
97-II	*Jp.*	Ten-dai-hok-ke-shū-gi-shū (天台法華宗義集)	2366
97-III	*Jp.*	Ken-kai-ron (顯戒論)	2376
97-IV	*Jp.*	San-ge-gaku-shō-shiki (山家學生式)	2377
98-I	*Jp.*	Hi-zō-hō-yaku (秘藏寶鑰)	2426
98-II	*Jp.*	Ben-ken-mitsu-ni-kyō-ron (辨顯密二教論)	2427
98-III	*Jp.*	Soku-shin-jō-butsu-gi (即身成佛義)	2428
98-IV	*Jp.*	Shō-ji-jis-sō-gi (聲字實相義)	2429
98-V	*Jp.*	Un-ji-gi (吽字義)	2430
98-VI	*Jp.*	Go-rin-ku-ji-myō-hi-mitsu-shaku (五輪九字明秘密釋)	2514
98-VII	*Jp.*	Mitsu-gon-in-hotsu-ro-san-ge-mon (密嚴院發露懺悔文)	2527
98-VIII	*Jp.*	Kō-zen-go-koku-ron (興禪護國論)	2543
98-IX	*Jp.*	Fu-kan-za-zen-gi (普勧坐禪儀)	2580
99–103	*Jp.*	Shō-bō-gen-zō (正法眼藏)	2582
104-I	*Jp.*	Za-zen-yō-jin-ki (坐禪用心記)	2586
104-II	*Jp.*	Sen-chaku-hon-gan-nen-butsu-shū (選擇本願念佛集)	2608
104-III	*Jp.*	Ris-shō-an-koku-ron (立正安國論)	2688
104-IV	*Jp.*	Kai-moku-shō (開目抄)	2689
104-V	*Jp.*	Kan-jin-hon-zon-shō (觀心本尊抄)	2692
104-VI	*Ch.*	Fu-mu-ên-chung-ching (父母恩重經)	2887

Vol. No.		Title	T. No.
105-I	*Jp.*	Ken-jō-do-shin-jitsu-kyō-gyō-shō-mon-rui (顯淨土眞實教行証文類)	2646
105-II	*Jp.*	Tan-ni-shō (歎異抄)	2661
106-I	*Jp.*	Ren-nyo-shō-nin-o-fumi (蓮如上人御文)	2668
106-II	*Jp.*	Ō-jō-yō-shū (往生要集)	2682
107-I	*Jp.*	Has-shū-kō-yō (八宗綱要)	蔵外
107-II	*Jp.*	San-gō-shī-ki (三教指帰)	蔵外
107-III	*Jp.*	Map-pō-tō-myō-ki (末法燈明記)	蔵外
107-IV	*Jp.*	Jū-shichi-jō-ken-pō (十七條憲法)	蔵外